PROSTITUTION, HARM AND GENDER INEQUALITY

CW00485938

Prostitution, Harm and Gender Inequality
Theory, Research and Policy

Edited by

MADDY COY
London Metropolitan University, UK

Routledge
Taylor & Francis Group

LONDON AND NEW YORK

First published 2012 by Ashgate Publishing

2 Park Square, Milton Park, Abingdon, Oxon OX14 4RN
711 Third Avenue, New York, NY 10017, USA

Routledge is an imprint of the Taylor & Francis Group, an informa business

First issued in paperback 2016

British Library Cataloguing in Publication Data
Prostitution, harm and gender inequality : theory, research
and policy.
1. Prostitution--Social aspects. 2. Prostitution--
Psychological aspects. 3. Prostitutes--Abuse of.
4. Prostitutes' customers--Attitudes. 5. Male domination
(Social structure) 6. Women's rights. 7. Prostitutes--
Legal status, laws, etc.
I. Coy, Maddy.
306.7'42-dc23

Library of Congress Cataloging-in-Publication Data
Prostitution, harm and gender inequality : theory, research and policy /
[edited] by Maddy Coy.
    p. cm.
Includes index.
ISBN 978-1-4094-0545-0 (hbk.) -- ISBN 978-1-4094-0546-7 (ebook)
1. Prostitution. 2. Women--Identity. 3. Sex role. 4. Sexual discrimination.
I. Coy, Maddy.
HQ118.P77 2011
306.74--dc23

2011053311

ISBN 13: 978-1-4094-0545-0 (hbk)
ISBN 13: 978-1-138-26820-3 (pbk)

Contents

List of Tables and Figures

Tables

Figures

List of Contributors

Dr Maddy Coy is Deputy Director of the Child and Woman Abuse Studies Unit (CWASU), at London Metropolitan University, UK. She worked for several years in a specialist residential centre for sexually exploited girls and as an outreach worker with women and girls in the sex industry. She has published articles and book chapters on: routes into prostitution from local authority care; women's experiences of prostitution; perspectives of men who buy sex; and the sexualization of women and girls in popular culture. Maddy has also conducted research on and evaluations of specialized violence against women support services.

Josefina Erikson has recently completed her PhD in the Department of Government at Uppsala University, Sweden. Her dissertation focused on Swedish prostitution policy, and she developed a dynamic frame analysis to conceptualize this process of policy formulation.

Maria Garner is a PhD student with the Child and Woman Abuse Studies Unit at London Metropolitan University. Her research interests centre around the gendered politics of media and cultural representation and consumption, specifically possible links between formations of gender and sexuality in popular culture and violence against women. Her doctoral research is an exploratory study of men's perspectives on, and experiences of, what has been termed the sexualization of culture.

Dr Miranda A.H. Horvath is a Senior Lecturer in Forensic Psychology at Middlesex University. Her PhD (2006) investigated the role of alcohol and drugs in rape. The majority of her research is focused on sexual violence working from an applied social psychological perspective. She co-edited the book, *Rape: Challenging Contemporary Thinking* (Willan, 2009) and co-authored a book *Understanding Criminal Investigation* (Wiley, 2009). She is currently co-editing the book, *Handbook on the Study of Multiple Perpetrator Rape: A Multidisciplinary Response to an International Problem* (Routledge, forthcoming 2013). Her current research interests include multiple perpetrator rape and the links between men's use of 'lad's mags', their attitudes towards women and paying for sex. She is an Associate Editor of the *Journal of Sexual Aggression*.

Professor Liz Kelly is the Director of the Child and Woman Abuse Studies Unit and Roddick Chair of Violence against Women at London Metropolitan University. She has been active in the field of violence against women and children for over three decades, has led CWASU since 1993, and is recognized as a leader in the field. She is the author of *Surviving Sexual Violence* (Polity, 1988), which established the concept of a 'continuum of violence', has written over 100 book chapters and journal articles, and given over 500 papers and workshops at local, national and international events. The topics range from overviews about violence against women and child abuse, to specific forms such as domestic violence, rape, sexual abuse in childhood and trafficking. Liz is co-chair of the End Violence Against Women Coalition, and an expert on VAW to the European Women's Lobby and EU Gender Institute.

Sheila Jeffreys is a Professor in the School of Social and Political Sciences at the University of Melbourne, where she teaches sexual politics and international feminist politics. She is the author of seven books on the history and politics of sexuality including, *The Industrial Vagina: The Political Economy of the Global Sex Trade* (Routledge, 2009). She is the founding member of the Australian branch of the Coalition against Trafficking in Women.

Marjut Jyrkinen, PhD, MPolSc., has published many co-authored and solo articles and book chapters on the sex trade, pornographization of media, and gendered violence. Her doctoral thesis 'The Organisation of Policy Meets the Commercialisation of Sex. Global Linkages, Policies, Technologies' (2005) focused on policies on the globalizing sex trade and the new information and communication technologies. Marjut's current research topics relate to gender, age and organizational policies and practices; gendered violations, organizations and managements; and, corporate social responsibility and global governance. Marjut is a part-time teaching fellow at the Department of Political and Economic Studies, University of Helsinki, and visiting research fellow at the Centre for Research on Relationships and Families, University of Edinburgh. She also works currently as an Affiliate Post-doctoral researcher at the Department of Management and Organisation, Hanken School of Economics, Finland.

Jody Raphael, Visiting Professor of Law at DePaul University College of Law (Chicago, Illinois), is the author of over 20 peer-reviewed research articles and a trilogy on violence and poverty published by Northeastern University Press (*Saving Bernice: Battered Women, Welfare, and Poverty* 2000; *Listening to Olivia: Violence, Poverty, and Prostitution* 2004; and *Freeing Tammy: Women, Drugs, and Incarceration* 2007.) In the past three years she has completed research projects that interviewed 100 Chicago girls in prostitution under the control of a pimp, and 25 ex-pimps who trafficked girls and women in Chicago.

Mary Lucille Sullivan is an author and public policy consultant. She has lectured extensively and provided policy advice on Australia's experience in relation to prostitution, both in Australia and internationally. She has a PhD in Political Science from the University of Melbourne and a Masters Degree in Public History from Monash University. Mary's publications on prostitution include *Making Sex Work: A Failed Experiment with Legalized Prostitution* (Spinifex, 2007) and *What Happens When Prostitution Becomes Work: An Update on Legalized Prostitution in Australia* (Coalition Against Trafficking in Women Australia, 2006). Her other works on prostitution include a contribution to *Not For Sale: Feminists Resisting Prostitution and Pornography* (Spinifex, 2004).

Jackie Turner is a lawyer now working as an independent consultant in the fields of human trafficking and violence against women. She has undertaken research and consultancy, nationally and internationally, on behalf of the European Women's Lobby, the European Commission and the Council of Europe. She has taught at the International Institute of Higher Studies in Criminal Sciences in Siracusa, Italy, and is currently undertaking doctoral research on human trafficking at the Child and Woman Abuse Studies Unit, London Metropolitan University, UK.

Dr Meagan Tyler is lecturer in the School of Social Sciences and Psychology at Victoria University, Australia. Her research on prostitution, pornography and sex therapy has been published in *Women's Studies International Forum* and *Women and Therapy* as well as the edited collections *Everyday Pornography* (Routledge, 2010) and *Big Porn Inc.* (Spinifex, 2011). Her first book: *Selling Sex Short: The Pornographic and Sexological Construction of Women's Sexuality* was released in 2011 (published by Cambridge Scholars).

Josephine Wakeling is a UK practitioner who has worked alongside women affected by prostitution/trafficking for 16 years. She is currently a consultant/ trainer to NGOs and projects delivering support services both in the UK and internationally. Josephine is also studying for an MA in Woman and Child Abuse at London Metropolitan University.

Acknowledgements

Many women have provided much valued support, inspiration, advice and challenging questions as the thinking that informed this collection developed, including Maggie O'Neill, Liz Kelly, Miranda Horvath, Linda Regan, Heather Cole, Nicole Westmarland, Jenny Pearce, Natalia Dawkins, Marai Larasi, Julie Bindel, Holly Dustin, all the women from the SAFE project, CWASU students, and many more in policy and practice networks. The images reproduced in Chapter 6 would not have been possible without the women and girls who shared their experiences in the arts workshops and interviews, the skills and empathy of Kate Green, and support from Walsall Youth Arts. I would also like to thank all the contributors for their enthusiastic and patient engagement, the team at Ashgate Publishing for their commitment and support, and finally Peter for unwavering love, especially during the final stages of bringing this together.

Introduction:
Prostitution, Harm and Gender Inequality

Maddy Coy

This collection brings together theoretical, research and policy perspectives that explore harms of prostitution as a practice of gender inequality. While there is an often disguised consensus across different positions that prostitution is a 'conducive context' (Kelly 2007) for violence, questions about long-term visions and approaches revolve around whether prostitution is itself harmful. Emergent awareness of trafficking of women and children for sexual exploitation, and urgency to formulate law and policy interventions, have thrown these 'fault lines' of debate into the spotlight (Miriam 2005: 1; Kelly 2003). There are at least two contested layers here: the first relates to the question of whether prostitution itself is harmful for the bodily integrity and autonomy of women who sell sex, or harms are created by the conditions in which prostitution operates. For many, including contributors here, there is no simple dichotomy, no either/or, rather it is a both/and; criminalization and stigmatization of women involved in prostitution intensifies harm and discrimination. The second layer of contestation is about what it means for women's bodies to be commodified in order to serve men's sexual desires, and thus to what extent the existence of prostitution is an obstacle to gender equality. Both layers are addressed throughout chapters in this collection.

There is, however, no single critique of prostitution. Just as there is a range of perspectives and voices within a framing of prostitution as work, there are more nuanced questions and explorations at stake than the term 'oppression paradigm' (Weitzer 2009) allows for. Not least, reactionary right-wing moral discourses are all too often conflated with critical feminist analyses. This collection offers space for progressive perspectives grounded in analyses of gendered power inequalities. Linked through this overarching lens, there are, however, differing vantage points among the authors. As Karen Boyle (2010: 5) has noted with respect to feminist critiques of pornography, to share a value position, or make contributions that are relevant to one, is not to follow a 'party line'. The platform for differing voices offered by *Prostitution, Harm and Gender Inequality* is similarly recognition that it is 'important to give visibility to the possibility of resistance' (Boyle 2010: 5).

The term 'prostitution' here refers to the activities that comprise the majority of commercial sex: 'heterosexual sexual exchanges, with men buying the sexual services of women, within a set of social relations implying unequal power relationships between the two sexes' (Outshoorn 2004a: 3). For the most part, analysis of prostitution in this collection centres on 'sexual services' in terms of physical sexual activities – the purchase of access to women's bodies – although some contributors, particularly Marjut Jyrkinen in her opening chapter, take a wider view of the sex industry.

Theorizing and researching prostitution is complex since practices differ according to local contours. Rapidly evolving technological advances and ways in which sexual consumerism is increasingly knitted into mainstream capitalism are also transforming the organization of prostitution (Campbell and O'Neill 2006; Hearn 2006; Jeffreys 2009; Jyrkinen: Chapter 1). Such is the potential for variation in the ways that sex markets are constituted and collide with individual circumstance that routes into, and experiences of, prostitution are multi-faceted. What connects these 'glocalized' individual experiences is a primarily gendered pattern; it is 'with few exceptions ... a market for men' (O'Neill 2001: 155). Joyce Outshoorn's definition thus illuminates two issues at the core of this collection: that most prostitution is markedly gendered, and that it occurs within a context of material inequalities between women and men. These inequalities, present across the globe even in contexts where aspects of formal equality have been achieved, include men's greater economic capital, disproportionate share of political decision-making, and violence against women and girls that occurs across and in all communities (Walby 2011). Holding gendered inequalities in plain sight, as Liz Kelly (2003) has pointed out, orientates analytic attention to a continuum across which women are coerced and pressured into prostitution, and denied meaningful alternatives to capitalizing on use of the body as economic resource.

Evident in much discourse on prostitution, however, is a focus on women's individualized agency and decision-making, which Melissa Farley (2003)[1] has argued serves to invisibilize harm at individual and social levels. Angela McRobbie (2009) suggests this focus on individual choices reflects negativity about radical perspectives that are 'concerned with social criticism rather than with progress of improvement in the position of women in an otherwise more or less unaltered social order' (p. 14; see also Miriam 2005). Again, with respect to prostitution, it is possible to aim for both/and, rather than either/or. Decriminalization of the sale of sex and specialized support services are essential to redress gender inequality in legislative and policy frameworks and address women's safety. Building pragmatic alliances over these vitally important issues (O'Neill 2008) need not detract from belief in the possibility of 'an alternative world' (McRobbie 2009: 49; O'Neill 2008): a social order that is altered in the sense that it is without prostitution. This message continues in many local, national and transnational campaigning and activism networks (Miriam 2005), including those established by survivors of prostitution. In 2011, the European Women's Lobby launched a 'Together for a

---

1   See also www.prostitutionresearch.com, the website for Prostitution Research and Education, a nonprofit organization established by Melissa Farley to conduct research and provide training and consultancy on prostitution, pornography and trafficking.

Europe free from Prostitution' campaign (EWL 2011). Tackling men's demand is a key plank of this value position as a means to transform social (gender) orders.

Yet within academia, US philosopher Kathy Miriam (2005) has argued that radical feminist perspectives which imagine an alternative world without prostitution are marginalized, perhaps chiming with what Sylvia Walby (2011) identifies as a 'neoliberal turn' in the academy – 'a shift in intellectual enquiry about systems of power to that of agency ... [which] functions in practice towards deflecting analytic interest away from the powerful and from systems of power' (p. 23). Thus one intention throughout this collection is to re-engage an 'analytic gaze' (ibid) on systemic gendered power inequalities with respect to prostitution. Through this analytic gaze, aspects that are critically explored include: the organization of globalized sex industries and connections across sectors (Marjut Jyrkinen); trafficking as a means of delivering women into sex industries, and human rights responses (Jody Raphael and Jackie Turner's chapters); how agency has become a dominant lens for theorizing prostitution (Sheila Jeffreys); the 'sex of prostitution' (Meagan Tyler), and harmful impacts for body and self experienced by women involved in prostitution (Maddy Coy); male entitlement to women's bodies and intersections with sexual consumerism in accounts of men who pay for sex (in the chapter by Coy, Horvath and Kelly); what have been termed 'prostitution policy regimes' (Kelly, Coy and Davenport 2009) in Australia and Sweden (Mary Sullivan and Josefina Erikson, respectively); and finally sexual consumerism as an increasingly globalized socio-cultural motif, where commercial sexual practices are repackaged as leisure and entertainment (in Coy, Wakeling and Garner's chapter).

While seeking to offer space for these multiple perspectives connected by a focus on unequal gender orders (Connell 1987, 2009), the collection does not comprehensively address inequalities linked to social locations. Gender is influenced and transformed as it intersects with race, ethnicity, class, age (Crenshaw 1991). Studies indicate that women who are most marginalized in social hierarchies are over-represented in prostitution, particularly on the street – a context acknowledged to be the most dangerous and harmful (e.g. Farley et al. 2005; Kramer and Berg 2003; Nelson 1993). Unequal distributions of social and economic capital, and sexualized and racialized stereotypes in the eroticization of 'otherness' are factors that narrow women's 'space for action' (Kelly 2003). Yet how prostitution is constructed by, and flourishes within, intersections of gender with other dimensions of inequality is currently under-theorized and under-explored (Valandra 2007), and filling these gaps and silences is a critical task for future research.

Before introducing the content of the book in more detail, I elaborate on the theme of prostitution as an obstacle to gender equality, and suggest it is possible to conceptualize prostitution as a gender regime,[2] using the work of Raewyn Connell

---

2   I am grateful for discussions with Liz Kelly during which this framing was refined.

(1987, 2009), and with potential to connect with Kimberle Crenshaw's (1991) concept of intersectionality.

Prostitution as an Intersectional Gender Regime:
Individual and Systemic Harms

Many, from varying approaches, have sought to explore tensions of accounting for individual capacity to act while recognizing contexts of gender inequality; between a 'critical respect' (Gill 2007) for women's decisions while interrogating the conditions in which such decisions are made (e.g. Brison 2006; Jeffreys: Chapter 4; Miriam 2005; Matthews 2008; Munro and Della Giusta 2008; O'Connell Davidson 1998; O'Neill 2001, 2008; Phoenix 1999; Westmarland and Gangoli 2006). Here, I draw on Connell's (1987, 2009) model of gender orders, gender regimes and gender relations as a conceptual framework to also explore this complexity, and propose that prostitution can be framed as a glocalized gender regime, where intersections of race/ethnicity, class/caste and age are also crucial to applying the concept to particular places in and over time.

'Gender orders' are overarching hierarchical social arrangements and patterns. A gender regime, for Connell (1987, 2009),[3] is the organization of gender within social institutions; commonly cited examples are families, schools, the military. Both are formed by, and form, 'gender relations'; ways in which individuals interact with each other, which are 'always being made and re-made in everyday life' (Connell 2009: 73). Gender regimes and gender relations may therefore be harmonized, or not, with gender orders; the latter are not conceived as necessarily determinants (Connell 2009). With respect to prostitution, the contention is here that if framed as a gender regime, it reflects and reproduces unequal gender orders even though there may be variation at the level of everyday gender relations between women who sell, and men who buy, sex.

In Connell's formulation (2005, 2009), gender as social structure falls into four interlinked categories. The first is production and consumption, including how certain occupations are segregated on gender lines. The second category is power, where use of control and coercion follows a gendered pattern. Third are emotional and human relationships, and Connell specifies sexuality and Arlie Hochschild's (1983) concept of 'emotional labour' as core components. The fourth dimension is symbolic, comprising cultural meanings attached to gender. Following Connell's (2005) suggestion that this 'fourfold model provides a template for analyzing any gender regime' (p. 7), how might it apply to prostitution? Social and historical data are key to understanding how variation in contexts will make some elements more or less relevant. Connell consistently emphasizes that gender orders, regimes and

---

3   Sylvia Walby has also developed the concept of a gender regime in her extensive theorizing on gender, and uses it in a similar way to Connell's gender order (see Walby 2011).

relations can and do change. Yet given the extensive and rich knowledge base on prostitution, a 'structural inventory' of prostitution as a gender regime (Connell 1987: 99) can be undertaken using these four fundamental contours, whilst mindful that deeper analysis would be needed to address specific contexts.

A gendered division of labour is perhaps the most straightforward, since prostitution disproportionately involves men buying access to women's bodies. Power is the most contested, and here refers first to prostitution 'as an institution which allows certain powers of command over one person's body to be exercised by another' (O'Connell Davidson 1998: 9). This raises questions about how such a power of command creates a 'conducive context' (Kelly 2007) for violence, and may undermine women's bodily integrity and autonomy. Power also operates in the form of structural inequalities heightened by globalization which deny sustainable livelihoods to most of the world's women, making prostitution a strategy for economic survival and/or independence. Emotional dimensions of prostitution as a gender regime are evident in the emotional labour required of women to fulfil men's requests (including performance of femininity), minimization of self and potential disruption to relationships with the body. Normative constructions of masculinity which reproduce notions of men's biological need to sex in/on a woman's body are also relevant here. Constructions of sexuality are therefore crucial, insofar as prostitution can be viewed as an institution that primarily relies on, and reproduces, heteronormativity (see Turner: Chapter 2). Finally, at a symbolic level, 'othering' and stigmatization of women in prostitution persists. Gendered meanings attached to women who sell sex are reflected in derogatory language and practices of social marginalization. These are possible starting points for conceptualizing prostitution as a gender regime. Each dimension is integrally linked to each other (Connell 2009); a gendered division of labour requires women's emotional labour; how power operates in male entitlement to women's bodies is connected to heteronormative constructions of sexuality and masculinity; these constructions are related to symbolic and material practices of othering. Intersections with race/ethnicity, class/caste, and context/setting will inflect each dimension, and the ways in which prostitution as a gender regime is constituted and experienced across space and time.

If, however, analysis of prostitution remains at the level of everyday gender relations between women and men, the kaleidoscope of interactions can be shaken to fall in a range of combinations. Within these, individual capacity for decision-making will be present to different degrees for some women (although not all), as will the extent to which selling sex is experienced in terms of personal power, but the organization of prostitution and its location within unequal gender orders, as a gender regime, will continue to be opaque. When analysed in this way the harms of prostitution are both individual and systemic: prostitution as a gender regime reproduces gender as a hierarchy (Connell 1987, 2009; Jackson 2006), and thus undermines movements towards gender equality. This framing underpins *Prostitution, Harm and Gender Inequality*.

Content of the Book

Chapters offer multiple starting points into theory, research and policy approaches that explore prostitution as a practice of gender inequality and/or seek to illustrate its harms. The voices of contributors, and thus the language and terms they use, varies. None, however, opts to use the term *sex work*, as this framing 'de-genders and de-sexualizes the issue' (Outshoorn 2004b: 190), and contributors aim to focus attention on gendered and sexualized inequalities. In addition, many are particularly mindful of Johanna Niemi's (2010) observation that the language of markets normalizes 'unequal and commercialized sexual practices' (Walby 2011: 115), which are antithetical to feminist commitments to 'mutualism and equality' (ibid: 21), instead reflecting neoliberal economics and politics which reproduce, and in the eyes of some, deepen inequalities.

Marjut Jyrkinen's opening chapter explores the organization and mainstreaming of sex industry with reference to globalization, which she refers to as 'McSexualization'. She outlines links between sectors of the sex industry and discusses the gendered commercialization of bodies and sexualities, before turning to the concept of McSexualization and how it extends George Ritzer's (1993) 'McDonaldization' to understand the sex industry in terms of his four key elements: control; efficiency; calculability and predictability. Concluding that while the sex trade functions in many ways on the rationalization model of contemporary businesses, there is much 'irrationality' for gender equality and the lives of women and girls, Marjut introduces key themes that are developed by subsequent contributors: globalized patterns of men buying access to women's bodies; implications of expanding sex industries, including links with trafficking and the normalization of sexual consumerism; the necessity for critical examination of policy approaches.

Chapter 2, by Jackie Turner, challenges the argument that prostitution and trafficking for the purposes of sexual exploitation are separate issues, and critiques international human rights approaches which have focused on addressing only the 'means of delivery' (trafficking) rather than the sex industries into which women are delivered. She begins with locating trafficking conceptually on a continuum of harms and violences (extending Kelly 1988) along with migration and smuggling. Underpinning this chapter is the argument that contemporary discourses on trafficking, including migration and crime control, fail to adequately acknowledge unequal gender orders that form conducive contexts for prostitution and trafficking, domestically and internationally. Whilst recognizing that human rights approaches have some potential, Jackie proposes that until they, too, adequately acknowledge and address the reality of unequal gender orders and, within them, systems of prostitution, efforts to strengthen gender equality, and to combat gender-based violence and trafficking will remain 'long on rhetoric but short on decisive action'.

Jody Raphael's chapter also focuses on trafficking but with a view to extending understandings of it to encompass movement within domestic borders.

She draws on three strands of empirical research on how young women are recruited into prostitution in the US. From research with 71 young women who were recruited into prostitution, and five men who identified as ex-pimps, she documents coercive recruitment processes and ongoing violences that are used as means to exploit young women for profit. Data from 113 men who paid for sex in Chicago (Durchslag and Goswami 2008) is also included to illustrate the extent to which they also viewed women as commodities. Jody's analysis rests on two key points: that domestic trafficking in the form of coercive recruitment is often obscured by discourses of choice and the focus on transnational trafficking; and that interventions with young women, and indeed with coercers, will be ineffective where demand for prostitution is not also tackled.

Developing these themes theoretically, in Chapter 4 Sheila Jeffreys focuses on the origins, use and meanings of concepts of agency and choice and their limitations for theorizing women's involvement in prostitution. She unravels how notions of agency have been developed in different disciplines, then defined and applied to women's decision making processes with respect to prostitution. The consequences of this focus on agency are that structural gender inequalities are made invisible, and men's demand for women in prostitution is accepted as inevitable. Sheila sets out a challenge for these aspects to be made the subject of analytic gaze.

Chapter 5 by Meagan Tyler blends research on harms experienced by women in prostitution with radical feminist theory to present and develop the concept of the 'sex of prostitution'. She outlines four interlinked characteristics of the sex of prostitution: the requirement to sexually service the desires of another, typically women in the service of men; gendered power inequalities that enable this to be conceived of, and commercialized; objectification/derivatization (drawing on Cahill 2011), where the self is subordinated to accommodate the fantasies/desires of sex buyers; and finally, demands for women to perform enjoyment. Meagan concludes that a focus on prostitution as economic exploitation has obscured this harmful model of sex that lies at its heart.

In Chapter 6, my research explores how prostitution disrupts women's relationship with their bodies. This chapter presents key themes from life story interviews with a small sample of women in prostitution and digital arts images created in arts workshops with women on the theme of '*MyBody MySelf*', using a methodology developed by Maggie O'Neill (2001, 2002 et al., 2008, 2010) to represent women's lived experience. Women's verbal and visual accounts demonstrate challenges of retaining a sense of belonging in the body and autonomy over its boundaries. For some, this originated in templates of disembodiment from earlier sexual abuse, yet for most women who participated, prostitution also led to disconnection from an embodied sense of self. Participatory arts offered a space to explore harmful impacts with women as well as practices of coping, resistance and survival.

Chapter 7 moves attention onto men who pay for sex. Adding to the growing knowledge base on demand, I, with my colleagues Miranda Horvath and Liz Kelly, draw on a large UK survey we conducted that explored men's motivations and decision-making processes. The key themes of 'confessing', 'consuming' and 'boasting' that emerged from the data are discussed, along with the unexpected finding that some men are uncomfortable and unfulfilled. While a common theme was viewing paying for sex as a form of sexual consumerism, expressions of ambivalence, guilt and shame led us to suggest that one way to reduce demand is to engage with men about their own unease. We conclude that men's accounts reveal a complex picture of how male entitlement to women's bodies for sexual release is constructed and drawn on by men who buy sex.

In Chapter 8, Mary Lucille Sullivan turns to policy approaches and impacts of legalizing/decriminalizing prostitution in some states of Australia. She uses the state of Victoria as a case study, with reference to others, and raises questions about how successful the aims and objectives of such legislative models have been. Mary updates her argument that legalization has primarily benefitted sex buyers and prostitution business owners, and contends that legalization/decriminalization endorses the commodification of women and girls bodies to serve men's demand, with implications for the civil status of all women. She also explores the limitations of improvements in safety for women in prostitution by noting that these benefits appear to be present only in legal/regulated settings, which comprise a minority of prostitution businesses since illegal sectors have flourished. Notions of safety also have deeper meanings and implications from Mary's perspective, where prostitution itself is viewed as a form of violence against women.

Chapter 9 takes a different approach to policy responses, as Josefina Erikson explores the path to Sweden becoming, in 1998, the first country in the world to prohibit the purchase of sexual services on the grounds that prostitution is incompatible with gender equality. Using a dynamic frame analysis, she traces how prostitution was problematized as a social and criminal issue, the nuances between these frames and the critical junctures where directions for policy were cemented. Throughout this policy trajectory, concern about the gendered dimensions and connections to wider inequalities was more or less visible. This chapter provides a detailed analysis of how social and criminal framings of prostitution influenced law and policy formulation. With a concluding section on findings from the 2010 Swedish government inquiry into the impact of the law and contemporary debates, Josefina notes that struggles for meanings of prostitution continue.

The final chapter reprints an article I co-authored with Josephine Wakeling and Maria Garner (published in *Women's Studies International Forum*, 2011). Here we analyse representations of prostitution in contemporary Western sexualized popular culture, and suggest that many constitute a form of what philosopher Pierre Bourdieu (1990) refers to as 'symbolic violence', concealing (misrecognizing) gendered power relations. This chapter contrasts the glamorization of prostitution with empirical realities that include violences and psychosocial harms. The mainstreaming of pimp and ho chic in popular culture provides an example of how prostitution has become normalized as a cultural motif and marketing device, while its existence as cause and consequence of gender inequality is unchallenged.

References

Bourdieu, P. (1990) *The Logic of Practice.* Cambridge: Polity Press.

Boyle, K. (2010) 'Introduction: Everyday Pornography' in Boyle, K. (ed.) *Everyday Pornography.* London: Routledge.

Brison, S.J. (2006) 'Contentious Freedom: Sex Work and Social Construction'. *Hypatia* 21(4): 192–200.

Cahill, A. (2011) *Overcoming Objectification: A Carnal Ethics.* New York: Routledge.

Campbell, R. and O'Neill, M. (2006) 'Introduction' in R. Campbell and M. O'Neill (eds), *Sex Work Now.* Cullompton: Willan.

Connell, R.W. (1987) *Gender and Power: Society, the Person, and Sexual Politics.* Cambridge: Polity Press.

Connell, R.W. (2005) 'Advancing Gender Reform in Largescale Organizations: A New Approach for Practitioners and Researchers'. *Policy and Society* 24(4): 5–24.

Connell, R.W. (2009) *Gender.* Cambridge: Polity Press. 2nd edition.

Crenshaw, K. (1991) 'Mapping the Margins: Intersectionality, Identity Politics, and Violence against Women of Color'. *Stanford Law Review* 43(6): 1241–99.

European Women's Lobby (2011) *EWL Campaigns: Together for a Europe Free from Prostitution.* Available at: http://www.womenlobby.org/spip.php?rubrique187 [accessed: 5 July 2011].

Farley, M. (2003) 'Prostitution and the Invisibility of Harm'. *Women & Therapy* 26(3/4): 247–80.

Farley, M., Lynne, J. and Cotton, A. (2005) 'Prostitution in Vancouver: Violence and the Colonization of First Nations Women'. *Transcultural Psychiatry* 42(2): 242–71.

Gill, R. (2007) 'Critical Respect: Dilemmas of Choice and Agency in Feminism (A Response to Duits and Van Zoonen)'. *European Journal of Women's Studies* 14(1): 69–80.

Durchslag, R. and Goswami, S. (2008) *Deconstructing the Demand for Prostitution: Preliminary Insights with Chicago Men who Purchase Sex.* Chicago Alliance Against Sexual Exploitation.

Hearn, J. (2006) 'The Implications of Information and Communication Technologies for Sexualities and Sexualised Violences: Contradictions of Sexual Citizenship'. *Political Geography* 25(8): 944–63.

Hochschild, A. (1983) *The Managed Heart: The Commercialization of Human Feeling.* Berkeley: University of California Press.

Jackson, S. (2006) 'Interchanges: Gender, Sexuality and Heterosexuality: The Complexity (and Limits) of Heteronormativity'. *Feminist Theory* 7(1): 105–21.

Jeffreys, S. (1997) *The Idea of Prostitution.* Melbourne: Spinifex Press.

Jeffreys, S. (2009) *The Industrial Vagina: The Political Economy of the Global Sex Trade.* London: Routledge.

Kelly, L. (1988) *Surviving Sexual Violence.* Cambridge: Polity Press.

Kelly, L. (2003) 'The Wrong Debate: Reflections on Why Force is Not the Key Issue with Respect to Trafficking in Women for Sexual Exploitation'. *Feminist Review* 73: 139–44.

Kelly, L. (2007) 'A Conducive Context: Trafficking of Persons in Central Asia' in M. Lee (ed.), *Human Trafficking.* Cullompton: Willan.

Kelly, L., Coy, M. and Davenport, R. (2009) *Shifting Sands: A Comparison of Prostitution Regimes across Nine Countries.* London: CWASU.

Kramer, L. and Berg, E. (2003) 'A Survival Analysis of Timing of Entry into Prostitution: The Differential Impact of Race, Educational Level, and Childhood/Adolescent Risk Factors'. *Sociological Inquiry* 73(4): 511–28.

Matthews, R. (2008) *Prostitution, Politics and Policy.* Oxon: Routledge-Cavendish.

McRobbie, A. (2009) *The Aftermath of Feminism: Gender, Culture and Social Change.* London: Sage.

Miriam, K. (2005) 'Stopping the Traffic in Women: Power, Agency and Abolition in Feminist Debates over Sex-Trafficking'. *Journal of Social Philosophy* 36(1): 1–17.

Munro, V. and Della Giusta, M. (2008) 'The Regulation of Prostitution: Contemporary Contexts and Comparative Perspectives' in V. Munro and M. Della Giusta (eds), *Demanding Sex: Critical Reflections on the Regulation of Prostitution.* Aldershot: Ashgate.

Nelson, V. (1993) 'Prostitution: Where Racism and Sexism Intersect'. *Michigan Journal of Gender and Law* (1): 81–9.

Niemi, J. (2010) 'What We Talk About When We Talk About Buying Sex'. *Violence Against Women* 16(2): 159–72.

O'Connell Davidson, J. (1998) *Prostitution, Power and Freedom.* Cambridge: Polity Press.

O'Connell Davidson, J. (2002) 'The Rights and Wrongs of Prostitution'. *Hypatia* 17(2): 84–98.

O'Neill, M. (2001) *Prostitution and Feminism: Towards a Politics of Feeling.* Cambridge: Polity Press.

O'Neill, M. with Giddens, S., Breatnach, P., Bagley, C., Bourne, D. and Judge, T. (2002) 'Renewed Methodologies for Social Research: Ethno-mimesis as Performative Praxis'. *The Sociological Review* 50: 69–88.

O'Neill, M. (2008) 'Sex, Violence and Work: Services to Sex Workers and Public Policy Reform' in G. Letherby, K. Williams, P. Birch and M. Cain (eds), *Sex as Crime?* Cullompton: Willan.

O'Neill, M. (2010) *Asylum, Migration and Community.* Bristol: Policy Press.

Outshoorn, J. (2004a) 'Introduction: Prostitution, Women's Movements and Democratic States' in J. Outshoorn (ed.), *The Politics of Prostitution*. Cambridge: Cambridge University Press.

Outshoorn, J. (2004b) 'Voluntary and Forced Prostitution: The 'Realistic Approach' of the Netherlands' in J. Outshoorn (ed.), *The Politics of Prostitution*. Cambridge: Cambridge University Press.

Ritzer, G. (1993) *The McDonaldization of Society*. Thousand Oaks: Pine Forge Press.

Valandra (2007) 'Reclaiming Their Lives and Breaking Free: An Afrocentric Approach to Recovery From Prostitution'. *Affilia* 22(2): 195–208.

Walby, S. (2011) *The Future of Feminism*. Cambridge: Polity Press.

Weitzer, R. (2009) 'Sociology of Sex Work'. *Annual Review of Sociology* 35: 213–34.

Westmarland, N. and Gangoli, G. (2006) 'Introduction: Approaches to Prostitution' in G. Gangoli and N. Westmarland (eds), *International Approaches to Prostitution: Law and Policy in Europe and Asia*. Bristol: Policy Press.

Chapter 1

McSexualization of Bodies, Sex and Sexualities: Mainstreaming the Commodification of Gendered Inequalities

Marjut Jyrkinen

This chapter explores how the commercialization of bodies, sex and sexualities that is widely present in late modern societies interlinks with the sex trade. I discuss how sex industries relate to the current consumption culture of everyday life, including work life. I address here the wide range of activities within the sex trade, and people, groups and organizations involved directly and/or indirectly in such businesses, with or without their own willingness to do so. I develop the concept of McSexualization to discuss the 'relational rationality' in the industrialized and globalized sex markets and the impact of these developments.

The sex trade, embodied in the international sex industry, is a phenomenon present in multifaceted forms in nearly all parts of the world (Jeffreys 2009a, 2009b). By the 'sex trade' I refer to economic transactions where people's bodies and sexualities are offered for sale, and are sold, bought or delivered further and (ab)used in the name of clients' sexual wishes and desires (Hearn and Jyrkinen 2000; Jyrkinen 2005). The generic term sex trade includes many forms of sex businesses; some forms are criminalized in most countries (e.g. abuse of children in prostitution), and others are under constant debate (e.g. 'adult' pornography and prostitution) in many parts of the world. There are obviously many different kinds and levels of actors in sex markets, from individual sellers of sex to international listed companies. However, commercialization of the body and desire is the basis for the functioning of local and international sex markets, which are significantly gendered: the bodies which are offered for sale are mainly women's and children's, and the buyers and consumers of commercialized sex and sexualities are mostly men – local men as well as international travellers, military men and businessmen. The sex trade and trading of other assets by sex are not new phenomena, but industrialization, globalization and virtualization of commercial sex have radically changed the situation: multiplied the volume and the forms of commercial sex, and increased the speed of the trade and profits available (for some) in the field (Hughes 2002). Sex markets tend actively and artificially to create new needs in its existing clientele, and also to draw attention of new potential clients to its products and services. At the same time, the sex trade, like other forms of the commercialization of bodies, sex and sexualities, reproduces and (re)constructs sexualities and understandings of gender/sex relationships. The sex trade blurs the limits of acceptable and unacceptable, and the borders of legal and illegal. It also actively reformulates the attitudes in societies and internationally towards deregulation of its actions, away from being illicit towards legal business.

In order to explore the functioning of the sex trade, it is important to open up its global and local linkages, which are manifold, complex and often hidden. These linkages are overlapping and intermingled – connections, alliances and bonds of, and in, the sex trade, which facilitate the functioning and expansion of such trade locally and globally. Thus the linkages of the sex trade fall into, at the minimum, the following four categories: substantive, economic and organizational; temporal, spatial and cultural; technological; and, legislative and policy related linkages. These are central for the functioning of its various businesses: the sex trade needs business, public sector and political contacts, through which lobbying for their interests can take place (see Jeffreys 2009). The embedded complexity and often the illegal or semi-legal nature of sex businesses cover many of these connections and alliances. The sex traders also seek to create a web of linkages with other sex industry enterprises, which are often covert and hidden from the responsible officials. Thus focusing on the linkages of and in the sex trade enables re-evaluation and critical reading of the existing policies on the sex trade, and the sex trade and the new information and communication technologies (ICTs) worldwide.

Exploring the Linkages

The linkages of the sex trade are, firstly, *substantive, economic and organizational.* Many sex(ualized) businesses are connected to each other through the 'substance', namely the bodies, sex and sexualities they sell, market, promote and profit from. Various sub-areas of the sex trade are more or less tightly connected to each other. For instance, pornography uses fantasies of prostitution, and its producers introduce women in pornography into prostitution markets (Barry 1995; Jeffreys 1997). Trafficking in persons delivers (mainly) women into sex markets as prostitutes, who can be introduced to clients as 'erotic dancers' in sex clubs or through escort services' advertisements on the Internet (Group of Specialists 2003). On the other hand, sexualities which are produced in and marketed through pornography, are increasingly spread amongst general public by glorifying 'careers' in the sex trade as glamorous, well-paid and international work opportunities, for instance in and through pornography (Dines 2010). Substantive linkages between forms of sexualized business are crucial for the normalization of prostitution and other forms of the sex trade.

Economic gains of the sex trade concentrate much into large sex enterprises, whether legal and/or illegal and comprise supply of multiple services and products. For example, a producer of *Hustler* in Finland states that 'one cannot survive only with selling porn. Contacts are important. A human being wants to rub elbows with another person', reflecting the interconnectedness of different sectors of sex trade (cited in Hänninen 2010). The same organization can profit from printed and web-based pornography, telephone sex, sex chats, text-television contact advertisements, and sale of sex equipments through the Internet. Illegal sectors, such as trafficking in persons for prostitution, interlink with procuring of prostitution services in sex bars and massage parlours, as well as non-criminalized sectors, for example strip tease shows on stage. Sex businesses need a constant flow of consumers who buy and consume the products and services that are brought into markets, which creates linkages between the non-criminalized and illegal sectors and consumers, even if indirectly so.

Organizational linkages include many areas, such as sports, where organizers of big events encounter questions of how to react on the increase in the sex trade before and during the event. Examples of sports-related increase in sex trade cover for example football World Cups in Germany 2006 and South Africa 2010, and Jyväskylä Rally in Finland 2010. Another area is international conferences and political and business summits crowded with male professionals which have increased significantly the turnover of local sex industries and thereby trafficking in women for prostitution (see Jeffreys 2009a, 2009b).

In short, substantial, economic and organizational linkages of the sex trade enable normalization of sex industries locally and globally. Economic gains as well as losses from the sex trade are reflected in the formal sectors of societies; linkages between formal sector organizations and the sex trade (for instance, official tourist services and sex enterprises[1]) are crucial for survival of and increase in the sex trade. Official sector and legal businesses which benefit from the sex trade through taxation or as 'side-effects' (e.g. boost for other businesses, such as restaurants and hotels because of annual 'sex exhibitions' or well-known sex trade services in bigger cities) tend to keep silent on these linkages. In addition, the same sex enterprise may take care of (open or secret) brothels, run street prostitution rings, and produce and deliver pornography. International sex businesses are often connected to (other) organized crime groups which can facilitate recruitment of new women into prostitution and, at the same time, run other forms of criminality, such as drug trafficking.

Secondly, with the *temporal, spatial and cultural* linkages of the sex trade I refer to the globalizing of the phenomena of commercializing of sex and thereby to the issues of local cultures. In the westernized world, 'Otherness' is interpreted often in a simple and non-questioned way – other cultures are interpreted to be 'lower' than one's own, which in the context of the sex trade means that 'the Others' are eroticized, exoticized and naturalized as available for (ab)use of international sex tourists and travellers. In many developing areas and countries

---

1 General tourist brochures of many bigger cities, available free of charge at the Tourism Information Bureaux, hotels, foreign embassies, bars and restaurants, include advertisements of the sex trade.

in transition the sex trade is fuelled by sex tourism, but also by the presence of foreign military troops. Military rest and recreation (R&R) centres in foreign countries entice prostitution services. In fact, military occupations and bases have often preceded organized sex trade and sex tourism in various parts of the world. This has entrenched prostitution into local cultures in, for example, in Southeast Asia. An earlier example of military and war impacts originates from the Second World War and Japanese invasion to Korea and China, when altogether 200,000 Korean women and girls were recruited and kidnapped to become prostitutes, 'military comfort women' by and for the Japanese Imperial Army[2] (Enloe 1989; 2000; Kazuko 1994; Soh 2001). The military has been and is still tightly linked to various forms of the sex trade. According to Dennis Altman (2001: 109) 'the ready availability of prostitutes has been a major concern of military commanders as a way of both maintaining the morale of their troops and restricting possible homosexuality among their troops'.[3] The linkages of the sex trade and traders with the military are significant, and they extend to international peace-keeping operations (ibid).

Thirdly, *technological* linkages are of outmost importance for the evolvement of the sex trade. As the information and communication technologies are developing, the sex traders are keen to use these new possibilities to progress their businesses. In fact, it could be claimed that the sex trade has been in an innovative side of the ICTs and early adapter of new technology to market current and create new 'services'. Technological linkages of the sex trade involve the use of older versions of technologies with new, multiple and complex technologies. Constantly developing ICTs have several characteristic features: time/space compression, instantaneousness, asynchronicity,[4] (sometimes) affordability, easy access, reproducibility of image production, the creation of virtual bodies, and the blurring of the 'real' and the 'representational' (Hearn and Parkin 2001; Hearn 2006; Hughes 2002).

Fourthly, *legislative and policy* related linkages are crucial for the existence and expansion of the sex trade. Ideological bases of policies regarding sex industries vary from one country and culture to another, which reverberate in legislation and implementation of policies in practice. For example, prostitution

---

2   In addition to Korean women, comfort women originated also from Japan, China, Taiwan, the Philippines, Indonesia, and even the Netherlands. Comfort women were sent to the front lines and military bases in order to 'keep up the fighting spirit' of the solders. Many of these women were killed in the fighting or were massacred by the Japanese army; many killed themselves after returning home because of the harsh memories and shame. Some women had to continue in prostitution in post-war Japan. See Kazuko (1994).

3   For example, the Dutch government provided copies of sex magazines to its peacekeepers in the former Yugoslavia (Altman 2001: 119).

4   Asyncronicity is (here) connected to easy access and anonymity: ICTs offer possibilities to e.g. pre-order prostitute(s) via Internet to be (ab)used when travelling abroad for a holiday or business; catalogues of women are easily available on the web, as well as evaluations of sex services by other buyers.

policies vary from harm reduction policies to elimination of prostitution and policies towards reduction of prostitution and its demand (Kelly et al. 2009). Thus the sex trade operates in many different legislative environments. Its interests are best accomplished in contexts where there is tolerance of rather than bans that restrict sex businesses (Sullivan: Chapter 8; Jeffreys 2009b). Lobbying for decriminalization and/or legalization takes place in many forms and through different channels. Linkages with favourable politicians, officials and NGOs offer routes to impact (in)directly on policy-making processes. Often the agenda is hidden through arguing for human rights, freedom of choice and liberties. This debate is the core of drafting policies nationally as well internationally. Connections between pro-prostitution lobbyists and the sex trade have been acknowledged by NGOs and activists – there are large economic interests concerning legalizing prostitution which would open up sex trade markets in new areas and forms.

Policy related linkages may be built also on more dubious interconnections, such as blackmail of officials who have been involved in the sex trade and who wish to conceal this. The creation of useful, even necessary contacts can take place through 'business and leisure prostitution' (Jeffreys 2010). Thereby shared identity and friendships are built in through male bonding within combined business/policy and sex trade contexts. This can take place through, for example, organizing meeting and post-meetings in sex bars, and offering of prostitution services as bonuses and gifts (Holgersson and Svanström 2004; Jeffreys 2009b; Jeffreys 2010; O'Connell Davidson 1998).

Commercialization of Bodies, Sex and Sexualities

The many levels of linkages of the sex trade, as described above, build up the basis for the global and local forms of sex consumption and profiteering. In most Western(ized) countries, and also increasingly in developing countries, the visual and textual worlds and spaces are organized, structured, restructured and powered by images that are sexualized. Often this happens in a very traditional way: businesses (ab)use in their marketing and advertisement strategies mainly (young) women's sexualized bodies in order to sell various kinds of products and services. In addition to the sale of material and immaterial goods by bodies and sex through the sexualization of women's bodies, this phenomenon is increasingly extending also towards the eroticization of the (young and/or 'fit') male body (see for example, Gill et al. 2003). The capturing of the attention by sexualized bodies is mostly directed towards the male viewer, whether the male gaze is understood to be heteronormative or homoerotic. Women are also targeted increasingly to become consumers of sexualized material as well as paid sex itself (Halmekoski 2002; O'Connell Davidson 1998).

Sex as a Form of Commercial Consuming

In the sale of sex, the body becomes an article of the exchange of (sex) services for (usually) economic compensation, the value of which varies by the place, status of the seller, and content of transactions. Until recently, academic research on buying of sex has been relatively elusive compared to the extent and impacts of the phenomenon globally. What is clearly known is that consuming sex is heavily gendered: most clients of prostitution, globally and locally, are men (Coy, Horvath and Kelly: Chapter 7; Kleiber and Velten 1994; Månsson 1996, 2001; Monto 2002, 2004; O'Connell Davidson 1998, 2001; Sandell et al. 1996). Consuming sex and sexual services seem to accumulate, and according to a survey in Finland, those men who, for example, consume sex magazines also seem to consume other sexual products, such as sex videos (Lammi-Taskula 1999).

Commercialization of sex can be looked at from the perspective of a sovereign (sex) consumer with his (her) individual needs: the needs are 'there', and because the consumers express their desire to consume (on) sex, the markets are ready to fulfil this wish (see Coy et al.: Chapter 7). The understanding that people have sexual 'needs' rather than wants or desires and that human sexual behaviour is formed by biologically based sexual appetites or drives is predominant in many Western societies and underpins many defences of commercial sex. Uncontrollable needs refer mainly to 'male' sexuality, which is underestimation of men as sex/ gender and their wants and wishes. Sexual needs are not exactly comparable to needs such as hunger – people do not die from the lack of sex as they do because of malnutrition and famine[5] (O'Connell Davidson 2001). Libertarian consumption culture is clearly represented in and through the sex trade, based on the 'right' to maximize individual sexual pleasure. A more complex issue is to address the origin of men's sexual 'needs', which appear to be his own, but as this chapter will go on to demonstrate, are built on the marketing and advertising campaigns of the sex trade.

The understanding that the buyers of sex are somehow deviant, 'other' than normal people is a popular common-sense notion. On the contrary, in general sex buyers do not differ from non-clients on their socio-economic status (Coy et al.: Chapter 7; Hanmer 2000; Lammi-Taskula 1999; Sandell et al. 1996). Many buyers do not limit their sex consuming only to the local sphere, but instead reach out for (sex) destinations far away from home in order to avoid 'getting caught', but also in order to fulfil their racialized and sexualized fantasies which construct the Other (Mullings 2000; O'Connell Davidson 1998, 2001).

In addition to many forms of sex consumerism by individuals in their home countries or abroad, there are other, more organized forms of consumption including

5   It could be argued, using a restricted understanding of sexuality, that one of the most 'sexually unsatisfied' part of the population would be older women (rather than male sex clients), whose spouses have often died earlier. However, elderly women are not often seen in the barricades in order to promote the sex trade.

the involvement of business organizations that can function between (some) men in management and high positions as part of homosociality or 'male bonding'.

Profiting from the Commercialization of Bodies, Sex and Sexualities

The sex trade is estimated to be a third rapidly expanding grey zone[6] business area in the world, after the illegal drug and weapon sales. Compared to the fast food industries, the mode of organizing the monetary flows is quite similar: the amount of money which is gained from the selling of products and services, accumulates mainly to the owners, and the actual workers gain a very small share of the profit (Banerjee and Linstead 2001; Hughes 2002).

There are many kinds of direct and indirect profiteers of the sex trade (see Table 1.1). Direct profiteers consist of those who gain economically from sex businesses, and who themselves either offer sex services (sellers) or own or run sex business organizations (intermediaries). However, not all sellers of sex gain economically – for instance, in the case of trafficking or debt-bondage, where the economic gains are directed to the organizers. Indirect profiteers cover a large group of business organizations and individuals who vicariously earn from the sex trade. The profits can be in the form of tips (information delivery for access to sex trade services, e.g. doormen, bar personnel, taxi drivers), paid services for travels and accommodation in sex trade destinations (hotels, airlines), advertising costs (media), profits from medical treatments or services (clinics, NGOs), profits through payment systems (banks, credit card companies), and taxation (national economies). The biggest profits, both direct and indirect, are therefore gained by large sex business companies and illegal organizations. Thus the substantial, economic and organizational linkages underpin the successes of the sex trade, often interpreted as freedom of speech and liberty.

In order that the gains from the sex trade are guaranteed for the profiteers, there are at least four essential elements; 'products', clients, effective marketing, and normalization of sex businesses. In this sense, the sex trade functions as any other branch of business, even though it is obvious that there are differences: the 'products' or 'assets' are human beings, whose bodies and sexualities are sold and (ab)used. To attract clients, there is a need for marketing and advertising. Organized marketing takes many forms which are used also in non-sex trade businesses. An important part of marketing is informal knowledge sharing, for instance, about access to brothels or choice of 'best' sex bars; between clients and informants that can indirectly profit. ICTs have radically changed advertising of the sex trade, which can currently reach nearly unlimited publics on the web, and offer possibilities for targeted advertising directed to specific audiences. Traditional marketing channels of the sex trade, such as sex magazines and advertisements in

---

6   This refers to areas of business activities where legislation, rules or regulations are unclear or not followed, and/or where omissions in legislation and its implementation are purposefully abused.

media and public spaces (e.g. leaflets on notice boards, telephone boxes and car parks) co-exist with the ICT-related marketing channels.

Successful and profitable running of sex businesses require that the sex trade is accepted as much as possible as a normal business. Processes of the normalization of the sex trade are linked with other forms of the commercialization of bodies and sex(ualities), which facilitate sex businesses to become inextricable phenomena in late modern life (Barry 1995). Table 1.1 presents the stakeholders of the sex trade, i.e. the persons, groups, organizations, and in the longer run, the system(s) and/or institutions which affect or can be affected by the actions of the sex trade.

Table 1.1   Stakeholders of the sex trade

Sellers	Women, girls (and to a lesser degree men/boys, transgender and transsexuals) in prostitution and pornography, indoor and outdoor, including mail order brides, escorts.
Buyers	Men (and to a lesser degree women) singly or in groups; nationals, (locals), foreigners; travellers, tourists, businessmen, military men.
Inter-mediaries	Pimps, pornographers, 'producers', sex club and brothel owners, traffickers.
Indirect profiteers	Travel agencies, airlines, hotels, motels, restaurants and doormen, taxi drivers and companies; media (including newspapers and television companies); Internet providers; banks and credit card companies; national economies.
Bystanders (knowing and unknowing)	Children, partners and spouses of sellers and buyers of sex; people living in nearby prostitution/sex trade milieu or districts.
Policy agents	Local, regional and national governments, NGOs and INGOs.

In addition to those who are directly involved in the sex trade, i.e. sellers and buyers of sex or other sex services or direct profiteers (intermediaries), there is a large group of people who cannot necessarily avoid encounters with the sex trade, such as family members and those living in or nearby the red lights districts. In addition to these levels of stakeholders, there are many policy agents, such as ministries, parliaments, non-profit organizations and co- and self-regulating bodies of the sex trade, which have an important role in defining the limits for its functioning. The policy-making is under constant change, not least because of active lobbying by direct actors and profiteers of the sex trade.

Consumer Sovereignty, Needs and Consuming Sex

The consumption of paid sex services fulfils an idealized ideology of freedom of and through consumption, and thereby the need and argumentation for the commercialization of bodies, sex and sexualities that I will discuss in the next section using the concept of McSexualization. The current 'eroticized' consumption culture is difficult to avoid: the cultural patterns of consumerism developed in the middle of twentieth century in Western countries have been distributed nearly all over the world. Consumption is also symbolic, it 'becomes the main form of self-expression and the chief source of identity'; not only *material* but also *non-material* items, are consumed and commodified (Waters 1995: 140, emphasis original). Material and non-material consumerism as a part of everyday life is reflected in the consumption of commercial sex: material products (for example, pornographic magazines or videos) have been followed by the exchange of non-material and virtual forms of services (such as 'sexy' voices on the telephone line; interactive live-sex show on the Internet).

Table 1.2 gives examples of forms of sex commodities. Commodification of sex includes marketing of an enormous variety of 'body/sex products' which are offered for sale/purchase. For example, the client can define criteria for the purchase, and choose his consumable 'object', on the basis of the skin or hair colour or of the age of the prostitute from a catalogue or from the stage in a sex club. After the sex trip, the sex client can and often will exchange his experiences with other sex (ab)users, such as of functioning of 'teenage sex niche' in a chat group on the Internet. The sex client can build up a bond with other buyers through websites and Internet forums. The regulating bodies and policy-makers often lag far behind the newest innovations and applications, for instance, through ICTs.

Table 1.2   Examples of trade commodities and sex trade services

Physical contact: touching; masturbation; intercourse (vaginal, anal, oral); etc.	Prostitution, 'intimate massage', lap-dancing, private strip-tease, S/M services.
Voice: speech, sounds.	Telephone sex (live or recorded).
Visual: published images; live; visual recordings.	Pornography, catalogues of women, strip tease shows, peep shows, sex videos, DVDs, films, CD-roms, television shots/ads.
Writing: print media.	Sex magazine texts, sex advertisements, catalogues.
Virtual: Internet browsers (for example, through PC-keyboard); television; mobile telephone.	Interactive striptease and sex shows on the Internet, interactive PC-games, chats (blogs and posts by buyers and sellers of sex).

The borders between these categories presented in Table 1.2 are blurred, and, for example, the virtual commercial sex encounters can include writing (emails or chatting), visual forms of consumption of sex (pornography browsing, downloading and use), interaction by talking as well as meeting with a seller of sex and physical contact. Pornographic magazines include visual and written forms of sex descriptions and advertisements, and sometimes enclose a pornographic DVD as a free gift. 'Sex exhibitions' which have become widely spread in major cities include a substantial variety of sex products and services, and function as normalizers of the trade.

The basis for the globalizing consumption culture is in the liberal assumption of unlimited, privatized 'right' to consume (Waters 1995). In this sense, late modern consumption reflects hedonistic and narcissistic values. 'I shop, therefore I am', or, 'I consume, therefore I am', describe the newest version of the Cartesian understanding of existence, which dominates the Western world and increasingly also other parts of the globe (see Edwards 2000; Slater 1997). Critics of liberal and hedonistic reasoning for unlimited and increasing needs of consumption point out that the consuming culture is also reproducing and artificially creating 'needs', and accordingly, consumption is to be interpreted only as an image of freedom. Therefore, advertising and marketing reaches the potential consumers who deliberately or unconsciously response (only) to the stimulus. The 'rational' consumer aims for maximum results and enjoyment with minimal costs and efforts (Slater 1997). It is embedded in the characteristics of consumerism that when an individual consumes something, he or she is keen on that at that very particular moment, but soon the interest is directed to another product or service, which reflects the 'constant cycle of desire' (Miles 1998: 151). This is one aspect of what Miles names as a *consuming paradox*. Thus to consume more does not satisfy the 'needs' of the consumer, but instead leads to new desires of consumption.

Promotion and production of desire and needs are the core mechanisms of capitalist consumption culture, where every thing and everything has its price if individuals express a demand for it. Markets do not have any morality, which Slater (1997) refers to as 'economic amoralism'. The ability to pay for assets or services defines what is offered for sale. Liberal economics and market ideology defines consumers as sovereign: individuals are the best ones to decide what they want and need. Their decisions and wishes should not be judged or criticized, whether the desires are for drugs, weapons – or even human bodies, body-parts or sexualities (Slater 1997).

The power and (imagined) freedom embedded in buying of sex can be realized only if the experience is shared with others. Therefore, it is important to consume particular commodities in the company of others or to tell others about the (ab)uses one has experienced/committed (Urry 1995). Sharing of (commercial) sex experiences has 'traditionally' been possible through bragging in men's safeguarded networks, such as in talking to other (assumed) users or other trustworthy and interested partners[7] in pubs or bars, or by writing to sex magazines. The Internet is increasingly a crucial media for sharing of the adventure(s) with other sex buyers, and it enables building up homosocial[8] fraternity and male bonding. The buyer expects that his 'conquests' are enjoyed and secretly envied by other members of the community (Earle and Sharpe 2007; Månsson and Söderlind 2004; Mullings 2000). For instance, there are websites created for and used by sex buyers, such as Punternet or Sihteeriopisto, which include discussion forums and chats (also) for evaluations of experiences of prostitute use nationally and internationally. Many of the same sites advertise and sell pornography in different forms and offer tips, advices and contact addresses for prostitution use.

From McDonaldization to McSexualization

Western rationalization – as identified by Weber[9] – can be understood as a basis for the formation of (the) globalizing consumption culture model. George Ritzer (1993: 1) argues that the world is 'afflicted' by a process that he calls 'McDonaldization', that is 'the process by which the principles of the fast food restaurant are coming to dominate more and more sectors of American society as well as of the rest of the world'. McDonalds is an example and a metaphor of a globalization process of Westernized consumption model, extending its reach to all over the world. McDonalds formula and its applications to other spheres of life are represented not only in the food culture, but its impacts have spread on other aspects of the lives of people, their (our) spending of time, money, and whole lifestyles.

According to Ritzer (1993), there are four main characteristics and methods by which McDonald's has sought to construct and rationalize systems to gain higher profits, namely, through efficiency, calculability, predictability and control. McDonaldization as a theoretical framework has been applied to various sectors of social and organizational lives, such as work ('McWork', Royle 2000, 2002; 'McJobs', Ritzer 2002; 'McDonaldization of Social Work', Dustin 2007), leisure-time activities ('McDonaldization of Sport Store', Miles 2002; 'Disneyization of Society', Bryman 2002), family life ('McDonaldization of the Family', Dennis 2002) and universities ('McUniversity', Hayes and Wynyard 2002a, 2002b).

---

7 During my research on the sex trade, I have met various sex buyers, who have been enthusiastic to talk about their sex consumption; see also Coy et al. 2007; Chapter 7.

8 Homosociality has been discussed particularly in critical men's studies. Homosociality can be defined as solidarity between and exclusive networking of men in patriarchy and paternalistic power structures. See Lipman-Blumen (1976) and Hearn and Parkin (2000).

9 Rationalisation can be defined to mean the process by which nature, society and individual action are increasingly mastered by an orientation to planning, technical procedure and rational action.

The characteristics of McDonaldization (efficiency, calculability, predictability and control) are spread as norms to many areas of the world.

In the context of the sex trade, McDonaldization can be interpreted to mean, for instance, easy access for clients to a guaranteed supply of commercial sex locally and when travelling abroad. According to Sven-Axel Månsson (2001: 144), some sex buyers compare sex 'to a consumer product rather than an aspect of intimate relationships. This kind of self-focused sexuality and the idea of shopping for a sex partner leads to what Blanchard calls McSex'.[10] This McDonaldization framework has been applied to the sex industry by Kathryn Hausbeck and Barbara Brents (2002: 106), particularly in the context of the United States. Accordingly, '[a] McDonaldized sex industry is convenient for some consumers, safer and more lucrative for some workers, and profitable for owners, but it also threatens to entrap us in Weber's fearsome iron cage: coldly colonizing our imaginations and brushing up against our skin' (ibid: 106). The apparent ease and freedom within sex industries obscure the ultimate rational of profit-making of the business owners and abuses of those involved in selling sexual services; at the same time, buyers and consumers of sex commerce are accustomed to polished images of the businesses and access to these worldwide.

In developing and extending Hausbeck and Brent's argument, I use the term 'McSexualization' in order to refer to the mainstreaming and industrialization of sex as business(es) and the commercialization of bodies, sex and sexualities. McSexualization, as sale and consumption of sex and sex(ual) services like any other asset or service, can involve, for instance, the following:

1. *Control*: The potential to control the body has increased through the use of new innovations and advances in technologies, such as cosmetic plastic surgery, in vitro fertilization and transplant surgery (Shilling 2003: 32–3). The medicalization of the mind and body has been followed by various innovations enabling control of the (female) body developed particularly for aesthetic purposes (Schilling 2003; Wolf 1990). Gendered body makeover industries, including the use of cosmetic surgery, have becomes normalized and mainstreamed. Control is present also in sex industries, as the owners of the businesses tend to control the sellers of sex in order to guarantee maximum profit.

2. *Efficiency*: Sex businesses offer clients a way to satisfy his(her) needs with very little effort and time. Brothel owners and the prostitute usually gain more money if the sex act is over quickly, and a new customer is being serviced. Or, the efficiency can be maximized in the street prostitution where the buyer may be serviced even without him leaving the car. Efficiency is inbuilt to the sale and marketing of everyday products by the use of sexualized imagery and bodies to capture consumer. Such marketing is

---

10   'McSex' was originally used in a non-academic article by K. Blanchard on young men buying sex in 1994 and thereafter cited in Monto (2000).

targeted in particular to male viewers, whether the male gaze is understood to be heteronormative or homoerotic.

3. *Calculability*: The larger the supply and markets of paid sex, e.g. in countries where prostitution is legalized, the better is the possibility for sex buyers to calculate and negotiate low price for paid sex. Men may count that buying of sex is cheaper than 'wining and dining' non-prostitute women, who might not in the end of the day be willing to have sex with him (see Coy et al. 2007; Chapter 7). The thread of calculability is present in sex industries as well as in ordinary McSexualized worklife: body remoulding through cosmetic surgery is common in sex industries for maximizing the profits, but also in non-sex industry worklife; investing in appearance has become increasingly common for many women in jobs in highly competitive areas and/or work with customers or media.

4. *Predictability*: the sex buyer can be sure that 'the sexual relief and satisfaction' which he is searching for is offered to him in a prostitution contact, or in a private sex club. For instance, one crucial marketing trick of the sex advertisements published in Finnish newspapers and on text-television pages is a clearly expressed 'guarantee' for satisfaction: '100% satisfaction guaranteed'; or, 'Quick relief of your pressures promised' (Laukkanen 2000). The client 'knows' that the act what he orders is what he gets, whether in his own hometown or abroad. Thus through the industrialization of the sex trade, the consumer's wishes are fulfilled, and the price and contents predictable.

Contradictions and Irrationalities of McSexualization

Following rationalization and the McDonaldization model, the sex trade functions nearly as many other businesses in the contemporary world: effectively managed and organized, and carried out by low-paid labour. However, the rationalizing model according to Ritzer needs to be critically evaluated because of the embedded 'irrationality of rationality'.

In order to look at the ir/rationalities of the sex trade, there is a need to underscore the gendered nature of the business in that field locally and globally. Global research shows that most sex buyers are male, and the sellers are mainly female (see, for instance, Lammi-Taskula 1999; Månsson 1996, 2001; Monto 2000, 2004; O'Connell Davidson 1998). Trafficking in human beings is a clear example of the operation of global gendered sex markets, too: international trafficking removes hundreds of thousands of women annually from their home villages and towns into brothels and sex bars to serve sex clients in bigger cities, whether in their own or neighbouring countries or even on other continents[11] (see Raphael: Chapter 3; Turner: Chapter 2). Therefore, globally, trafficking means potential population catastrophes in which the poor areas lose their younger female population and the sex trade centres and cities become over-populated with disadvantaged, vulnerable women and international sex tourists.[12]

Through McSexualization, beauty and sexual attractiveness as defined and advertised in western(ized) media and society have become highly valued assets worldwide. Interests in face and body moulding through cosmetic surgery have increased rapidly in many developing countries. Poor families may invest in the looks of the girl child to be able to increase her possibilities to find a wealthy husband; for instance, 'eye-jobs' have become popular school graduation gifts presents by parents and relatives in Asian countries (Ko 2006). Similarly, the mainstreaming of the sex trade increases feminization of poverty, because girl-children are sent or sold to sex industries instead of schooling them – when girl children are valued as tradable assets, the interest in schooling of girls decreases. In addition, women's lack of education in many countries of origin as well as men's (continuing) subordination of women increases the risks of HIV-infections. In particular, prostitute women with low positions in the prostitution hierarchy are often obliged, tempted or coerced by men offering more money, to sell sex without condom use (see Farley 2004). Illiterate or otherwise less educated women and girls are (often) easier to be even more severely abused – which might be 'rational' in considering the interests of the sex trade, but irrational from the point of view of women's rights or sustainable development.

Consuming commercial sex can reflect traditional gender roles where women are understood to be owned as other forms of property by the father and later on by the husband. The sex buyer becomes an additional metaphorical 'shareholder' of the female body, even though his ownership is temporary. Thereby, subordinate customs of traditional and/or current societies are transferred into the modern and late modern consumer cultures: 'I consume sex, therefore I am'. The irrationality from women's rights perspective is embedded in very serious ways in the trade: women and girls entering into sex industry face the risk to lose their health, even their lives, for example, because buyers may prefer unprotected sex (at least for a better price); the condoms may break; or, the unsatisfied client or procurer may use violence.

---

11   Trafficking of a person can start first 'locally', i.e. through the recruitment and transport of a person from (mainly) her own context into larger cities in the same country for the exploitation, and then further on to other countries and continents. See Galiana 2000; Raphael: Chapter 3; Turner: Chapter 2.

12   The population crisis is not based only on the functioning of the sex trade, but on complex, structural level problems, such as poverty and postcolonialism, which in turn are linked to the growth of sex industries.

Conclusion

During the last few decades, the sex industry has become one of the largest grey-zone business activities worldwide, which effectively and increasingly uses new and older forms of technologies for running and marketing its businesses, and creates new forms of products and services based on gendered commercialization(s) of the body and desire. The sex trade or trading of other sexualized assets are not new phenomena, but industrialization, globalization and 'virtualization' of commercial sex have radically changed the situation: multiplied the volume and the forms of commercial sex, as well as the speed and profits in the field. At the same time, the sex trade, like other forms of the commercialization of bodies, sex and sexualities, reproduces and (re)constructs sexualities and understandings of gender/sex relationships.

These developments are framed here through the concept of McSexualization, which refers to the mainstreaming and industrialization of sex as business(es) including and interlinking with commercialization of bodies, sex and sexualities as a part of globalizing western consumer culture. The consequences of the expansion and normalization of the sex trade extend to many areas of societies in wealthy/late modern, and developing countries as well as those under transition phases. Sex markets seek to actively and artificially create new needs in its existing clientele, and to draw new potential clients to its products and services. There is a significant amount of people and organizations directly involved in these increasing business activities, but the impacts reach out to other agencies and individuals indirectly, often without agreement and permission. As policies on the sex trade vary from country to another, sometimes within a country, sex industries emerge in different forms. A common ground is that the implications are deeply gendered as reflected in the structures and power relations of the trade itself. The mainstreaming of the sex trade blurs the limits of acceptable and unacceptable, and the borders of legal and illegal. In seeking normalization, those profiting from sex industries also actively and internationally reformulate social attitudes towards deregulation of its actions, away from being illicit towards legal business. Yet the gendered inequalities of the roots, realities and implications of McSexualization require re-analysis, and critical discussion and revision of policies and practices.

References

Altman, D. (2001) *Global Sex.* Chicago: The University of Chicago Press.

Banerjee, S.B. and Linstead, S. (2001) 'Globalization, Multiculturalism and Other Fictions: Colonialism for the New Millennium?' *Organization* 8(4): 683–722.

Barry, K.L. (1995) *Prostitution of Sexuality: Global Exploitation of Women.* New York: New York University Press.

Blanchard, K. (1994) 'Special Report: Young Johns'. *Mademoiselle* 100: 131.

Bryman, A. (2002) 'The Disneyization of Society'. In George Ritzer (ed.), *McDonaldization. The Reader.* Thousand Oaks: Pine Forge Press, 52–9.

Coy, M., Horvath, M.A.H. and Kelly, L. (2007) *'It's just like going to the supermarket': Men Buying Sex in East London.* London: Child & Woman Abuse Studies Unit, London Metropolitan University.

Dennis, J.P. (2002) 'McDonaldization of the Family'. In George Ritzer (ed.), *McDonaldization. The Reader.* Thousand Oaks: Pine Forge Press, 107–15.

Dines, G. (2010) *Pornland: How Porn Has Hijacked Our Sexuality.* Boston, Massachusetts: Beacon Press.

Dustin, D. (2007) *The McDonaldization of Social Work.* Aldershot: Ashgate.

Earle, S. and Sharp, K. (2007) *Sex in Cyberspace: Men Who Buy for Sex.* Aldershot, Burlington: Ashgate.

Edwards, T. (2000) *Contradictions of Consumption. Concepts, Practices and Politics in Consumer Society.* Buckingham: Open University Press.

Enloe, C. (1989) *Bananas, Beaches and Bases. Making Feminist Sense of International Politics.* Berkley: University of California.

Farley, M. (2004) '"Bad for the Body, Bad for the Heart": Prostitution Harms Women Even if Legalized or Decriminalized'. *Violence against Women* 10(10): 1087–125.

Galiana, C. (2000) *Trafficking in Women.* Civil Liberties Series LIBE 109 EN. Brussels: European Parliament.

Gill, R.H. Karen and McLean, C. (2003) 'A Genealogical Approach to Idealised Male Body Imagery'. *Paragraph* 26(1/2): 187–201.

Group of Specialists on the Impact of the Use of New Information Technologies on Trafficking in Human Beings for the Purpose on Sexual Exploitation. *Final Report* (2003). EG-S-NT (2002) 9 rev. Council of Europe: Strasbourg. Available at: http://www.coe.int/t/dghl/monitoring/trafficking/Source/EG-S-NT(2002)09revE.pdf [accessed: 5 January 2011].

Halmekoski, T. (2002) 'Erotiikan markkinat – nyt myös naisille' [Markets of erotics – now also for women]. *Anna-magazine* 35–6/2002: 24–7.

Hanmer, J. (2000) 'Buying Sex: Responding to Kerb-Crawlers' in Laura Keeler (ed.) Recommendations of the E.U. Expert Meeting on Violence Against Women. *Reports 2000:13. Helsinki: Ministry of Social Affairs and Health*, 98–104.

Hausbeck, K. and Brents, B.G. (2002) 'McDonaldization of the Sex Industries? The Business of Sex'. In George Ritzer (ed.), *McDonaldization. The Reader.* Thousand Oaks: Pine Forge Press, 91–106.

Hayes, D. and Wynyard, R. (eds.) (2002a) *The McDonaldization of Higher Education.* London: Greenwood Publishing Group, Bergin & Garvey.

Hayes, D. and Wynyard, R. (2002b) 'Whimpering into the Good Night: Resisting McUniversity'. In George Ritzer (ed.), *McDonaldization. The Reader.* Thousand Oaks: Pine Forge Press, 116–25.

Hearn, J. (2006) 'The Implications of Information and Communication Technologies for Sexualities and Sexualised Violences: Contradictions of Sexual Citizenships'. *Political Geography* (25)8: 944–63.

Hearn, J. and Jyrkinen, M. (2000) 'Uudet teknologiat, globalisaatio ja seksiteollisuus' [New Technologies, Globalisation and Sex Industry.] *Naistutkimus-Kvinnoforskning* 4: 67–71.

Hearn, J. and Parkin, W. (1995) *'Sex' at 'Work': The Power and Paradox of Organisation Sexuality.* Revised edition. Hemel Hempstead: Prentice-Hall; New York: St. Martin's Press.

Hearn, J. and Parkin, W. (2001) *Gender, Sexuality and Violence in Organizations: The Unspoken Forces of Organization Violations.* London: Sage.

Hedlund, E. (1999) 'Experiences with Treating Men with Compulsive Sexual Behavior'. In Laura Keeler and Marjut Jyrkinen (eds), *Who's Buying? The Clients of Prostitution.* Helsinki: Ministry of Social Affairs, Council for Equality, 4: 73–81.

Holgersson, C. (2003) *Rekrytering av företagsledare. En studie I homosocialitet* [The Recruitment of Managing Directors – A Study of Homosociality]. Stockholm: Ekonomiska Forskningsinstitutet vid Handelshögskolan i Stockholm.

Holgersson, C. and Svanström, Y. (2004) *Lagliga och olagliga affärer – om sexköp och organisationer* [Legal and Illegal Businesses – On the Sex Trade and Organisations]. Stockholm: Ref.No 020513, Norfa rapportering.

Hughes, D.M. (2002) 'The Use of New Communications and Information Technologies for Sexual Exploitation of Women and Children'. *Hastings Women's Law Journal* 13(1): 129–48.

Hänninen, J. (2010) Porno 2.0. [Porn 2.0.] *Helsingin Sanomat* 15.8.2010.

Høigård, C. and Finstad, L. (1992) *Backstreets: Prostitutio, Money and Love.* Cambridge: Policy Press.

Jeffreys, S. (1997) *The Idea of Prostitution.* Melbourne: Spinifex Press.

Jeffreys, S. (2009a) *The Industrial Vagina. The Political Economy of the Global Sex Trade.* Oxon: Routledge.

Jeffreys, S. (2009b) 'Outsourcing Women's Subordination: Male buyers in Business and Leisure Prostitution', in Jeff Hearn (ed.), *GEXcel Work in Progress Report, Vol. V: Proceedings GEXcel Theme 2: Deconstructing the Hegemony of Men and Masculinities.* Tema Genus Report Series No 9. Linköping: University of Linköping, 111–22.

Jeffreys, S. (2010) 'The Sex Industry and Business Practice: An Obstacle to Women's Equality', *Women's Studies International Forum* 33(3): 274–82.

Jyrkinen, M. (2005) *The Organisation of Policy Meets the Commercialisation of Sex – Global Linkages, Policies, Technologies.* Economics and Society 146. Helsinki: Hanken School of Economics. Available at: http://hdl.handle.net/10227/118 [accessed: 5 August 2010].

Kazuko, W. (1994) 'Militarism, Colonialism and the Trafficking in Women: "Comfort Women" forced into Sexual Labor for Japanese Soldiers'. *Bulletin of Concerned Asian Scholars* 26(4): 2–17.

Keeler, L. and Jyrkinen, M. (1999) 'On the Invisibility of the Buyers in the Sex Trade'. In L. Keeler and M. Jyrkinen (eds) (1994), *Who's Buying? The Clients of Prostitution.* Helsinki: Ministry of Social Affairs, Council for Equality, Publications on Equality, 4: 6–12.

Kelly, L., Coy, M. and Davenport, R. (2009) *Shifting Sands: A Comparison of Prostitution Regimes Across Nine Countries.* London: Child & Woman Abuse Studies Unit (CWASU): London Metropolitan University.

Kinnunen, T. (2008) *Lihaan leikattu kauneus. Kosmeettisen kirurgian ruumiillistuneet merkitykset* [Beauty Cut into Flesh. Embodied Meanings of Cosmetic Surgery]. Helsinki: Gaudeamus.

Kleiber, D. and Velten, D. (1994) *Prostitutionskunden.* Eine Untersuchung über soziale and psychologische Charakteristika von Besuchern weiblicher Prostituierter in Zeiten von AIDS [Clients of Prostitution]. Band 30, Bundesministerium für Gesundheit, Baden-Baden, Nomos-Verlagsgesellschaft.

Ko, C. (2006) 'Peer Pressure Plastics: Kids Gotta Have it Too', *Time Magazine Asia.* Available at: http://www.time.com/time/asia/covers/1101020805/plastics.html [accessed: 4 May 2011].

Lammi-Taskula, J. (1999) 'Clients of the Sex Industry in Finland. The Habitus Study 1995'. In L. Keeler and M. Jyrkinen (eds), *Who's Buying? The Clients of Prostitution.* Helsinki: Ministry of Social Affairs, Council for Equality, Publications on Equality, 4: 82–8.

Laukkanen, M. (2000) *Suomalainen päivälehdistö seksikaupan foorumina.* [The Finnish Daily Press as a Forum for the Sex Trade]. Helsinki: Reports of the Ministry of Social Affairs and Health, 12.

Lipman-Blumen, J. (1976) 'Towards a Homosocial Theory of Sex Roles: An Explanation of the Sex Segregation of Social Institutions', in M. Blaxall and B. Reagan (eds), *Women and the Workplace. The Implications of Occupational Segregation.* Chicago: University of Chicago Press.

Marttila, A. (2004) 'Seksiä ilman rajoja? Kansainvälistyvä seksiteollisuus ja suomalaiset prostituution asiakkaat' [Sex without Limits? Internationalising Sex Industry and Finnish Sex Clients]. *Naistutkimus-Kvinnoforskning* 1: 22–35.

Miles, S. (1998) *Consumerism – As a Way of Life.* Guildford, Surrey: Sage Publications.

Miles, S. (2002) 'McDonaldization and the Global Sports Store: Constructing Consumer Meanings in a Rationalized Society'. In George Ritzer (ed.), *McDonaldization. The Reader*. Thousand Oaks: Pine Forge Press, 171–7.

Monto, M.A. (2000) 'Why Men Seek Out Prostitutes'. In Ronald Weitzer (ed.), *Sex for Sale. Prostitution, Pornography and the Sex Industry*. London: Routledge, 67–83.

Monto, M.A. (2004) 'Female Prostitution, Customers and Violence'. *Violence against Women* 10(2): 160–88.

Mullings, B. (2000): 'Fantasy Tours: Exploring the Global Consumption of Caribbean Sex Tourisms'. In M. Gottdiener (ed.), *New Forms of Consumption. Consumers, Culture, and Commodification*. Maryland: Rowman & Littlefield Publishers, Inc., 227–50.

Månsson, S. and Söderlind, P. (2004) Sexindustrin på nätet: Aktörer, innehåll, relationer och ekonomiska flöden. Stockholm.

Månsson, S. (1996) 'International Prostitution and Traffic in Persons in Relation to Costs and Benefits of Europeanization'. In Marjut Jyrkinen (ed.), *Changing Faces of Prostitution. Conference Book*. Keuruu: Unioni, the League of Finnish Feminists, 14–31.

Månsson, S. (2001) 'Men's Practices in Prostitution: The Case of Sweden'. In B. Pease and K. Pringle (eds), *A Mans' World? Changing Men's Practices in a Globalized World*. London: Zed Books, 135–49.

Månsson, S. and Söderlind, P. (2004) *Sexindustrin på nätet: Aktörer, innehåll, relationer och ekonomiska flöden* [Sex Industry on the Web: Actors, Contents, Relations and Economic Flows]. Stochkholm: Ègalité.

Nurmi, R. (2002) 'Prostitution at the Limits of Risks'. In Ursula Aaltonen, Ali Arsalo and Minna Sinkkonen (eds), *Being Positive. Perspectives on HIV/AIDS in the EU's Northern Dimension and Finland's Neighbouring Areas*. Saarijärvi: Stakes, Sosiaali- ja terveysalan tutkimus- ja kehittämiskeskus, 175–85.

O'Connell Davidson, J. (1998) *Prostitution, Power and Freedom*. Cornwall: Polity Press.

O'Connell Davidson, J. (2001) 'Punter Fiction – Stories Clients Tell about Their Prostitute Use'. In M. Jyrkinen and K. Leena (eds), *Minors in the Sex Trade*. Hamina: Programme for the Prevention of Prostitution and Violence against Women, 35–46.

Raymond, J.G. (2001) *Guide to the New UN Trafficking Protocol*. North Amherst: Coalition Against Trafficking in Women.

Ritzer, G. (1993) *The McDonaldization of Society*. Thousand Oaks: Pine Forge Press.

Ritzer, G. (2002) 'McJobs: McDonaldization and Its Relationship to the Labor Process'. In G. Ritzer (ed.), *McDonaldization. The Reader*. Thousand Oaks: Pine Forge Press, 141–7.

Royle, T. (2000) *Working for McDonald's in Europe: The Unequal Struggle?* London: Routledge.

Royle, T. (2002) 'McWork in Europe'. In George Ritzer (ed.), *McDonaldization. The Reader*. Thousand Oaks: Pine Forge Press, 148–50.

Sandell, G., Pettersson, E., Larsson, J. and Kuosmanen, J. (1996) *Könsköparna* [Buyers of Sex]. Falun: Natur och Kultur.

Shilling, C. (2003) *The Body and Social Theory.* Second edition. London: Sage.

Slater, D. (1997) *Consumer Culture and Modernity.* Cornwall: Polity Press.

Urry, J. (1995) *Consuming Places.* New York: Routledge.

Watanabe K. (1994) 'Militarism, Colonialism and the Trafficking in Women: "Comfort Women" forced into Sexual Labor for Japanese Soldiers', *Bulletin of Concerned Asian Scholars* 26(4): 2–17.

Waters, M. (1995): *Globalization.* London: Routledge.

Weber, M. (1930) *The Protestant Ethic and the Spirit of Capitalism*. London: Allen and Unwin.

Wolf, N. (1990) *The Beauty Myth. How Images of Beauty are Used Against Women*. London: Vintage.

Chapter 2

Means of Delivery:
The Trafficking of Women into Prostitution,
Harms and Human Rights Discourse

Jackie Turner

Over the past several decades, debates on the trafficking of women for the purposes of sexual exploitation have developed alongside an evolving discourse on human rights. Whilst this has shed light on the considerable and numerous harms and human rights violations suffered by those who fall under the control of traffickers, human rights discourse has been long on rhetoric but short on decisive action against the conditions which create and sustain the conducive contexts for the sex trafficking of women: women's subordination within patriarchal cultures and pervasive violence against women.

Violence against women was described by the current secretary-general of the United Nations, Ban Ki-moon, in his launch of the UNiTE campaign,[1] as 'a global pandemic', and by the former secretary-general, Kofi Annan, as 'the most atrocious manifestation of the systematic discrimination and inequality women continue to face, in law and in their everyday lives, around the world'.[2] This chapter will frame trafficking of women into prostitution and other forms of sexual exploitation as gender-based violence against women. Structural and other factors intersect with multiple layers of inequalities to increase women's risk of trafficking – internationally and domestically – into sex markets around the world. This is not to say that all women in prostitution are there as a result of trafficking as it is currently defined. Yet for many women, the 'choice' to enter prostitution is vitiated by dire economic necessity and/or the absence of other viable choices (see Jeffreys: Chapter 4). For trafficked women, there is not even the semblance of choice. If trafficking is the method and the means of delivery, prostitution is the end game. The two are not easily de-coupled. Issues of choice and agency in prostitution, however, remain highly contested within feminist scholarship,

---

1 Launched in 2008, United Nations Secretary-General Ban Ki-moon's *UNiTE to End Violence against Women* campaign is a multi-year effort aimed at preventing and eliminating violence against women and girls in all parts of the world. See: http://www. un.org/en/women/endviolence/about.shtml.

2 From Secretary General Kofi Annan's 2005 message on the International Day for the Elimination of Violence against Women. See http://www.un.org/womenwatch/daw.

and have long embedded themselves in discourses on trafficking, such that there can no longer be discourse on one without discourse on the other. And multiple discourses there have been, to which this chapter seeks to make a contribution. The following pages discuss contemporary framings of sex trafficking and conclude with a cautionary note to those who appeal for resolution by resort to human rights.

The UN Approach

Current international anti-trafficking law in the form of the United Nations (UN) Optional Protocol to Prevent, Suppress and Punish Trafficking in Persons, Especially Women and Children (known as the Palermo Protocol), is not a human rights instrument. It is one of three Protocols to supplement the UN Convention Against Transnational Organized Crime (TOC). This is, as the title suggests, the main international instrument binding ratifying states to cooperate in the fight against transnational organized crime. In supplementing TOC, the Palermo Protocol defines what is meant by the crime of trafficking, in the following terms:

> Trafficking in persons shall mean the recruitment, transportation, transfer, harbouring or receipt of persons, by means of the threat or use of force or other forms of coercion, of abduction, of fraud, of deception, of the abuse of power or of a position of vulnerability or of the giving or receipt of payments or benefits to achieve the consent of a person having control over another person, for the purpose of exploitation. Exploitation shall include, at a minimum, the exploitation of the prostitution of others or other forms of sexual exploitation, forced labour or services, slavery or practices similar to slavery, servitude or the removal of organs.[3]

The achievement of international consensus on the definition of trafficking paves the way for member states to draft and implement compliant national laws covering key elements. However, the UN approach has been critiqued on a number of grounds, not least that in appending the Palermo Protocol to an instrument dedicated to the fight against transnational organized crime, this detracts from the diverse and even legitimate, or semi-legitimate facilitators of the trade, such as travel operators, employment- and overseas marriage agencies – what Skeldon (2000) calls a 'continuum of facilitation' in both regular and irregular flows of migrant workers. Furthermore, focus on the 'transnational' nature inextricably links

---

3   United Nations Convention Against Transnational Organized Crime, Protocol to Prevent, Suppress and Punish Trafficking in Persons, Especially Women and Children, Article 3(a). The United Nations Convention Against Transnational Organized Crime was adopted in 2000 and entered into force in September 2003. The Protocol to Prevent, Suppress and Punish Trafficking in Persons, Especially Women and Children, entered into force shortly thereafter in December 2003.

it with migration (see also Raphael: Chapter 3) and, hence, with migration control strategies which, however, rarely take account of the 'tensions, disjunctures and inequalities associated with globalization and a differential freedom of movement' (Lee 2011: 6) characterized by Bauman (1998: 87–8) as a 'hierarchy of mobility', as states distinguish between wanted and unwanted migrant workers. This, in turn, has contributed to a 'criminalisation of migrants' (Melossi 2003, 2005; Welsh 2003) with 'profound consequences for trafficked victims and other border crossers' (Lee 2011: 6), but especially for women trafficked into prostitution, as the chapter will go on to discuss.

The trafficking of women for sexual exploitation has attracted particular and increasing attention over the last couple of decades. Whilst this has led to considerable lacunae, in the United Kingdom and elsewhere, in policy developments and concrete measures to tackle other forms of trafficking – for example, the trade in human organs, but also trafficking for the purposes of other forced labour – there is good reason to maintain focus on the trafficking of women for sexual exploitation. Although there are no confirmed numbers indicating the scale of the phenomenon, a study undertaken on behalf of the International Labour Organisation (ILO) suggests that at any given time there are a minimum of 2.45 million people globally trapped in situations of forced labour as a result of trafficking (Belser et al. 2005: 4–6; ILO 2005: 14). Of these, just under half – 43 per cent – are believed to have been trafficked for the purposes of commercial sexual exploitation. As for reported cases, according to the UN Office on Drugs and Crime (UNODC 2006: 33), 87 per cent concern the trafficking of women and children for sexual exploitation. It is of course possible – even probable – that many cases of trafficking in men go unidentified and/or unreported, but it is equally probable that all identified and reported cases of trafficking in any event represent 'just the tip of the iceberg' (Di Nicola 2007: 53). Hence, while these figures may not paint the whole picture, they do indicate that the sex trade in women is on a significant scale. But the traffic in women is not just a question of numbers, important though it is to obtain estimates which are as accurate as possible to better inform intervention strategies. As traffickers adapt to the conditions and new opportunities of the twenty first century, the supply of women and girls into prostitution, nationally and internationally, remains an enduring feature of the trade, moreover, it is one which international law – despite its express focus on women (and children) – has impacted only minimally, if at all. This begs the question of whether the UN and international law – and, hence, the laws of nation states – have adopted an effective approach to tackling the problem of trafficking and the multitude of harms it brings in its wake for women trafficked into prostitution.

Trafficking – A Continuum of Violence and Harms

The concept of a continuum of violence was introduced by Liz Kelly (1988) in relation to sexual violence to identify, *inter alia*, 'the common character underlying the many different forms of violence [as being] the *abuse, intimidation, coercion, intrusion, threat and force men use to control women* (ibid: 76) (emphasis in original). It is used in similar fashion here to convey the range of violences traffickers employ throughout the trafficking process to control those they have targeted as their victims. The concept is also used, as it was originally intended, to establish connections across forms of violence and which cannot be readily distinguished, but which result in multiple harms to women trafficked into prostitution. These harms have been well documented (see, for example, Zimmerman et al. 2003, 2006; Silverman et al. 2007). They include physical and sexual harms, harms to mental health and to social and economic well-being, and are similar to those experienced by women in prostitution who have not been trafficked (see Tyler Chapter 5 for an overview). The trafficking process accentuates these harms, not just on arrival at a pre-determined destination, but at all stages. Prior experiences of violence may also increase women's risk of being trafficked and many harmful legacies persist beyond the trafficking process, whether women are detained, deported, involved in criminal proceedings and/or returned to their countries of origin.

The process of recruitment itself may involve abduction, or sale by parents or other guardians, but it may also, more typically in many cases, involve deception (UNODC 2006). There are numerous reasons, discussed below, why women may wish or need to leave their homes, their communities, and their countries. Migration, especially from poorer to richer countries, and from the global South to the global North, is a daunting undertaking, facilitated by many intermediaries, not just those already mentioned, but also public officials (some of them corrupt), document processors and checkers, financiers, smugglers and traffickers. Many traffickers typically recruit from within their own ethnic communities, where proximity, access, a shared language and culture all make it easier to establish a bond of trust (Shelley 2007: 126). The deception by traffickers – false promises of good jobs, love, even marriage – means that many women are unaware that they are in the hands of traffickers until later stages in the trafficking process. Indeed, some women may not know they have been trafficked until after arrival in a destination country. In such circumstances, '[t]he violation of trust which occurs in every trafficking case may be as devastating to the individual as the physical or psychological abuse applied to the victim' (ibid: 126). Travel and transit stages can also pose risk of significant harms to women – including violence – but others which derive from the conditions of transit themselves and the dangers associated with illegal border crossings. One European study (Zimmerman et al. 2003) reveals accounts of women forced to travel in refrigerated containers, swim across fast-moving rivers, or lie in the ceiling panels of trains. Accompanying this physical trauma is fear and anxiety. On arrival in destination countries, however, women rarely have the opportunity to recover or receive medical assistance. Instead, they are prostituted by their traffickers, or sold to local pimps, where rape and unsafe sex expose them to the harms of sexually transmitted infections, unwanted pregnancies, abortion, damage to internal organs such as the reproductive tract, kidney and bladder, infertility and miscarriage, as well numerous psychological harms (ibid). Another study of 49 trafficked women in the Philippines, found 82 per cent of the women reported suffering depression, with 40 per cent having suicidal thoughts (Raymond et al. 2002: 112).

The Migration-Smuggling-Trafficking Continuum

In light of this, it may seem somewhat remarkable that, outside of (some) feminist literature, trafficking is rarely expressly conceived as violence against women. Maggie Lee (2011: 10–11) identifies the six major conceptual approaches by which trafficking is variously understood 'as a modern form of slavery; as an exemplar of the globalization of crime; as synonymous with prostitution; as a problem of transnational organized crime; as a migration problem; and as a human rights challenge'. Clearly, some or all of these approaches are applicable to some or all forms of trafficking in persons – any victim of trafficking may be delivered into conditions of slavery through criminal networks which span the globe; women and girls are predominantly trafficked into prostitution by groups which may, or may not, operate as *transnational organized crime* groups;[4] international trafficking may involve legal and illicit migratory processes; and all forms of trafficking invariably involve violation of, at the very least, basic human rights such as the right to freedom of movement and the right to free choice of employment (as defined in the 1948 Universal Declaration of Human Rights).

The dominant way in which trafficking is conceived, however, will largely dictate the focus of international and national counter-trafficking measures. Hence, if trafficking is primarily understood, as it is in the United Kingdom for example, as a problem of 'organized immigration crime' (Home Office and Scottish Executive 2007), strict border controls will figure high in the government's anti-trafficking strategy. This association of trafficking with immigration crime can lead to a conflation of counter-trafficking measures with (im)migration control, which has specific implications for responses to migrant and trafficked women, some of which are explored here.

Whilst trafficking need not entail the crossing of borders, international trafficking plainly does and, where it does, the flow of traffic is most typically from poorer to richer countries, particularly, but by no means exclusively, from the

4   In addition to the problems already outlined, there is no common understanding of the term 'organized crime' or 'transnational' in the context of organized crime (for an overview, see Wright (2006)). Similarly, the applicability to, and relevance of, organized crime to trafficking operations is contested. See, for example, Shelley (2003) and Finckenauer (2001).

global South to the global North (UN Office on Drugs and Crime 2006). Migratory flows, like trafficking flows, tend to follow the money, and those with the least access to regular channels of migration are often among the most disadvantaged in the poorer countries of origin. Migration is frequently driven by social unrest and economic and political instability, by wars and conflicts, and by poverty and destitution. Much poverty, in particular, is attributable to the uneven impacts of globalization, as a result of which whole regions have been cut off from the prosperity, and the prospects of prosperity, which globalization has delivered to the richer North.[5] The UN estimates that 'women today make up a majority of the world's poor: some 70 per cent of those living below the poverty threshold are female' (Monzini 2005: 59–60). This is no coincidence. Structural and other factors – violence in the home or in the community (Turner and Kelly 2009), discrimination in the labour market, chronic under-employment, the privatization of state assets to men in economies in transition and the loss of welfare provisions, such as those that occurred in the former Soviet Union (Shelley 2000), low status and low education (Kelly 2005) – combine to produce a 'feminization of poverty'[6] which denies women local access to sustainable livelihoods, providing an 'imperative for them to be 'on the move' and to cross borders in search of physical and economic security' (Lee 2011: 152). These 'push' factors in turn combine with 'pull' factors – global demand for cheap and unskilled labour – to produce 'fertile fields for exploitation' (Kelly 2005). It is this dynamic, described by Sassen (2002) as the 'counter-geographies of globalization', which drives women into 'survival circuits'. Migration, however, exacerbates these gender-linked constraints. The same systems of discrimination which operate to deny women equal access to food, education and employment, also operate to deny women equal access to movement within and out of their homes, communities and countries. Denied equal access to regular migratory channels, women are forced into greater dependence on the array of intermediaries previously referred to. These are the conditions in which '[t]hose with limited prospects of security, survival or prosperity at home may see little option but to barter what few resources they, or their families, have and take their chances in the lottery of the assisted migration industry. And lottery it is, for the 'fertile fields' are also the hunting grounds of human traffickers, in their many deceptive guises' (Turner and Kelly 2009: 187).

If staying put is a poor survival choice, and migration a high risk lottery for poorer women, those risks are arguably further inflated by a border regime which frames trafficking as a subset of illegal migration, and which fails to take account of gender inequalities in access to regular channels of migration, exposing many women to the dangers of exploitation along a 'murky continuum of migration-smuggling-trafficking' (ibid: 193). The tighter the border controls, the greater the

---

5   Globalization is a highly contested term but is generally accepted to have produced 'winners' and 'losers'. See, for example, Beck (2000); Falk (2001); Giddens (1990); Held and McGrew (2007); Hillyard et al. (2004).

6   See Baden (1999) for a presentation of the data and an analysis of this concept.

market for 'assisted' border crossing. Not all trafficked women, however, enter a country illegally. They may have obtained temporary work permits, spousal, student or tourist visas. Even those who enter illegally, for example, with false documents, may not know they are in the hands of traffickers and, hence, collude with their traffickers in trying to secure undetected entry to a country. Those who fail to secure such entry are unlikely to be identified as victims of trafficking, and are more likely to face detention, prosecution and/or deportation as illegal immigrants. They then face the risk of return to their countries of origin and to the same conditions which compelled them to migrate in the first instance (IOM 2010). Now, however, they have the added burden of additional debt and may be in immediate danger of being re-trafficked. In those circumstances, they will again have to endure all the harms of travel and transit in unsafe and exploitative conditions. The fate of women who are successfully trafficked past the borders of, and into prostitution within, a destination country involves immediate exposure to the multitude of harms already discussed. Additionally, however, their avenues of escape may be compromised by a lack of understanding of their constrained circumstances and needs on the part of officials. In particular, there may be conflicts between immigration officials who regard a woman as an illegal immigrant and police who see her as a potential witness in criminal justice proceedings (Zimmerman et al. 2003: 78). Scepticism and disbelief of women's accounts, long documented with respect to sexual violence (see Jordan 2004; Kelly et al. 2005), may also narrow access routes to support and assistance. 'Police and others have, in a limited number of cases, expressed concerns about the veracity and authenticity of women claiming to have been trafficked. For example, there have been cases where women were suspected of being 'spies' or 'plants' placed in refuges or the social service system in order to inform traffickers about the actions of other women' (Zimmerman et al. 2003: 78). Moreover, prostituted women have to run the gauntlet of racial and gendered perceptions of 'victimhood', in which 'the typical victim of trafficking' is depicted as 'the naive, young, impoverished and disadvantaged woman from a developing country' (Segrave et al. 2009: 10). Women who do not measure up against this 'ideal', women who are angry, uncooperative and rejecting of 'rescue', are less likely to be regarded as 'legitimate' victims, especially those who are seen less as 'trafficked victims' and more as 'smuggled accomplices' (Green and Grewcock 2002). In crime discourse, this 'hierarchy of victimization' illustrates the elevated status enjoyed by 'innocent' victims whose experiences of victimization are taken more seriously, as against 'blameworthy' victims whose victimhood is not accorded high status and whose experiences of victimization are accordingly taken less seriously (Christie 1986). Maggie Lee (2011: 68) describes the consequences of this in relation to migration. 'The construction of a hierarchy of victimhood is evident in the different forms of irregular migration. 'In the case of refugees and asylum seekers, for example, their status as victims of political oppression and civil unrest is often sidelined by populist references to their racial otherness and perceived security risks to the global North'. In the context of trafficking, 'a migrant's degree of volition is set up as the determining factor that distinguishes trafficked victims worthy of support as opposed to 'voluntary' smuggled migrants, who are excluded' (ibid: 69). Hence, the harms and human rights violations endured by those women who are sufficiently 'othered' and/ or who are deemed to have been insufficiently compelled are treated less seriously (if at all) than those who fit the appropriate victim profile. For women, then, multiple forms of discrimination intersect with gender-based discrimination to create conditions which contribute to the need to leave their homes, communities and countries in order to find the means to provide for themselves and their families. Simultaneously, migratory processes themselves exacerbate gender-linked vulnerabilities, creating opportunities for exploitation along a continuum of migration, smuggling and trafficking, while conflation of anti-trafficking measures and migration control, racial and gender stereotyping and discrimination by border control officials and within migration management policy operate to further impede women's access to safety and sustainable livelihoods.

Framings of Trafficking and Prostitution: Unequal Gender Orders

These different factors revolving around degrees of 'choice' and harms coalesce in the conceptualization of trafficking as synonymous with prostitution and it is here, within feminist scholarship, that the framing of trafficking as violence against women is most contested. The controversy centres on the issues identified above, namely, *who* gets to be identified as a victim of trafficking and who, instead, gets caught up in immigration controls and criminalized, prosecuted and/ or deported for failing to meet preconceived standards of victimhood; in short, who is regarded, not as a victim of trafficking but rather as an actual, or at least potential, illegal immigrant (Green and Grewcock 2002; Lee 2011; Segrave et al. 2009). Notions of 'victimhood' jostle with the twin notions of 'free agents' and 'fallen women' in need of 'rescue'. These binaries, however, often drawn on by human rights activists, those seeking legitimization of prostitution as work, and 'moral crusaders' respectively – the latter described as including the religious right as well as abolitionist feminists (Weitzer 2007: 448) – do little (with the exception of abolitionist feminists) to point the finger at those who use women's bodies in, and consume the outputs of, the world's sex industries. Here, a biologistic model (Stanley 1995) of male sexuality prevails: prostitution is deemed a functional necessity, predicated upon a taken-for-granted 'natural' male (hetero)sexuality which must find an outlet. As Davis (1937: 755) once suggested: '[e]nabling a small number of women to take care of the needs of a large number of men, it [prostitution] is the most convenient sexual outlet for an army, and for the legions of strangers, perverts, and physically repulsive in our midst. It performs a function, apparently, which no other institution fully performs'.

This functionalist account of the necessity of prostitution persists in much contemporary discourse (though apparently without any consideration of its functional necessity to women – other than as a means of subsistence). Expansion of sex industries globally means it is no longer possible, if it ever was, to talk of 'a small number of women', though 'armies', and other 'strangers' remain legion, and each now has easy access to the bodies of women and girls anywhere, anytime, thanks to globalized transport and communication infrastructures and technologies which enable women to be trafficked with speed around the globe, their internet images preceding them across a borderless world wide web (see Jyrkinen: Chapter 1).

So normalized, therefore, is this sexual subordination of women that many commentators clamour to call it freedom (see Jeffreys: Chapter 4). Seen through this lens, prostitution is divorced from the wider context in which the exchange of women between men to afford men sexual and reproductive access, as well free labour is (and remains) the foundation of inequality – the basis of women's subordination – rooted within patriarchal cultures (Rubin 1975). Here, 'the stigmatization of prostitutes – rather than the structure of the practice itself – becomes the basic injustice to be redressed by pro-sex work advocates' (Miriam 2005: 7). Prostitution becomes an issue of women's personal choice and agency – as if unequal gender orders (Connell: 1987) did not exist. Segrave et al. (2009: 5) express the position of pro-sex work advocates as follows:

> Feminists within this scholarship argue that women, as adult and rational human beings, are capable of making their own choices. Prostitution is seen as a form of labour based on women's use of their bodies as a source of income. Sex work *per se* is not a violation of human rights: it is work, and sex workers do not have to be 'rescued', but enabled to exercise their labour rights.

On the face of it, this position is persuasive, but only if the many structural and deeply embedded systems of discrimination are disregarded. It contrasts sharply with the abolitionist position, which takes the non-existence of 'choice' in prostitution as its starting point. Again, in the words of Segrave et al. (2009: 3), '[t]his scholarship perceives prostitution as gender-based violence, a practice that de-humanizes and objectifies women. As such, sex work is considered coercive and consent is irrelevant (O'Connell Davidson 2006: 8; Rijken 2003: 60–61)'. This *does* locate prostitution within a wider context, and broader understanding, of violence against women as gender-based violence. As such, it acknowledges that unequal gender orders *do* exist.

These two oppositional approaches to prostitution have migrated into discourse on trafficking, where the violence against women agenda is particularly critiqued as 'amenable to neo-liberal agendas of control' (Bumiller 2008; Kapur 2005), and infected with the privilege of Western feminists, who peddle colonial views and patronize Third World Women (Altink 1995; Doezema 2000, 2001). Maggie Lee (2011: 63) is a little more circumspect, suggesting a need to guard against the appropriation of the violence against women agenda and the use of 'images of bodies in pain' (Aradau 2004) in counter-trafficking campaigns, which tend to produce stereotypical assumptions about who can be seen as a victim, the circumstances of trafficking in which they are found, and how victims look and behave.

At issue here is women's international mobility – the gendered modes, patterns, causes and consequences of women's migration – as well as what has been termed the 'increasingly sophisticated culture of control' (Segrave et al. 2009: 31) – or 'the violent logic of global trafficking control' (Lee 2011: 153) – which operates to place women at greater risk of trafficking, and to impede their exit from conditions of exploitation. These are vitally important issues and have profound implications for developments in law and policy if these are to more effectively address the problem of trafficking. Not all trafficking is cross-border, however, and increases in domestic trafficking – particularly of girls for the purposes of sexual exploitation – have recently been noted in a number of European countries (United Nations Global Initiative to Fight Human Trafficking 2009: 10). The failure by and large, to date, in detecting cases of internal trafficking has been attributed to different recording systems. Because law enforcement and criminal justice system personnel do not 'expect' to find their own citizens among the victims of trafficking, their traffickers are more likely to be charged with other crimes, 'such as sexual exploitation, kidnapping or forced labour. The difference in how the data is categorized may thus be masking similarities between countries' domestic trafficking situations' (ibid). Here, attempts to de-couple trafficking from prostitution, and to focus exclusively on international trafficking, risks the loss of important connections between domestic and cross-border sex trafficking – how each operates as a cause and consequence of gender inequality – with profound implications for domestic victims of trafficking (see Raphael: Chapter 3). Moreover, when internal trafficking is factored back in to the trafficking narrative, connections can be (re-)established between the push and pull factors which operate to drive women into international 'survival circuits', and those which operate closer to home to compel women into domestic 'survival circuits'. Economic downturns, prior experience of violence and abuse, and the dynamics of demand in local sex markets are the home-grown 'fertile fields' which create conditions conducive to the exploitation of women and girls nationally, and which may also increase their risk of being trafficked internationally. International and domestic sex trafficking are not two separate phenomena, although they may be differently impacted by the specificities of local gender orders. Hence, '[i]t is always necessary to examine how male privileges/entitlements operate locally' (Kelly 2007: 85), not only in terms of political and cultural, social and economic conditions, but also in terms of sexual privilege.

Much feminist scholarship has questioned and challenged the presumed 'nature' of male and female sexuality, to make visible not only the underlying assumptions which underpin the social construction of sexuality (see, for example, Jackson and Scott 2010), but the ways in which that construction reinforces the heteronormative attitudes and behaviours that are so apparent throughout the trafficking process. For example, the trafficking of women into prostitution is predicated on the assumption that prostitution is a 'functional' necessity for men. Similarly, notions of the 'ideal victim' derive from perceptions of gender-appropriate behaviours; women who fail to sufficiently conform to these preconceived notions are less likely to be identified as victims of trafficking and, hence, to fall foul of immigration laws. These assumptions are rooted in constructions of heterosexuality which are cause and consequence of gender orders predicated upon the subordination of women. Here, '[h]eterosexuality is not, as it appears to be, masculinity-and-femininity in opposition: it *is* masculinity (Holland et al. 1998: 11) (emphasis in original). Hence, understanding the gendered impacts of migration control strategies and criminal justice responses are key to a better understanding of the risks and harms facing women with few options but to cross borders in their search for sustainable livelihoods. Equally important, however, is an understanding of how gender orders and notions of heteronormativity operate to limit women's 'space for action' (Kelly 2007: 89) to forge sustainable livelihoods which are *not* predicated upon their sexual and other labour exploitation, at home or abroad.

Human Rights Responses Enter the Arena

Both Lee (2011) and Segrave et al. (2009) advocate a shift in focus from tight border control and criminal justice responses to trafficking which inhibit or penalize women's mobility, and to foreground instead trafficking as a social problem, the response to which should be rooted in a human rights-based approach. International law, however and, from the latter part of the last century, human rights law and discourse, have something of a chequered history in responding to violations of women's human rights. In Western societies, current debates about the trafficking of women for sexual exploitation can be traced back to nineteenth century concerns about a 'White Slave Trade', leading to international efforts to regulate and combat 'white slavery' (Saunders and Soderlund 2003). The resulting International Agreement for the Suppression of the White Slave Trade 1904 defined trafficking as the procurement through coercion or fraud of women or girls abroad for immoral purposes (Rijken 2003: 54). Whilst the term 'abroad' may be given a wide or restrictive meaning – bearing in mind the colonial histories of many states – the 1910 International Convention for the Suppression of White Slave Traffic expanded this for the avoidance of doubt to include internal trafficking within the borders of a nation state (Derks 2000; Doezema 2002). Other Conventions followed during the next several decades, among them the 1921 International Convention for the Suppression of the Traffic in Women and Children and the 1949 Convention for the Suppression of the Traffic in Persons and of the Exploitation of the Prostitution of Others of the, by then, re-constituted, post World War II United Nations, which respectively removed the need to show coercion and declared prostitution to be 'incompatible with the dignity and worth of the human person' (UNDAW 2002: 2). Hence, then, like now, trafficking was linked to migration – in particular women's migration – and then, like now, it was linked to the prostitution of women, and attempts to combat this perceived, though unsubstantiated, 'white slave trade' were unashamedly paternal, gendered and 'racialized' (Kempadoo 2005). This changed as contemporary discourse on human rights entered the international arena.

The 1949 Convention, in particular, has its roots in human rights discourse, although its position with respect to prostitution was to prove unsustainable. As the evolving language of human rights heralded a shift from the gendered and racialized language of former international law, so issues of gender and race slipped into the shadows. Race was the first to re-emerge, with the adoption and entry into force in 1969 of the International Convention on the Elimination of All Forms of Racial Discrimination (CERD).[7] In ratifying the treaty, and in accordance with its preambular language, states confirm they are '[c]onvinced that any doctrine of superiority based on racial differentiation is scientifically false, morally condemnable, socially unjust and dangerous, and that there is no justification for racial discrimination, in theory or in practice, anywhere'. As Mackinnon (2006: 11) points out, 'CERD's formulation does not just up the rhetorical heat. It grounds the politics of equality in the world of reality'. It was another 10 years before the Convention to Eliminate All Forms of Discrimination Against Women (CEDAW)[8] issued a similar invitation, albeit in somewhat less forceful preambular language and, perhaps therefore, principle. Whilst condemning discrimination against women, the closest CEDAW comes to the wholesale rejection of the falsehood on which such discrimination is based lies in '[r]ecalling that discrimination against women violates the principles of equality of rights and respect for human dignity, is an obstacle to the participation of women, on equal terms with men, in the political, social, economic and cultural life of their countries, hampers the growth of the prosperity of society and the family and makes more difficult the full development of the potentialities of women in the service of their countries and of humanity'. Where the 'existence of racial barriers is repugnant to the ideals of any human society', and race discrimination 'an obstacle to friendly and peaceful relations among nations' (CERD: preamble), gender barriers and discrimination on grounds of sex impede women's ability to participate in and contribute to the prosperity of society and the family. Whilst CEDAW does elsewhere address many of the material realities facing differently situated women, the intention is not to challenge any doctrine of superiority based on sexual differentiation, or to unequivocally acknowledge the harm of gender-based discrimination.

Indeed, exploring patterns of systematic gender discrimination in some Middle-Eastern countries, Mayer (2000) queries why the international community

---

7   CERD 1969: 660 UNTS (UN Treaty Series) 195.

8   Convention to Eliminate All Forms of Discrimination Against Women 1979, 1249 UNTS 13.

has failed to classify widespread gender discrimination as a form of apartheid. Acknowledging that racial apartheid is a special category but nevertheless part of the broader problem that is racism, she posits that '[g]ender apartheid, despite its direct analogies to racial apartheid, has largely been seen as a relatively benign phenomenon' (ibid: 238). Continuing her analysis, Mayer points to the 1973 Apartheid Convention,[9] Article 1.1 of which defines apartheid as a 'crime against humanity', conduct which includes, by virtue of Article 2.2, acts by private individuals. She further points to Article II which acknowledges racial apartheid as a scheme of domination of one group over another and refers to 'inhuman acts committed for the purpose of establishing and maintaining domination by one racial group of persons over any other racial group of persons and systematically oppressing them'. Mayer cogently argues that 'defenders' of or 'apologists' for gender apartheid 'have tried to turn the discussion away from actual patterns of oppression of women, endeavoring to depoliticize this phenomenon ...' (ibid).

Whilst the Apartheid Convention was never widely ratified, and racism remains widespread, the principles expressed by the international community are clear. The language of both CERD and the Apartheid Convention leaves no room for doubt. Such practices amount to 'oppression' and involve 'crimes against humanity', the purpose of which is 'to establish and maintain' the 'domination' of one group over another. So forcefully is it condemned that it is without 'justification, in theory or in practice, anywhere', and states are required to 'prevent, eradicate and prohibit' it – unequivocally. CEDAW, on the other hand, makes no mention of 'oppression', 'domination' or 'crimes against humanity'. At Article II of CEDAW, states do indeed 'condemn discrimination against women in all its forms', but they are left to 'pursue by all *appropriate* means and without delay a *policy* of eliminating discrimination against women' (author's emphasis). Seen in the context of the preamble, such language cannot be said to be unequivocal; quite the opposite, it is entirely prescriptive and qualified. Here, again, in the words of MacKinnon (2006: 11), '[s]ex equality inhabits the realm of the good idea, the right view, a guide to proper thought and action, rather than being the only position consistent with the evidence'. Unlike CERD, CEDAW prescribes equality – as if unequal gender orders did not exist.

This brief, and limited,[10] overview of early anti-trafficking law and human rights discourse is nonetheless telling. The shift from the explicit pre-occupation in the nineteenth and early twentieth centuries with particular forms of (white women's) morality and, hence, specific 'protections' for (white) women, to the universal, ungendered language of human rights has not, in fact, shifted the

---

9   G.A. Res. 3068, U.N.G.A.O.R., 28th sess. Supp. No. 30 of Article 2. UN Doc A/9030 (1973) ("Apartheid Convention").

10   For a more detailed overview see, for example, Picarelli (2007), who charts the evolution of various forms of slavery and servitude to present day trafficking which, he concludes, 'retains the legacies ... and core aspects of these historical forms while adapting to meet new realities' (p. 45).

pre-occupation of international law with the morality/protection of women or, indeed, made any significant inroads in combating the trafficking of women. The Palermo Protocol may be commended in its acknowledgement of the particular vulnerabilities of women and, hence, the need for particular 'protections', but where basic questions fail to be addressed – who and what do women require protection from, and why? – notions of equality will remain aspirational, and paternalism will continue to lurk just beneath the surface, along with deep-rooted gender-stereotypes determining which women are 'deserving' of protection. Where the two specialized instruments intended to address race and gender discrimination respectively are concerned, CEDAW's reach into the collective psyche of the international community is considerably less than that of CERD, with the consequence that the harms of gender discrimination continue to go largely unaddressed. Guarantees of equality based on sameness are inadequate when the human rights violations suffered by women are different to those suffered by men, and where notions of 'equality' are themselves embedded in the very regimes dedicated to the preservation of unequal gender orders. As Audre Lorde (1984) prophetically commented, '[t]he master's tools will never dismantle the master's house'.

Limitations of Current Human Rights Approaches

The Palermo Protocol may have found a compromise and achieved international consensus on the definition of trafficking in persons but it came at the cost of abandoning wholesale the earlier position which found prostitution to be 'incompatible with the dignity and worth of the human person'. Of the many 'genealogies and discontinuities in the commodification of people' (Lee 2011: 3), and international responses thereto, this *volte face* ranks among the more glaring 'discontinuities' in historical, international approaches to trafficking. Sex trafficking is the means by which women and girls are sourced, corralled and herded into the world's sex and marriage industries. It is among the means by which men in rich countries can sexually buy women from poor countries (Belleau 2003) on the streets or in the brothels of their localities, or acquire 'brides' by mail order, or in the wake of organized tours by marriage agencies. There, men get to 'pick' their 'brides' – in much the same fashion as pimps select the women of their choice at the 'slave auctions' of trafficked women taking place within the confines of British airports (Weaver 2007). Whilst trafficking has been criminalized in most countries of the world, however, prostitution has not or, where it has, bribery, corruption, and an array of 'temporary marriage' arrangements (IRIN 2005, 2006) divert the official gaze. Prostitution, it seems, can be tolerated, but the means of delivering women into prostitution cannot. Just as the international community ultimately 'acquiesced to the cultural relativist position on women's rights ...' (Mayer 1995: 179) in relation to CEDAW, so it has again in abandoning its position on prostitution in the Palermo Protocol, with the consequence that the supply chain can and does remain unbroken.

Thus, advocating a human rights approach as even a partial solution to the problem of the traffic in women must be regarded with caution. This is not to say that human rights do not have *some* potential to address the patriarchal systems and structures which underpin women's subordination and, in doing so, to offer a vision of what substantive equality might look like. Indeed, whilst CEDAW does not specifically address violence against women, Article 6 does provide that 'States parties shall take all appropriate measures' (*sic*), 'including legislation, to suppress all forms of traffic in women and exploitation of prostitution of women'. This acknowledgement of the harms of trafficking and of the exploitation of women in prostitution paved the way – nearly 15 years later – for the CEDAW Committee's ground-breaking General Recommendation No. 19 on violence against women, noted to be a 'manifestation of historically unequal power relations between men and women'. In its opening comment, the CEDAW Committee determined that the definition of discrimination in Article 1 of CEDAW, which makes no mention of violence, nevertheless 'includes gender-based violence, that is, violence that is directed against a woman because she is a women or that affects women disproportionately' (CEDAW Committee 1992: paragraph 6).[11] Article 6 was re-affirmed. Perhaps most significantly, however, in its comments on Articles 2 and 3, the Committee links unequal gender orders with prostitution and violence against women, in noting that 'traditional attitudes by which women are regarded as subordinate to men ... also contribute to the propagation of pornography and other commercial exploitation of women as sexual objects, rather than individuals. This in turn contributes to gender-based violence (ibid: paragraphs 11 and 12)'.

However, the continued use of circumspect language, such as 'traditional' or 'historical'[12] to refer to the attitudes or the power relations which operate universally to deny women their universal human rights, suggests that they have no contemporary relevance. Even the 1993 Declaration[13] treads a careful line to distinguish between forced and free prostitution, thereby obscuring political realities of global and local power relations. While women in prostitution are differently situated in different parts of the world and will, therefore, have diverse experiences of benefits, costs, consequences and harms, where multiple

11   CEDAW Committee General Recommendation No 19, *Violence Against Women*, 11th Session 1992.

12   In the most recent regional instrument addressing violence against women, the Council of Europe Convention on Combating and Preventing Violence Against Women and Domestic Violence, the preambular language refers to a recognition of 'violence against women as a manifestation of *historically* unequal power relations between women and men ...' (author's emphasis). The full test of the Convention can be accessed at: http://conventions.coe.int/Treaty/EN/Treaties/HTML/DomesticViolence.htm.

13   Vienna Declaration and Programme of Action, General Assembly, A/CONF.157/23, 1993, Article 18.

and intersecting systems of discrimination operate to constrain their 'space for action', distinctions between force and choice are difficult to maintain. The real world is one in which '[n]o political system has conferred on women both the right to and the benefit of full and equal participation' (CEDAW Committee 1997: paragraph 14).[14] It is a world in which, by almost 'every indicator of social well-being and status – political participation, legal capacity, access to economic resources and employment, wage differentials, levels of education and health care – women fare significantly and sometimes dramatically worse than men' (Steiner and Alston 2000: 163). This is the context in which women often have to negotiate routes to survival along exceedingly narrow paths. For trafficked women, and for many women in prostitution, the line between life and death can taper to a knife-edge.

Conclusion

It is undoubtedly necessary to re-focus the trafficking debate away from a crime agenda and the criminalization of migrants – to 're-imagine' trafficking as a problem which 'should take "the social" rather than organized criminality as the starting point of discussion' (Lee 2011: 151). However, 'the social' is a highly stratified arena, in which intersections of gender, race, ethnicity, caste, and class impede women's access to safe migration and to sustainable livelihoods. Prostitution is undeniably one of the few means available to many women to forge or supplement a meagre living. However, it is also a foundation stone of gender inequality, a form of 'violence directed at a woman because she is a woman or which disproportionately affects women'. Trafficking is a form of violence against women, and global trafficking is the primary delivery and distribution system for prostitution industries across the world. The Palermo Protocol criminalizes that delivery and distribution system but is silent, like all international law, on the very institution which is the raison d'etre of the trade. This contradiction cannot be rectified by a human rights approach – to migrant and/or trafficked women – and human rights are no simple panacea for women trapped in circuits of survival, domestically and around the globe. In declaring prostitution to be 'incompatible with the dignity and worth of a human being' in 1949, the international community *had* a road map pointing the way to women's freedom from exploitation and commodification. That map is now far less legible, criss-crossed as it is by a multiplicity of networks, routes and intersections which, instead, constitute many roads to women's unfreedom. Human rights may still – just – hold out some promise, but if they are to more effectively address cause and consequence of the human wrongs perpetrated against trafficked women, they must themselves

---

14 Cedaw Committee General Recommendation No 23, *Political and Public Life*, 16th Session, 1997.

undergo a transformation and become the tools to 'dismantle the master's house'. As this chapter has demonstrated, there is as yet little evidence of this occurring.

References

Altink, S. (1995) *Stolen Lives – Trading Women into Sex and Slavery.* London, New York: Scarlet Press, Harrington Park Press.

Baden, S. (1999) 'Gender, Governance and the Feminization of Poverty', Background Paper No. 2, *Women and Political Participation: 21st Century Challenges.* Meeting organized by the United Nations Development Programme, New Delhi, 24–6 March.

Beck, U. (2000) *What is Globalization?* Cambridge: Polity Press.

Belleau, Marie-Claire (2003) 'Mail Order Brides in a Global World'. *Albany Law Review* 67: 59–607.

Belser, P., de Cock, M. and Mehran, F. (2005) *ILO Minimum Estimate of Forced Labour in the World.* Geneva: ILO.

Bumiller, K. (2008) *In an Abusive State: How Neoliberalism Appropriated the Feminist Movement Against Sexual Violence.* Durham: Duke University Press.

Christie, N. (1986) 'The Ideal Victim' in E.A. Fattah (ed.), *From Crime Policy to Victim Policy.* Basingstoke: MacMillan.

Connell, R.W. (1987) *Gender and Power: Society, the Person, and Sexual Politics.* Cambridge: Polity Press.

Davis, K. (1937) 'The Sociology of Prostitution'. *American Sociological Review* 2: 744–55.

Derks, A. (2000) 'From White Slaves to Trafficking Survivors – Notes on Trafficking Debate', The Center for Migration and Development, Princeton University Working Paper No. 00-02, May, in Segrave, M., Milivojevic, S. et al. (2009) *Sex Trafficking: International Context and Responses.* Cullompton: Willan.

Di Nicola, A. (2007) 'Researching into Human Trafficking: Issues and Problems' in M. Lee (ed.), *Human Trafficking.* Uffcolme, Cullompton: Willan.

Doezema, J. (2000) 'Loose Women or Lost Women? The Rre-emergence of the Myth of "White Slavery" in Contemporary Discourses of "Trafficking in Women"'. *Gender Issues* 18(1): 23–50.

Doezema, J. (2001) 'Ouch! Western Feminists' "Wounded Attachment" to the "Third World Prostitute"'. *Feminist Review* 67(1): 16–38.

Falk, R. (2001) 'Resisting "Globalization from Above" through "Globalization from Below"', in B. Gills (ed.), *Globalization and the Politics of Resistance.* Basingstoke: Palgrave.

Finckenauer, J.O. (2001) 'Russian Transnational Organised Crime and Human Trafficking', in D. Kyle and R. Koslowski (eds), *Global Human Smuggling – Comparative Perspectives.* Baltimore: The John Hopkins University Press.

Green, P. and Grewcock, M. (2002) 'The War against Illegal Immigration; State Crime and the Construction of a European Identity'. *Current Issues in Criminal Justice* 14(1): 97–101.

Giddens, A. (1990) *The Consequences of Modernity.* Cambridge: Polity Press.

Held, D. and McGrew, A. (eds) (2007) *Globalization Theory: Approaches and Controversies.* Cambridge: Polity Press.

Hillyard, P., Pantazis, C. et al. (eds) (2004) *Beyond Criminology: Taking Harm Seriously.* London: Pluto Press.

Holland, J., Ramazanoglu, C., Sharpe, S. and Thomson R. (1998) *The Male in the Head – Young People, Heterosexuality and Power.* London: The Tufnell Press.

Home Office and Scottish Executive (2007) *UK Action Plan on Tackling Human Trafficking.* London: Home Office.

International Organisation for Migration (2010) *The Causes and Consequences of Re-trafficking; Evidence from the IOM Human Traafficking Database.* Geneva: IOM.

IRIN (2005) *Yemen: Social Impact of Temporary Marriages.* IRIN. UN Office for the Coordination of Humanitarian Affairs, 7 July.

IRIN (2006) *In Egypt, Minors Sold for Prostitution under Guise of Marriage.* UN Office for the Coordination of Humanitarian Affairs, 17 November.

ILO (International Labour Organisation) (2005) *A Global Alliance Against Forced Labour.* Geneva: ILO.

Jackson, S. and Scott, S. (2010) *Theorising Sexuality.* Berkshire: Open University Press.

Kapur, R. (2005) 'Travel Plans: Human Rights of Transnational Migrants'. *Harvard Human Rights Journal* 18: 107–38.

Kelly, L. (1988) *Surviving Sexual Violence.* Cambridge: Polity Press.

Kelly, L. (2005) *Fertile Fields: Trafficking in Persons in Central Asia.* Vienna: IOM (International Organisation for Migration).

Kelly, L. (2007) 'A Conducive Context: Trafficking in Persons in Central Asia', in M. Lee (ed.), *Human Trafficking.* Uffcolme, Cullompton: Willan.

Kelly, L. (2001) *From Marginal to Globalised Issue: Three Decades of Research and Activism on Violence Against Women.* Inaugural Professorial Lecture given at (then) University of North London on 4 July 2001. The full text can be accessed at www.cwasu.org [accessed: 11 May 2011].

Kempadoo, K. (2005) 'From Moral Panic to Global Justice: Changing Perspectives on Trafficking', in Kempadoo, K., Sanghera, J. and B. Pattanaik (eds), *Trafficking and Prostitution Reconsidered – New Perspectives on Migration, Sex Work and Human Rights.* Boulder, CO: Paradigm Publishers, vii–xxxiv.

Lee, M. (ed.) (2007) *Human Trafficking.* Uffcolme, Cullompton: Willan.

Lee, M. (2011) *Trafficking and Global Crime Control.* London: Sage Publications Limited.

Lorde, A. (1984) *From Sister Outsider.* New York: The Crossing Press Feminist Series.

MacKinnon, C.A. (2006) *Are Women Human? And Other International Dialogues.* Cambridge, Massachusetts and London: The Bellknap Press of Harvard University Press.

Mayer, E.A. (1995) 'Cultural Particularism as a Bar to Women's Rights: Reflections on the Middle Eastern Experience' in J. Peters and Andrea Wolper (eds), *Women's Rights Human Rights, International Feminist Perspectives.* London: Routledge.

Mayer, E.A. (2000) *A "Benign" Apartheid: How Gender Apartheid has been Rationalized.* The full text can be accessed at: http://www.law-lib.utoronto.ca/diana/fulltext/maye.htm [accessed: 11 October 2011].

Melossi, D. (2003) '"In a Peaceful Life": Migration and the Crime of Modernity in Europe/Italy'. *Punishment and Society* 5(4): 371–97.

Melossi, D. (2005) 'Security, Social Control, Democracy and Migration within the "Constitution" of the EU'. *European Law Journal* (11)1: 5–21.

Miriam, K. (2005) 'Stopping the Traffic in Women: Power, Agency and Abolition in Feminist Debates over Sex Trafficking'. *Journal of Social Philosophy* 36.1, Spring: 1–17.

Monzini, P. (2005) *Sex Traffic.* London: Zed Books Limited.

Pickering, S. (2004) 'Border Terror: Policing, Forced Migration and Terrorism'. *Global Change, Peace and Security* 16(3): 211–26.

O'Connell Davidson, J. (2006) 'Will the Real Sex Slave Please Stand Up?' *Feminist Review* 83: 4–22.

Picarelli, J. (2007) 'Historical Approaches to the Trade in Human Beings' in M. Lee (ed.), *Human Trafficking.* Uffcolme, Cullompton: Willan.

Raymond, J., D'Cunha, J., Dzuhayatin, S.R., Hynes, H.P., Rodriguez, Z.R. and Santos, A. (2002) *A Comparative Study of Women Trafficked in the Migration Process.* Amherst: MA. Coalition Against Trafficking in Women. Available at: http://action.web.ca/home/catw/attach/CATW%20Comparative%20Study%202002.pdf [accessed: 21 April 2011].

Rijken, C. (2003) *Trafficking in Persons – Prosecution from a European Perspective.* The Hague: Asser Press.

Rubin, G. (1975) 'The Traffic in Women: Notes of the "Political Economy" of Sex' in Reiter, R. (ed.), *Towards an Anthropology of Women.* New York and London: Monthly Review Press, 157–210.

Sassen, S. (2002) 'Women's Burden: Counter-geographies of Globalization and the Feminization of Survival'. *Nordic Journal of International Law* 71: 255–74.

Saunders, P. and Soderland, G. (2003) 'Threat or Opportunity? Sexuality, Gender and the Ebb and Flow of Trafficking as Discourse'. *Canadian Women's Studies* 22(3–4): 16–24.

Segrave, M., Milivojevic, S. et al. (2009) *Sex Trafficking: International Context and Responses.* Cullompton: Willan.

Shelley, L. (2000) 'Post-communist Transitions and Illegal Movement of Peoples: Chinese Smuggling and Russian Trafficking in Women'. *Annals of Scholarship* 14(2): 71–84.

Shelley, L. (2003) 'The Trade in People in and from the Former Soviet Union', *Crime, Law, and Social Change* 40: 231–49.

Shelley, L. (2007) 'Human Trafficking as a Form of Transnational Crime' in M. Lee (ed.), *Human Trafficking*. Uffcolme, Cullompton: Willan.

Silverman, J., Decker, M. et al. (2007) 'HIV Prevalence and Predictors of Infection in Sex-trafficked Nepalese Girls and Women', *Journal of the American Medical Association* 298(5): 536–42.

Skeldon, R. (2000) 'Trafficking: A Perspective from Asia'. *International Migration* 38(3): 7–29.

Stanley, L. (1995) *Sex Surveyed: From Mass-Observation's 'Little Kinsey' to the National Survey and the Hite Reports.* London: Taylor and Francis.

Steiner, H.J. and Alston, P. (2000*) International Human Rights in Context, Law, Politics, Morals (2nd ed.)*. Oxford: Oxford University Press.

Turner, J. and Kelly, L. (2009) 'Trade Secrets: Intersections between Diasporas and Crime Networks in the Constitution of the Human Trafficking Chain'. *British Journal of Criminology* 49(2): 184–201.

United Nations Division for the Advancement of Women (2002) *The UN Response to Trafficking Women and Girls.* New York: Department of Economic and Social Affairs (DESA), UN.

United Nations Office on Drugs and Crime (2006) *Trafficking in Persons: Global Patterns.* Vienna: UNODC.

United Nations Office on Drugs and Crime (2009) *Trafficking in Persons: Analysis on Europe.* Vienna: UN:GIFT.

Weaver, M. (2007) 'National Police Campaign to Target Sex Trafficking'. *Guardian*, 3 October 2007.

Weitzer, R. (2007) 'The Social Construction of Sex Trafficking: Ideology and Institutionalization of a Moral Crusade'. *Politics and Society* 35: 447–75.

Welsh, M. (2003) 'Ironies of Social Control and the Criminalization of Immigrants'. *Crime, Law and Social Change* 39: 319–37.

Wright, A. (2006) *Organised Crime.* Uffcolme, Cullompton: Willan.

Zedner, L. (2000) 'The Pursuit of Security' in T. Hope and R. Sparks (eds), *Crime, Risk and Insecurity.* London: Routledge, 200–214.

Zimmerman, C., Yun, K., Shvab, I., Watts, C., Trappolin, L., Treppete, M., Bimbi, F., Adams, B., Jiraporn, S., Beci, L., Albrecht, M., Bindel, J. and Regan, L. (2003) *The Health Risks and Consequences of Trafficking in Women and Adolescents: Findings from a European Study*. London: London School of Hygiene & Tropical Medicine.

Chapter 3
Meeting Gendered Demand:
Domestic Sex Trafficking in Chicago

Jody Raphael

Introduction

Women and girls brought to the United States from other countries for the sex trade have been viewed as innocent victims of trafficking deserving of support. But young women born in the United States, who may be similarly coerced and controlled, are treated as out-of-control juveniles deserving detention, or freely consenting to sell sex, whose choices should be honored and supported.[1] By reinforcing a free/forced distinction, these approaches obscure the complexity of harm and exploitation often present in the sex trade industry (Kelly 2003), and methods of recruitment that this chapter seeks to illustrate.

In the United States, Congress has defined sex trafficking as 'the recruitment, harboring, transportation, provision, or obtaining of a person for the purpose of a commercial sex act, in which a commercial sex act is induced by force, fraud, or coercion, or in which the person forced to perform such an act is under the age of 18 years' (Trafficking Victims Protection Act 2000). U.S. law makes no distinctions between international and recruitment of local girls, which is also referred to as 'domestic trafficking', and does not require the girls or women to be transported across state lines to qualify as a victim of trafficking. Within the last few years, local law enforcement officials, responding with sting operations to Internet advertisements of girls and women selling sex, have discovered many locally born girls and women who have been recruited to the sex trade industry and maintained there through coercion and violence, who meet the federal definition of trafficked victims.

---

1   For example, 12-year-old Nicolette, a victim of childhood sexual assault, who ran away and came under the control of an adult male pimp, was apprehended in New York State in 2004. Authorities noted multiple scars on her body, including cigarette and iron burns, and a recently fractured rib. Despite this, the judge committed her to a facility for juvenile delinquents. On appeal, the court found that even though Nicolette was 12 years old and incapable of consenting to any sexual act under the penal code, the statute defining prostitution contained no age requirement and did not prohibit her incarceration. In the Matter of Nicolette R. 9 A.D.3d 270 (2004).

Law enforcement officials throughout the United States have targeted Craigslist, one of the most popular websites that links buyers and sellers throughout the nation, because sting operations related to Craigslist have resulted in police officers meeting up with minors in the hotel rooms. In the Chicago metropolitan area, for example, sheriff's deputies responded to an advertisement that included a nude photograph of a teenager, a 16-year-old runaway who had been forced into prostitution by two men, who were then arrested in another hotel room (Chicago Breaking News 2008). In May 2010, police responded to an online advertisement and found an 18-year-old who stated she had only been in the sex trade industry for a week. The undercover officers saw 'obvious and visible signs that she had been a victim of repeated acts of violence'; she disclosed that two young men had pressured, threatened, and beaten her, taking her belongings and keeping the money she was forced to make in prostitution (Chicago Breaking News 2010). Reportedly, Craigslist's adult services advertisements were expected to bring in $36 million in profits in 2010 (Stone 2010).[2]

This is an important moment in time in the United States. Emerging awareness of domestic recruitment and trafficking has begun to catch the attention of the public, police officers, and elected officials. Using data from three recent Chicago research samples (100 pimp-controlled girls, 113 customers, and five ex-pimps), and supported by existing literature, this chapter explores recruitment practices and the harms young women in Chicago experienced during and after recruitment into the sex trade. The data indicate that it is necessary to look beyond the theoretical focus on empowerment and choice that has dominated discourses about prostitution (see Jeffreys: Chapter 4), and develop new legal and policy responses that recognize gendered dynamics, and harms.

A Limited Knowledge Base

There is little formal research literature specifically focusing on recruitment processes, although there is increasing awareness and knowledge of how young women are 'groomed' into prostitution by men posing as boyfriends. Existing research confirms that coercive recruitment has occurred for significant proportions of women and girls. When 26 homeless women were interviewed in Nottingham, UK, a third (nine) reported involvement in prostitution, and of these, all said they had been forced into the sex trade industry by their partners, typically abusive and violent men (Harding and Hamilton 2009). In one of the few research studies specifically studying pathways into prostitution, 54 women in or formerly in the sex trade were interviewed in Vancouver, Canada. Similar to the Chicago findings, 12 per cent reported being forced to participate on the streets by their mothers,

---

2   Section 230 of the U.S. Communications Decency Act of 1996 provides complete immunity to web providers like Craigslist for the content posted by others. Title V of the Telecommunications Act of 1996, codified at 47 U.S.C. Section 230. Craigslist shut down its Erotic Services Section in September 2010.

fathers, foster parent, or older sibling, and 16 per cent described being recruited by a boyfriend or a pimp to whom they had an emotional attachment and to whom they felt indebted for gifts, clothing, money, or drugs (Kennedy et al. 2007). Research with a sample of 222 Chicago women in prostitution found that almost 71 per cent said that someone had suggested to them that they should be involved in the sex trade industry; approximately 20 per cent stated they had entered prostitution through being urged by a boyfriend (Raphael and Shapiro 2002). In a study of 47 women, all of whom had been involved in street prostitution before the age of 18 in western Canada, 19 per cent said they had been forced, coerced, or intimidated into prostitution by pimps or abusive intimate partners (Nixon et al. 2002).

The Chicago Research

Following findings from previous research, this study hypothesized that a significant proportion of young women may not have decided on their own to be involved in the sex trade industry, but may have been actively recruited by pimps and traffickers to supply demand for paid sex, with their involvement in the industry maintained through coercion and violence. Thus we developed a research project to examine the recruitment process in metropolitan Chicago. By interviewing young women controlled by pimps, the research aimed to add to the knowledge base about recruitment methods and levels of coercion, control, deception, and violence. Between July and December 2007, a total of 100 young women up to the age of 25 were interviewed in Chicago, all of whom were under the control of a pimp or trafficker at the time of the study. Due to the clandestine nature of the sex trade industry, it is not possible to construct a representative sample, nor is it possible to accurately identify the number of domestic girls and women trafficked into prostitution. Thus the sample reported on in this chapter was neither random nor necessarily representative of all women and girls involved in prostitution in the Chicago metropolitan area.

The research employed two survivors of prostitution who were trained to verbally administer a face-to-face structured survey which lasted about 30 minutes. Questions explored experiences of violence and being controlled at recruitment into the sex trade and if and how this altered over time (see Raphael and Ashley 2008; Raphael, Reichert and Powers 2010 for more details). Approximately half (55) the interviews were conducted at the site of a court-mandated alternative to incarceration programme for women and girls in prostitution. Others were interviewed on the streets, in restaurants, nail spas, and hotels. That those conducting the structured interviews had also been involved in the sex trade enabled trust and rapport to be established. In addition, the survivors, who had long been active in prostitution in Chicago, could more readily identify young women in prostitution to interview, including those involved in off-street and more hidden settings. Survivors/surveyors and participants made decisions about the safety of their involvement and determined when and where they could be interviewed in locations that prioritized women's safety.

Ages in the sample ranged from 16 to 25 years, with 21 the mean age. Over half of the women were Black, 20 per cent were white, and 15 per cent Hispanic. Study participants included women and girls selling sex indoors as well as on the street. The next sections turn to the key findings from the study.

Recruitment into the Sex Trade

Confirming our hypothesis, almost three-quarters (71 per cent) of the sample said others recruited them into the sex trade; the remainder stated they became involved on their own.[3] Of those recruited by others, 10 per cent said a family member had enticed or ordered them, including sisters, brothers, uncles, and foster parents. A third (35 per cent) said they were persuaded or groomed into the sex trade by a man or pimp serving a 'boyfriend' function.

The average age upon entry to the sex trade was approximately 16-and-a-half, with a third (33 per cent) between 12 and 25 when they regularly began selling sex. This early age of entry is corroborated by at least one other piece of research, a study of 19 pimped women and girls in the UK (whose average age at the time of interview was 26), which also found an average age of first involvement to be 16 years (May et al. 2000).

Recruitment by Family Members

In our sample, family member recruitment generally fell into two different categories: coercion from parents or foster parents, and suggestions from sisters and other relatives already in the business. On average, girls who had been ordered into the sex trade by family members were over two years younger than those recruited by non-family members. Two young women in our sample began prostituting regularly at the age of 12. One of these said that her brother sexually abused her after their mother died of an overdose. They went to live with cousins and her brother coerced her into prostitution. 'He said he wouldn't tell anyone about our secret and if I got money he would take care of me, but he did neither', she said. 'He told our cousin who decided to put me out. Then he really used me'.

The other 12-year-old was coerced by her foster parent, who told the young teen that if she did as he asked, he wouldn't 'mess with' her sister, but he ultimately abused her sister anyway. 'He would bring his buddies by from work and they would take turns with me. My foster parent taught me what to do'. Another reported that at 14, when her mother went to jail, her stepfather forced her into the sex trade to support them both financially.

---

3   Of the women and girls who began involvement in prostitution without a pimp, all ultimately ended up with one.

One young woman's story describes a recruitment scenario involving her sisters. She reported living with her mother, eight siblings, and an aunt with another three children. They all lived in a three-bedroom apartment. Her sister had moved out when she was 17.

> She always had nice clothes she would let me wear sometimes. I asked her how she got them, and that's when she told me [she was a prostituted woman]. She said it was real easy. She said I could quit when I got ready but that wasn't true. I haven't been able to quit. First I am scared to leave my sister behind, and now I have a heroin habit.

She and her sister are pimped by the same man.

> I don't know anything else to do and I won't leave my sister. She needs me. If we could get clean and get a house in the country. I'm dreaming, huh?

Homelessness and Escaping Childhood Sexual Abuse

Approximately a quarter of the young women in our sample described abusive family situations forcing them onto the streets at early ages, where they were subjected to successful grooming by pimps posing as boyfriends. Others, needing money for basic necessities, were introduced by girlfriends or relatives already in the business. Two young women in our sample were recruited into the sex trade by girls who had run away from the same foster home and had become involved in prostitution. Another explained:

> I ran away from home and I needed money to live, so I started having sex for money. It is so easy to make $200–$300 a day. I can get me a room and buy some clothes.

One young girl became homeless when her boyfriend kicked her out of the house. As she walked down the street, a man in a car approached her and asked her if she wanted to make money. He regularly employed violence, from slapping and punching to forced sex, in order to keep her trading sex with 10 to 15 customers a night.

Running away from childhood sexual abuse led to some young women becoming homeless. One pimp, for example, helped a 15-year-old girl run away from home because her mother's boyfriend was abusing her. 'He was sleeping with me and no one would believe me, so I was out of there', she said. 'We ran out of money while on the road and he showed me how to work the truck stops'. Eight years later, she is still with him, having sex with nine customers a day on the street and in hotels. 'I am okay with what I have and do', she explained. 'It's better than where I came from'. Another ran away from foster care because of sexual abuse and met her pimp on the street when she was 15 years old.

After leaving home to escape sexual abuse from her father, another young woman began prostituting at age 16. To survive, she said she routinely sold sex to 15 to 25 customers a day in a variety of prostitution venues. Now 23, she has a drug habit. 'I feel like I want to commit suicide sometimes', she said. 'I want to get my life back'.

Several studies of women and girls in prostitution find high prevalence of childhood sexual abuse (Farley et al. 2003). In the western Canadian research, for example, 63 per cent of the girls had a child abuse history and 64 per cent had been involved with the child welfare system (Nixon et al. 2002). Fifty-three per cent of the women in prostitution in the Cook County (Chicago) Jail between 1991 and 1993 reported being sexually abused as children, as compared to 38 per cent of the entire sample of jailed women, and childhood sexual assault nearly doubled the odds of entry into prostitution during the lifetime of the respondent (McClanahan et al. 1999). Research has also documented how sexual abuse grooms girls for prostitution, teaching them that love, attention, and financial rewards follow from sex, and showing how sexual use of the body can be an asset (Finkelhor 1988). One study suggested that 'girls learn that their sexual favors are a commodity to be exchanged for what they need developmentally (intimacy, avoidance of physical assault, a sense of importance to someone), for survival (food, rent, money), and what they want socially (particularly drugs)' (Dunlap et al. 2003: 92).

Taking Care of Family Members

Some girls were compelled to sell sex to financially support family members. One of the young women joined an escort service at age 17 because she needed the money to keep her family together. 'Some [family members] are illegal and that's why me and my sister needed money to help them', she explained. One 14-year-old was recruited while trying to care for her young siblings. Her mother was in the streets most of the time, and for extra money, she cared for a male cousin's babies. She shared the following:

> One day when I asked him for money to pay for some food and to get our lights back on, he said he would set me up with something. He set me up with a trick. He would make me give him a cut even though he knew I really needed the money for my brothers.

Now she is 19 years old, and separated from her siblings. 'I really need someone to help me get my little brothers back and a place for us', she explained.

The Recruitment Process

The recruitment process documented by our research, and corroborated by other studies (Hodgson 1997; Kennedy et al. 2007; Williamson and Cluse-Tolar 2002), illustrates how many girls become involved with intimate partners/pimps who end up coercing and abusing them. Homelessness, or near-homelessness, and childhood sexual assault made young women receptive to the manipulation of the recruiters they met on the street. Their need for love, stability and protection enabled pimps to easily reel them in. For instance, offers of a place to stay, money, or drugs, usually cannabis, were common. Said one participant:

> He promised me everything and better. Clothes, cars, house, himself. I was just looking for someone to love and love me.

This young woman's statement reflected a common scenario reported by those who participated in the research:

> He told me how much he loved me and how he wanted the best for me. At first I was not working. He bought me clothes, jewellery, and furs. After about two months or less, he said if I loved him then I would date his friend, then another, and another.

Responses demonstrate how emotionally vulnerable young women were deceived, only later learning that the promises were hollow. 'He told me he would buy me a fur coat. He didn't', said one. 'He did not take care of me as promised. There were no clothes or shoes and there was hardly any money', explained another. Promises of protection from violence from customers were common, but often quickly exposed as untrue: 'He told me that I would be safe. That didn't happen. I got beat up a lot'. Said another: 'He told me that I would never get hurt. I get hurt on a regular basis'. 'He promised no violence. There is violence', remarked a third young girl. Another summed it up: 'Everything he said to me was a lie'.

Interviews with five ex-pimps in a pilot research project in Chicago confirm the focus of pimps/traffickers on vulnerable girls, with the typical initial strategy being fraudulent promises of love and support (see Raphael and Myers-Powell 2009; Raphael and Myers-Powell 2010). One ex-pimp said he targeted 'neighborhood girls who weren't doing well and had low self-esteem'. Another explained:

> I looked for girls who needed things, who would do what ever to come out of the messed up homes and escape from their messed up parents, and I pulled those girls. Women who had been abused by some sucker, who wanted better treatment and nice things.

One pimp said he was doing a favour for vulnerable young girls by offering them a survival strategy:

> I don't feel I forced anyone or made anyone do anything they didn't want to do. In fact, I helped girls no one else would, I picked up throwaways and runaways and dressed them up and taught them how to survive.

Pimps also described the deception and lies they used to manipulate.

> I would tell them I was an agent. I would say I designed clothes. I even told them I sang with certain bands. It was more challenging when I got girls who were older. I really became more creative the older the girls were.

Another, who expressed regret for his actions, said 'We eat, drink, and sleep, thinking of ways to trick young girls into doing what we want them to do'.

These ex-pimps in this small volunteer sample expressed derogatory feelings toward the young girls. They were 'stupid', they said. Another explained, 'Some women are made to be whores', attitudes that enabled them to justify their treatment of young women as disposable. Previous research on processes of pimping, although limited, has also highlighted these deceptive practices with emotionally vulnerable young women. The pretense of love, combined with material assistance, was documented by Williamson and Cluse-Tolar (2002), who spent six months on the streets undertaking in-depth interviews with six pimp-controlled women. Similar findings were found by Kennedy and colleagues (2007), as well as by Hodgson (1997), who interviewed 28 pimps in Canada and the United States. He noted:

> The psychological coercion and manipulation that is exercised during this method of procurement is most successful in motivating these vulnerable recruits. The seduction method of procurement bonds the woman not only to the pimp but to a lifestyle that is presented to her as having many beneficial and rewarding components (p. 56).

For many women in our sample, however, coercion and violence were also necessary at initial stages. Half (49 per cent) of those recruited into the sex trade reported being subjected to coercion, including threats (threats of being kicked out of the home, threats to end the romantic relationship, and threats of harm), verbal abuse, and denial of certain benefits (money taken, withholding of drugs) at the time of recruitment. Fifty-five per cent said they were coerced by means of verbal abuse at the time of recruitment. Money was taken from half (52 per cent), and almost the same proportion (45 per cent) were told they were indebted to the recruiters because of the provision of food, clothing, and gifts. Almost two-fifths (39 per cent) were threatened with harm, and a third (32 per cent) said the person recruiting them warned that he would end the romantic relationship. One young woman said her pimp menaced that he would hurt her younger sister, and another threatened to take her baby from her if she did not comply. This emotional manipulation was a powerful means to ensure compliance and acquiescence.

One young woman explained, 'I knew no one would like me or talk to me if I did not do what they asked. I just wanted to be loved'.

Post-recruitment Violence

For the young women in our sample, involvement in the sex trade represented a downward spiral of exploitation and violence. There was, for example, at the time of participation in the research, an average increase of almost four customers per day from initial recruitment, from an average daily number of customers of 6 to 10, and greater violence from pimps and traffickers. In addition, there was for some young women a correlation between an increase in number of customers and heightened levels of violence and coercive control from pimps over time. After recruitment the young women were more than three times as likely to be pinched or kicked, twice as likely to be punched, kidnapped, or to have clothing ripped, and more than twice as likely to be forced to have sex with their pimps. Young women were also more likely to be transported to customers (58 per cent during recruitment to 67 per cent afterwards). These data indicate that the processes of luring young women into prostitution may not involve explicit harm and abuses, but that later violence escalates once women have been emotionally manipulated.

After recruitment, three-quarters (76 per cent) experienced slapping, half (51 per cent) punching, and rape (52 per cent). One was attacked with brass knuckles and a baseball bat, and had been tied up with a rope by her pimp. This young woman, who became involved in street prostitution on her own at age 14, connected with a pimp after being beaten and robbed. She could not leave him, she said, out of fear and a lack of a safe place to go. Another, who began in the sex trade industry at age 18 on her own, said her pimp attacked her with a hammer and screwdriver. She was required to have sex with 10 to 15 customers a day on the streets. When asked if she wanted to leave prostitution, she explained she was prevented by fear of having little or no money, and no one to watch over her. One young woman, who reported having sex with 20 to 30 customers a day at various prostitution venues, had been subjected to suffocation with pillows. She said 'fear of what he would do, and fear of being alone' prevent her from leaving. Another, who reported having sex with 15 customers a day at various prostitution venues, revealed that her pimp had put her in the trunk of a car and had threatened to kill her.

Those young women selling sex in indoor locations, often considered to be less violent venues, were not immune from pimp violence. Just over a quarter (28 per cent) of women and girls in our study started as escorts. Of these, almost all (93 per cent) said they had a pimp from the beginning, and a quarter experienced violence from them. At the time of the interview (post-recruitment), 41 per cent of the women were escorts. More than two-thirds of these had experienced violence at the hands of their pimps (67 per cent), and more than half had to turn their earnings over to the pimp (56 per cent). Pimps transported almost 80 per cent of the escorts to their customers. Nearly two-fifths (37 per cent) of women said they could not or were unsure if they could leave the sex trade without harm.

Post-recruitment Coercion

After recruitment, young women were also subject to coercion (in terms of emotional and psychological abuse) at higher rates. Threats to end the romantic relationship had risen to 69 per cent (from 32 per cent), and 69 per cent of the sample reported their money was taken, up from 52 per cent at the time of recruitment.

Women's lives became more and more constricted; two-thirds said they had to live in a certain place. Thirty-seven per cent of participants were not allowed to leave to visit friends and family. Forty per cent said their pimp watched them when they were not trading sex with customers, and another fifth (20 per cent) were not sure if they were under surveillance. These women were also transported beyond state lines in a process of domestic trafficking. Twenty-eight per cent of the sample said at the time of the interview they were being taken to neighbouring states such as Indiana and Wisconsin, but also to other locales including California, Atlanta, Georgia, Florida, Las Vegas, Nevada, and the Illinois state capital in Springfield.

Fear of what the pimp might do was what kept many girls in the sample from escaping or attempting to escape. Forty-three per cent of the sample reported they could not leave without physical harm and an additional 20 per cent said they were unsure if they could leave without physical injury. 'He said I can only leave in a box', said one, a statement that captures the experiences of the majority of women who participated. 'I need immediate help to stop this lifestyle', said another. 'I don't want to continue this in fear that I may not survive'. In addition, the research found that coercive control (Stark 2007) and violence went hand in hand; that is, few girls who experienced coercive control did not also experience violence from their pimp.

It is also important to note that these young girls were not passive or without some sense of power. Rather, they were strong and resourceful young women, coping with adversity, but in ways constrained by limited 'space for action' (Lundgren 1998, cited in Kelly 2003), making decisions in circumstances that reduced how they could exercise their self-determination. This quote from a young woman interviewed for the study illustrates the resilience expressed by many:

> I used to turn two to three tricks after I left school when I was a freshman with some guys in my neighborhood so I could eat and buy clothes. My mom was on drugs. She never had money to feed or clothe me. Once you get out here you are lost and you don't know any other way. People should know that us girls are not different. If anything, we are better because we didn't give up.

Violence from Customers

Data reported so far refer to violence that girls experienced at the hands of the pimp/trafficker. Customers can also perpetrate violence against women and girls in prostitution, and many participants also made reference to this. Studies document physical violence from customers at greater levels in outdoor venues (the street), but the amount of violence in indoor prostitution venues is not insignificant. In a sample of 222 women in prostitution in Chicago in 2002, of 113 women who operated on the streets, almost 20 per cent stated that customers had frequently (more than 10 times) threatened them with a weapon, 22 per cent frequently had sex forced on them, 39 per cent reported being slapped frequently, and 33 per cent were frequently punched. Those involved with escort services experienced frequent rape at the same rate (21.4 per cent), 29 per cent said they were frequently slapped, 18 per cent frequently punched, 32 per cent frequently had their hair pulled, and 21 per cent said their clothes were frequently ripped. Almost 29 per cent of women in escort services had fingers or objects forced into them frequently (more than 10 times) as compared to 18 per cent of women on the streets. Customers were the most frequently identified perpetrators of this violence across all types of prostitution (Raphael and Shapiro 2002).

Interviews with 113 men who buy sex in Chicago document that the ability to inflict violence may be part of the allure of prostitution for some buyers (Durchslag and Goswami 2008). The men's comments also illustrate the extent to which they view the girls and women as commodities or objects, which exist solely for their own pleasure. Although not representative of all sex buyers, the volunteer sample is notable in that significant proportions of men who came forward to talk about prostitution were frequent users. Approximately 40 per cent had paid for sex with between 1 to 10 women, but a quarter had purchased sex from between 11 to 20 women, and another 15 per cent had bought sex from between 21 to 40 women in the course of their lives. Just over 40 per cent purchased sex either monthly (20 per cent) or several times a month (21 per cent), and 27 per cent bought sex a couple of times a year.

Almost half of interviewees said they purchased sex to obtain acts they either felt uncomfortable asking of their partner or which their partner refused to perform, including anal and oral sex, using sex toys, and group sex, among others. 'I want to pay someone to do something a normal person wouldn't do', said one, 'to piss on someone or pay someone to do something degrading who is not my girlfriend' (p. 12). One man described his trip to Las Vegas where he and a friend bought sex: 'It was a threesome of me and my play bro … we came on her face at the same time, like in the porn movies' (p. 13).

Some of the men were straightforward about their interest in violence. Nineteen per cent of the interviewees told researchers they had raped a woman, and one in six (13 per cent) said they would rape a woman if they knew they could get away with it. Some, in answers to other questions, made clear that they sought out women in prostitution in order to commit acts of violence against them: 'She feels a lot of force between her legs, because I'm not going to be lenient. I'm going to give her everything I've got. You can pound them, she don't mind' (p. 15).

What emerged from this study was how some respondents compared women in prostitution to objects. For these men, women ceased to be individuals and instead became 'products' that could be bought and used. Some compared the women they bought to food, perhaps also indicating that women are something to which these men believed they were entitled, like food or water. 'Prostitutes are like a product, like cereal. You go the grocery, pick the brand you want, and pay for it. It's business', said one. Explained another, 'I usually call for a girl, you know, like a pizza' (p. 16). Yet another framed it thus, 'Like a grocery store where the food is tested and regulated, they should regulate prostitutes' (p. 16).

Men's comments also demonstrated negative and pejorative views of all females, not just women in prostitution. Since 60 per cent of the men believed that all women can be bought, they saw no perceived harm when purchasing a woman in prostitution since they all are viewed as 'for sale'. The only dissimilarity was that a man must buy a woman who is not in prostitution dinner and/or gifts in order to obtain sex from her. 'Women are all the same, they all make you pay', said one. 'I see no difference in women as a whole' (p. 16). Explained another: 'When you take a woman to dinner or the movies, it's basically the same thing. There's the cost of flowers, dinner, a show, dancing – it's $150–$200. By that point you might as well call a prostitute when the girl finally gives in' (p. 17). Many of these comments are nearly identical to those obtained in a recent research project in the UK, in which some men explicitly conceptualized women as commodities (Coy 2008; Coy et al.: Chapter 7). Violence from pimps and customers illustrates how both view the girl or woman as a commodity to be manipulated and exploited for their own use.

Exiting the Sex Trade Industry

Exiting and escaping prostitution were highlighted by women and girls as difficult due to a combination of material and emotional factors, as illustrated by the following comments: 'I don't have anybody else who cares about me'. Explained another, 'Me being homeless and my mother not caring for me'. 'Fear of him and of being alone in the world. I have nowhere to go', commented a third. Pimps are well practised in using isolation, violence, coercion, and love to bind young women to them. The imagined loss of love and protection are strong factors keeping girls and women bound to pimps and traffickers. One young woman said:

> Where would I go? What would I do? In the midst of what I endure, I'm in love
> with my man. He wants me more than any other woman.

However, involvement in prostitution also carries with it a powerful social stigma that increases isolation, and for some young women this served to prevent them from seeking support. Brenda Myers-Powell, a 25-year survivor of pimp-controlled prostitution, explains the complex nature of this entrapment. After Brenda's mother died when she was six months old, she was raised by an alcoholic grandmother, abused at the age of four or five, frequently beaten and verbally abused, and began in prostitution at age 15. Her experience is worth quoting at length here in order to give voice to how combinations of abuse, emotional vulnerability and coercive control reduced her 'space for action' (Lundgren 1988, cited in Kelly 2003):

> Low self-esteem and looking for love in all the wrong places. Low self-esteem even when you seem strong. I look at the kid that I have now and I try not to make the mistakes that were made with me. Because this stuff started early, very early. Being yelled at all the time, being spanked all the time for anything I did, never being encouraged, never being told that I was special, all those things led up. And during that same time I was being molested. There was a piece of me that was destroyed and that was the piece that the pimps play on. They are offering me everything that was taken from me.

> And they give it to me in the beginning, and then they gradually take it back because they know that I'll do anything to get it back from them. I want to get it back from them. I want you to treat me like you treated me when I first went with you. What did I do wrong? You see, because it is always my fault. What did I do wrong for you not to treat me like that? Do I need to make more money for you? Do I need to do this for you? What do I need to do, to take more chances on my life for you in order to make you love me? I'll take the beating, I'll take the whooping, but I just want you to say you love me, that you care for me, because you did in the beginning and it was wonderful and I like that feeling. And all the time I am trying to get that fix back, I want that feeling. I want you to treat me like that again. I am the one that's wrong when you don't. So I want you to treat me like that again.

> Why does she stay? Because we are trying to get something we never got from anybody and we had maybe ten minutes of it from him and we want it back. We don't have what it takes inside of us to know, until someone can talk to us and let us know that you can be free.[4]

After being rejected and stigmatized during multiple attempts to seek support from medical professionals, Brenda was finally referred to a specialist service for women in prostitution, who supported her to build a new life away from the sex trade.

---

4 Brenda Myers-Powell, author interview, 9 September 2009.

Implications and Conclusions

The young women in this Chicago study meet the definition of sex trafficking as defined by U.S. law, as they were recruited into prostitution by force, fraud and coercion, and/or under the age of 18 years old. When viewed in this way, these girls and women should not be prosecuted under state prostitution laws as many are at present.[5]

Abstract debates about legalization of prostitution, based on concepts of consent and individual choice, have diverted attention from these patterns of coercion. Notions of consent and agency obscure the role of the recruiter, who is linked to an organized industry, which is creating and profiting from the demand for women's bodies (see also Jeffreys: Chapter 4). Findings from the studies conducted in Chicago demonstrate that girls and women in prostitution are viewed by many as necessary cogs in a machine or industry that must, in turn, increase the degree of coercion and force to maintain their continued participation. Approaches that focus on agency and individual empowerment have also contributed to legalization or acceptance and normalization of prostitution, which, as others argue in this volume, may increase demand, and hence more recruitment, trafficking, and exploitation.

Current responses in the United States are limited to identification of trafficked girls and women and a new focus on arresting and prosecuting pimps and traffickers. Support for individual girls and women, including safe shelter instead of their arrest and incarceration, is vitally necessary. Arresting pimps and traffickers is also important but also beset with difficulties since it requires girls and women to divulge the identity and location of their pimps and to cooperate with prosecutions, a complex request given their fears for safety and emotional attachments to pimps/traffickers. As strategies to end trafficking, however, both come up short. Neither will end recruitment of vulnerable girls into prostitution, for others will be recruited to take their places to meet men's demand. The ex-pimps in our study explained that recruitment 'never stopped. It is part of the daily routine'. Every girl and woman, they said, was a potential recruit.

A number of U.S. groups and organizations have suggested that reducing demand is the only method to reduce pimping, trafficking, and exploitation of

---

5   Several states have recently passed legislation prohibiting prosecution of young people who have been prostituted. The Safe Harbor for Exploited Children Act went into effect in New York State in April 2010. It creates a presumption of trafficking for any person selling sex who is under 16 years of age, and Connecticut has similar legislation. http://actioncenter.polarisproject.org/take-action/advocate-for-policy/227. With a new state law, The Illinois Safe Children Act, Illinois has ended the practice of prosecuting anyone under the age of 18 for selling sex. Information about the Illinois law can be found at www.sharedhope.org/what/documents/sb647points.pdf. Training for law enforcement officials on the provisions of the Act should also include addressing myths around consent, in order to reorient classification of many girls and women in prostitution from offenders to victims controlled by pimps who are, in fact, traffickers.

vulnerable girls and women described in these Chicago studies.[6] Tackling demand involves a variety of strategies, which include law enforcement and prosecuting customers who buy sex from minors with charges of child abuse and/or statutory rape. The research reported here has clearly demonstrated how the profitable sex industry often rests on the exploitation of girls and women by pimps, traffickers, and customers.

References

Chicago Breaking News (2008) *Men Prostituted Teen, Police Say.* Available at: www.chicagobreakingnews.com/2008/11/100000-bail-for-2-men-accused-of-pimping-teen-girl.html [accessed: 18 May 2010].

Chicago Breaking News (2010) *Cops: Dolton Brothers Tried to Pimp Teen Girls.* Available at: www.chicagobreakingnews.com/2010/05/cops-dolton-brothers-tried-to-pimp-girlfriends.html [accessed: 26 May 2010].

Coy, M. (2008) 'The Consumer, the Consumed and the Commodity: Women and Sex Buyers Talk about Objectification in Prostitution' in Vanessa E. Munro and Marina della Giusta (eds), *Demanding Sex: Critical Reflections on the Regulation of Prostitution.* Aldershot: Ashgate.

Dunlap, E., Golub, A. and Johnson, B. (2003) 'Girls' Sexual Development in the Inner City: From Compelled Childhood Sexual Contact to Sex-for-Things Exchanges'. *Journal of Child Sexual Abuse* 12(2): 73–96.

Durchslag, R. and Goswami, S. (2008) *Deconstructing the Demand for Prostitution: Preliminary Insights from Interviews with Chicago Men Who Purchase Sex.* Chicago: Chicago Alliance Against Sexual Exploitation. Available at: http://www.chicagohomeless.org/files/images/Deconstructing_the_Demand_For_Prostitution.pdf [accessed: 10 January 2009].

Finkelhor, D. (1988) 'The Trauma of Child Sexual Abuse: Two Models' in G.E. Wyatt and G. Powell (eds), *Lasting Effects of Child Abuse.* Newbury Park, CA: Sage.

Harding, R. and Hamilton, P. (2009) 'Working Girls: Abuse or Choice in Street-Level Sex Work? A Study of Homeless Women in Nottingham'. *British Journal of Social Work* 39(6).

Hodgson, J. (1997) *Games Pimps Play: Pimps, Players and Wives-In-Law: A Qualitative Analysis of Street Prostitution.* Toronto: Canadian Scholars Press.

Kelly, L. (2003) 'The Wrong Debate: Reflections on Why Force is Not the Key Issue with Respect to Trafficking in Women for Sexual Exploitation'. *Feminist Review* 73: 139–44.

---

6   End Demand Illinois is a new state coalition whose work is described at www.enddemand.org. One national group is The Polaris Project, www.polarisproject.org.

Kennedy, M.A., Klein, C., Bristow, J.T.K., Cooper, B.S. and Yuille, J.C. (2007) 'Routes of Recruitment: Pimps' Techniques and Other Circumstances that Lead to Street Prostitution'. *Journal of Aggression, Maltreatment & Trauma* 15(2): 1–19.

May, T., Harocopos, A. and Hough, M. (2000) *For Love or Money: Pimps and the Management of Sex Work.* London: Home Office.

McClanahan, S.F., McClelland, G.M., Abram, K.M. and Teplin, L.A. (1999) 'Pathways into Prostitution among Female Jail Detainees and Their Implications for Mental Health Services'. *Psychiatric Services* 50(2): 1606–13.

Nixon, K., Tutty, L., Downe, P., Gorkoff, K. and Ursel, J. (2002) 'The Everyday Occurrence: Violence in the Lives of Girls Exploited through Prostitution'. *Violence against Women* 8(2): 1016–104.

Raphael, J. and Ashley, J. (2008) *Domestic Sex Trafficking of Chicago Women and Girls.* Chicago: DePaul University College of Law and the Illinois Criminal Justice Information Authority.

Raphael, J. and Myers-Powell, B. (2009) *Interviews with Five Ex-Pimps in Chicago.* Chicago: DePaul University, College of Law.

Raphael, J. and Myers-Powell, B. (2010) *From Victims to Victimizers: Interviews with 25 Ex-Pimps in Chicago.* Chicago: Schiller DuCanto & Fleck Family Law Center of DePaul University College of Law.

Raphael, J., Reichert, J.A. and Powers, M. (2010) 'Pimp Control and Violence: Domestic Sex Trafficking of Chicago Women and Girls'. *Women & Criminal Justice* 20(1).

Raphael, J. and Shapiro, D. (2002) *Sisters Speak Out: The Lives and Needs of Prostituted Women in Chicago.* Chicago: Center for Impact Research.

Stark, E. (2007) *Coercive Control: The Entrapment of Women in Personal Life.* Oxford: OU Press.

Stone, B. (2010) 'Sex Ads Seen Adding Revenue to Craigslist'. *The New York Times*, 25 April 2010.

Trafficking Victims Protection Act of 2000, Pub. L.No. 106–368, Division A, Section 103(8), 114 Stat. 1464 (signed into law on October 29, 2000); codified as amended at 22 USC 7102 Section 103(8).

Williamson, C. and Cluse-Tolar, T. (2002) 'Pimp-Controlled Prostitution: Still an Integral Part of Street Life'. *Violence against Women* 8/9: 1078–85.

Chapter 4

Beyond 'Agency' and 'Choice' in Theorizing Prostitution

Sheila Jeffreys

Feminists who take the 'sex work' position on prostitution see this harmful practice as a form of women's 'work' that should be respected. The idea that prostituted women express their 'agency' and 'choice' in stripping and prostitution is fundamental to these arguments. Such approaches focus on the motivations for individual sexual acts, without acknowledging either the highly industrialized and harmful context in which they take place, or the effects of prostitution industries on the status of women and on communities.

Prostitution has been industrialized in the last two decades, through an increase in scale and intensity. National sex industries and the global sex industry are presently experiencing startling growth and profit levels (IBISWorld 2007; Jyrkinen: Chapter 1; Poulin 2005). In consonance, the many problems that are now being recognized as intrinsically linked to the industry, harms to the health of women and girls in the industry (Jeffreys 2004), organized crime and corruption (Sullivan 2007), trafficking (Farr 2004; Monzini 2005), are growing apace. The growth of the industry is having an increasing influence on the culture in which all women live, on fashion, sports, the music industry, streetscapes, the possibility of equality in sexual relations, and the mental and physical health of teenage girls (American Psychological Association 2007). Yet prostitution is mainly discussed in the academy from the point of view of a decontextualized individualism, which talks of women being empowered, of women being entrepreneurs, and being able to make rational choices to be prostituted. This is the language of neo-liberal economics which underlies the policy of either legalizing or tolerating the industry of prostitution. The context in which women are prostituted is rarely factored into neo-liberal analyses. In fact, the brothels, strip clubs, porn merchants, prostitution tourism operators, control prostitution, largely through organized crime, and make the profits (Jeffreys 2009), whilst the individual prostituted women who are exploited in this industry see little profit and suffer considerable harms to their health and lives (see Coy: Chapter 6; Raphael: Chapter 3). This chapter will contrast these facts of the organization of the industry of prostitution, and the harms that accompany it, with the inadequacies of the choice and agency perspectives with which many feminist scholars approach the topic.

Neo-liberal Language in the Industry of Prostitution

The language of feminist theorists on prostitution was affected by the normalization of the industry in the last decades of the twentieth century. Though some remained critical (see for example Barry 1995; Jeffreys 1997; Stark and Whisnant 2004), many started to use a language more in tune with the neo-liberal economists, such as Milton Friedman, who were calling for the decriminalization of prostitution and its treatment as just like any other industry. They began to use terms such as agency, entrepreneurship, rational choice and empowerment, to describe the experience of prostituted women. The concept of 'agency' has been widely adopted by feminist theorists in the fields of development, and postcolonial feminism in particular as a way of paying respect to women's strengths and survival skills. Kalpana Wilson, writing about the ways in which the concept of 'agency' has been used in relation to gender and development, explains that 'agency' 'has historically been rooted in the construction of the individual in Enlightenment thought, within which agency can be understood ... as "socially unfettered" free will' (Wilson 2007: 126). Individuals have 'agency', she explains, to the extent that they are able to exercise 'rational choice'. Marxist philosophers have criticized the notion of agency for ignoring the material constraints of class relations and ideology, and as a foundational concept of capitalist ideology. Wilson explains that when some feminist theorists began to take up the concept of 'agency', they did so in a specific context and for a specific purpose. They adopted it to counter the idea of the naturalness of an active/passive dichotomy in relation to men's and women's roles under patriarchy. They sought to emphasize that women were not just passive victims of historical forces. But in particular they sought to show that women could engage in resistance to the structures of power, not just individually, but collectively in social movements. Unfortunately the concept proved to be a poisoned chalice. Its individualist and capitalist associations could not be dislodged.

In gender and development theory, as Wilson explains, 'agency', which was supposed to show women's ability to stand up against the forces of colonialism, came instead to stand for women's ability to seize the opportunities that development agencies wedded to capitalist and neo-liberal ideology presented to them, such as microfinance. 'Agency', she points out, came to mean, in many contexts, little more than the attempt to survive, by finding any possible way to avoid penury and sustain life, for instance. Survival is not the same thing as resistance, or an attempt to transform the relations of power, that some socialist feminist theorists thought the concept of 'agency' should encompass. Survival tactics and agency have come, however, in such understandings, to mean the same thing.

The concept of 'agency' has been taken up with particular enthusiasm by anthropologists of women. The anthropologist Saba Mahmood uses the term 'agency', for example, in her research on women in Egypt who are caught up in a new wave of Islamic religiosity (Mahmood 2001). Her work shows one extreme of the way the term 'agency' is now deployed in relation to women, that is to mean the embrace of subordinate status. Mahmood seeks to gain respect for the exercise of 'agency' by her research subjects who teach each other about Islam in mosques and are extremely pious, praying the required amount of times per day, and engaging in veil wearing and various bodily practices that remind them to be modest and shy. She says that they express their 'agency' in the wearing of the veil, and Mahmood is critical of feminists who do not understand that 'agency' can be expressed in submission to God's will, 'The veil ... is seldom entertained as an expression of and a means to a Muslim woman's submission to God's will, despite repeated evidence that for many veiled women this understanding is central' (Mahmood 2001: 208). She is critical of what she sees as the poststructural understanding that the exercise of agency needs to be understood as being related to 'resistance'. She doesn't agree with that, and says that agency can be understood as women seeking to tie themselves more firmly into dominant practice, 'we might think of agency not only as the capacity for progressive change but also, importantly, as the capacity to endure, suffer, and persist' (Mahmood 2001: 217). Wilson identifies two big problems with this use of the concept of 'agency'. It serves to mystify or hide relations of power, with its tendency to individualism, and it sidesteps or renders unnecessary, collective movements of resistance (Wilson 2007; Gill 2007). The Mahmood example makes it clear that agency can be used by anthropologists specifically to mean the embrace of relations of subordination, the very opposite of the dynamics of resistance that it was expected to encompass.

The language of 'agency' alongside the concepts of 'choice' and even 'entrepreneurship', has become dominant within academic feminist discussion of prostitution. The neo-liberal language is accompanied by euphemisms in which prostitution becomes 'sex work', women who are prostituted are called 'sex workers' or even 'service providers', and the men who buy them are called 'clients'. Joanna Niemi has shown that even in Sweden, which has model legislation penalizing the male buyers of prostituted women, this 'commercial' language has been adopted. Men are penalized for the 'purchase of sexual services' (Niemi 2010). The main vectors of neo-liberal language are the sex work agencies set up or funded by governments to supply condoms to prostituted women and men against the transmission of HIV (Murphy and Ringheim 2001). This 'AIDS money' has created a powerful force of sex workers' rights organizations which take the 'sex work' position, i.e. that prostitution is just a job like any other, and now a useful market sector that must be decriminalized (Doezema 1998; Kempadoo 1998). With the advent of AIDS funding, sex worker activists gained platforms and an authority, as experts in a supposed public health crisis, that enabled the creation of a strong, international pro sex work lobby group. The influence of the sex work position has been most marked in international health politics, UNAIDS and the International Labour Office (ILO) (Oriel 2006). The position is a comfortable one for governments and UN agencies to adopt because it offers no challenge to the rights of men to buy women for sex, and promotes the ideology of entrepreneurship and individualism that melds with the interests of governments wedded to neo-liberal economic policies. The neo-liberal language of the 'sex work' position has also been adopted by many who are concerned to ameliorate the harms experienced by prostituted women. Funding and recognition may now depend upon a willingness to appear, through this language, in tune with the now dominant ideology on prostitution.

The work of Ratna Kapur demonstrates the enthusiasm for using the language of 'agency' in the field of postcolonial feminist studies. Kapur says that those who 'articulate' the 'victim subject', such as suggesting that prostituted women are oppressed or harmed, base their arguments on 'gender essentialism' and generalizations which reflect the problems of privileged white, Western, middle-class, heterosexual women (Kapur 2002: 6). This accusation implies that those who identify women as being oppressed are 'classist' through the very fact of making that identification. Such arguments are based on 'cultural essentialism' too, portraying women as victims of their culture, Kapur says. Those guilty of these racist and classist practices are those involved in working against violence; she identifies Catharine MacKinnon and Kathleen Barry in particular, and anti-trafficking campaigners who 'focus on violence and victimisation'. Campaigns against violence against women, she says, 'have taken feminists back into a protectionist and conservative discourse' (p. 7). Anti-violence feminists are accused of using 'metanarratives' and erasing the differences between women, and of a lack of complexity that 'sets up a subject who is thoroughly disempowered and helpless' (p. 10). However, it is not just 'western' feminists that Kapur criticizes for these solecisms, but Indian ones too who happen to be anti-violence campaigners. They too negate the 'very possibility of choice or agency' by saying that 'sex work' in south Asia is a form of exploitation (p. 26).

In relation to prostitution the meaning of the concept of 'agency', as drawing on free market capitalism, is easy to identify. Alys Willman-Navarro uses the idea of 'rational choice' to describe women making the decision to enter prostitution (Willman-Navarro 2006). She looks at research literature showing that prostituted women in Calcutta and Mexico engage in sex with male buyers without condoms because they know 'sex workers who are willing to perform unprotected sex will be compensated for doing so, while those who prefer to use condoms earn less', a loss which can be as much as 79 per cent of earnings (Willman-Navarro 2006: 18). Such research, she says, shows 'sex workers' as 'rational agents responding to incentives' (p. 19). The 'choice' that the women face is between the chance of death from HIV/AIDs and the ability to feed and school their children. There are no realistic alternatives. Nonetheless, Willman-Navarro remains upbeat in her approach, 'In Nicaragua I have met sex workers who are barely making ends meet. I have met others who send their children to some of the best schools in the capital ... They didn't do this by cashing in on one lucky night, but through years of rational choices' (Willman-Navarro 2006: 19). Women in prostitution, this account tells us, can be successful entrepreneurs if only they act rationally, though this is contradicted by the woefully low earnings that prostituted women actually achieve, as indicated later in this chapter (DeRiviere 2006).

The representation of prostituted women as 'entrepreneurs' is another example in literature from the sex work position that demonstrates the embrace of neo-liberal values and language. Bandana Pattaniak, in a volume on 'transnational prostitution' for instance, suggests that 'There is also a formulation that sex-workers should be seen as entrepreneurs ... According to this way of conceptualizing sex work one does not need to have an employer' (Pattaniak 2002: 224). 'Entrepreneur' is a very positive term, especially under neo-liberal conditions in which such enterprise is much respected, but it is particularly unsuitable for prostitution. There is no evidence that the vast majority of prostituted women lack 'employers'. Such a category could only include 'callgirls' working on their own, women in brothel cooperatives, or those street prostituted women who do not have pimps, or boyfriends who, to support their own drug habits, pimp their partners. In legalized prostitution in Australia, for instance, the vast majority of prostituted women are in legal or illegal brothels or 'escort' agencies, where the pimps are the business owners (see Sullivan: Chapter 8). Even 'exotic dancers' commonly have dependent male partners who live off their earnings. A study on 'exotic dancers' and their partners showed that the men that the women are involved with are most frequently unemployed, financially dependent, and generally verbally and emotionally abusive (Bradley-Engen and Hobbs 2010). It is an irony that the language of 'agency', which implies that the women are independent workers, is used to describe the prostituted women in legal brothels in Australia, in order to justify the exploitation to which they are subjected. Women who are the raw material for the trade are described as 'agents' by the brothel and strip club owners so that they do not have to pay wages or benefits, and have no responsibility for their welfare (Sullivan 2007). There are no scheduled breaks, women must tip valets and bouncers, and they can be fined for supposed wrongdoing. The 'agents' have to wait in brothels for many hours to see if they can attract a buyer, and get no money if they do not attract one. This is not an 'empowering' situation, and use of the term 'agent' is a deceit, as is the term 'entrepreneur'.

The language of 'agency' is used in relation to prostitution tourism as well. Kemala Kempadoo takes a sex work approach and positions the prostituted women and men of the Caribbean as having 'agency', when engaged in prostitution tourism, and being involved in acts of transgression which free them from oppressive relations rather than subjecting them to oppression. Too many studies, she considers, emphasize the problems associated with prostitution, and obscure the 'agency and subjectivity' of sex workers (Kempadoo 2001: 41). The language of 'agency' is even used by academics in relation to child prostitution, a situation that might seem to be particularly unsuited to this approach, since children are powerless in many respects. Thus Julia O'Connell Davidson, in her book on children in the global sex trade, criticizes what she calls 'anti-prostitution feminists' who, she says, ignore the 'diverse and complex realities' of those who are prostituted and deny their 'autonomy and agency' (O'Connell Davidson 2005: 3). Through stressing that children can have 'agency', she joins a growing stream of researchers who are arguing that both children and adult women express agency and choice in prostitution, and that showing special concern for children infantilizes them. Thus Heather Montgomery, for instance, writing about prostituted children in a tourist resort in Thailand, says that children's 'agency' and 'choices' need to be acknowledged (Montgomery 1998). One of the children whose experience she discusses was sexually used in masturbation by 'James' from the age of six until he started to penetrate her when she was eight and she was pregnant by twelve. It is hard to see the usefulness of drawing attention to the children's 'choice' in such situations.

Dianne Otto takes the 'agency' approach to what she calls 'survival sex' by young girls in refugee camps who are prostituted by camp staff (Otto: 2007). Otto is extremely critical of the fact that the UN has introduced a policy which bans staff from paying girls for sexual use when they are desperate for food and other privileges, and emphasizes the importance of the children's 'agency'. She starts her critique with examples of three girls, aged 13–17 who engage in survival sex in West African refugee camps. The 13-year-old does this to get scraps of food that will enable her to have the strength to look after her six-month-old baby. She points out that if payment is made for 'survival sex' it is 'often not even enough to buy a full meal' and there is always the risk of no payment at all. The girls, she acknowledges, had 'little or no power to negotiate the rate or to determine the kind of sexual exchange that took place, including whether safe sex was practiced' (Otto 2007: 6). But this practice should not, she considered, be banned. The girls' 'stories' 'offer an opportunity to question overdetermined representations of powerlessness and to respect the rational calculations they are making ... but it is poverty that is the main harm, not sex' (p. 10). The girls are involved in 'rational choice' as well as 'agency'. The prohibition of the activities covered in the directive, Otto argues, 'drains agency' from those involved (p. 12). In this case the girls were unable to control what was done to them, what recompense they received, whether they were infected with STIs, and had to accept these conditions in order to acquire food to eat. Otto's approach is an example of the determination by some of those who take a sex work position to find 'choice' and 'agency' even in the most unlikely situations. The application of concepts such as choice and agency to situations in which girls and women submit to serious abuse because they have no realistic alternatives, shows up the deceptiveness of these terms.

Prostitution as a Global Industry

By focusing on the individual woman who is prostituted, the neo-liberal approach excludes consideration of the context in which women are prostituted. Prostitution, in the 'agency' approach, takes the form of empowered entrepreneurs doing prostitution independently and on their own. This is a misconception. The most significant factor affecting the choices and experience of prostituted women at present is the industry in which they are prostituted. Whereas it might once have been the case that prostituted women worked at home, or on the street with or without a pimp, the industry is now much more concentrated. The profits from the industry do not mostly go to the women but to the pimps/brothel owners and a number of other industries that feed off prostitution. Prostitution is not just a naturally occurring opportunity that women may exploit, but socially constructed out of male domination and women's subordination. For women to make the 'rational choice' to be prostituted, or exercise their 'agency' in this regard, prostitution must exist as an established practice. The 'idea of prostitution' must exist amongst men and in the culture (Jeffreys 1997) so that there is a demand from male buyers. Usually, there must be pimps or traffickers to acquire the women and girls, and offer them for sale (see the website of the UK organization Coalition for the Removal of Pimping; Jeffreys 2009; Raphael: Chapter 3). In brothels in India a third of prostituted girls and women were placed there by relatives who take the profits that accrue (Tambe 2006). The majority of women work for brothel, escort agency or strip club owners who live on the earnings of prostitution. The industry of prostitution has increased hugely in the range of its practices, its scale and reach over the last two decades in which some governments have actively legalized or decriminalized the industry or in other ways provided the conditions for its growth (Jyrkinen: Chapter 1). It is in this context of the industrialization and globalization of the industry, that sex work analyses have been enabled to grow in influence make their arguments as to choice and agency. Yet the idea that prostituted women act as independent agents is less and less suited to the context in which this practice takes place.

Many scholars who see themselves as postmodernist, or postcolonial, anti-imperialist and generally of the left, have taken up the neo-liberal approach to prostitution with such enthusiasm, yet have not done this in relation to other forms of labour. As Carole Pateman points out, when socialist feminists adopt this approach to prostitution they end up being rather more positive and context blind in relation to prostitution than they would be towards other kinds of work, which are understood to be carried out in employment relations of domination and subordination (Pateman 1988). It is striking that concepts of agency and choice are not applied to workers in other immensely harmful industries, such as asbestos mining, for instance. Similarly no outpouring of outrage from the left is encountered in relation to the abolition or diminution of other harmful industries, such as the logging of old growth forests which destroys the environment, or the tobacco industry which destroys health. It is prostitution which is defended as necessary to empowerment, choice and agency, despite the clearest evidence that for the majority of those involved, sale or coercion by family, boyfriends, pimps, traffickers, experience of severe sexual violence, and privation, are involved in the entry of girls and women into prostitution (Barry 1995; Jeffreys 1997). Prostitution can be seen by its apologists as an ordinary or even positive way to survive for those gendered female, in a way in which labouring in an asbestos mine would not be seen as a form of empowerment for male workers.

Prostitution is now a significant market sector within national economies, though the worth of domestic sex industries is hard to estimate, considering the size of the illegal industry and the general lack of transparency that surrounds it. The industry of prostitution is most developed and entrenched in those countries in which militaries such as the US and Japan in the 1930s and 1940s, set up prostitution systems on a scale and with a precision which is industrial, such as Korea, the Philippines and Thailand (Moon 1997; Tanaka 2002). An ILO report a decade ago estimated the sex industry to account for from 2–14 per cent of the worth of economies in the four counties studied, the Philippines, Malaysia, Thailand, and Indonesia (Lim 1998). The Korean government estimated in 2002 that one million women were in prostitution at any one time in the country (Hurt 2005). The industry was estimated to be worth 4.4 per cent of GDP, more than forestry, fishing and agriculture combined (4.1 per cent). This was said to be a conservative estimate since many forms of prostitution were untrackable. It was estimated that 1 in 6 to 1 in 10 of women in the country have worked in some capacity in prostitution (Hurt 2005). In China the boom in the prostitution industry since the move towards a market economy from 1978 onwards, has been particularly notable since it has developed off a low base in the Maoist era when prostitution was not tolerated. There are now an estimated 2–300,000 prostituted women in Beijing alone and anywhere between 10 and 20 million prostituted women in China as a whole (Zhou 2006). The industry of prostitution is estimated to account for eight percent of the Chinese economy, and be worth about 700 billion USD (Zhou 2006).

Moreover, in most of these contexts prostitution is illegal. Crime groups organize trafficking of women and girls, run protection rackets on the venues in which they are prostituted, provide 'security', deliver drugs through the brothels, launder money through brothels and strip clubs, and run international franchises for strip clubs (Jeffreys 2009). Legalization of the industry has no effect in reducing these operations and leads to growth of the industry which provides a profitable environment for crime groups that are engaged in trafficking of drugs and women, money laundering and protection rackets. In Victoria in Australia, for instance, the Chief Commissioner of Police, Christine Nixon, told a parliamentary committee that organized crime gangs are entrenched in the state's legal brothel industry (Moor 2007). In states where brothel prostitution is legalized, such as Victoria, the majority of the industry is illegal because the criminals involved in organizing it do not wish to be regulated (Sullivan 2007; Chapter 8). A concentration in feminist theory on the 'agency' of the women who are prostituted, rather than the industry itself, diverts attention from those who control prostitution and make serious profits from it.

Industry Profits Do Not Go to the Women

Though women may, in the sex work approach, be seen as exercising 'agency' this is unlikely to bring them great economic benefits. Though they may earn more than other unskilled women whilst they are being prostituted, other long-term negative effects on their health and future earnings may need to be factored in. The approach which emphasizes the rational choice of women to enter prostitution on the grounds of the earnings they can make therein (Willman-Navarro 2006), is contradicted by some more critical and carefully calculated analysis. Research is just beginning to take place into the economics of prostitution from the point of view of the women who are prostituted. Though prostitution forms an increasingly profitable global economic sector, the profits are largely going to those who control the business rather than to the individual prostituted women themselves. Prostituted women in Hong Kong, for instance, barely make enough money to survive. Zi Teng (2006), writing about Chinese migrant 'sex workers' in Hong Kong, explains that there is a redundant labour force of 150 million people in the Chinese countryside. The higher unemployment rates among women cause them to move to Hong Kong and into prostitution, where they earn meagre wages of $20 per 'service' and have an average of three customers per day. Teng describes the physical abuse they suffer and the problem of being robbed. As is common, they engage in sex without condoms in order to get the few customers they are able to attract. She found that the majority of the prostituted women she studied would 'not absolutely insist their customers to use condoms'. A 2007 report on the legalized brothel and strip club industry in Australia, while positive about the increased profitability of the industry, quotes a Sydney survey which found that after brothel charges, one-third of women earned up to $500 each week, about 20 per cent earned $800–1,000 and another 20 per cent earned more than $1,000 (IBISWorld 2007). In the same year the average weekly earnings in Australia were $1,106 (Queensland Government 2011). These are certainly not high earnings, and are likely to be restricted to the short number of years that the women remain in the industry. They do not reveal what the women are able to earn on leaving. The report also states that average wages have decreased in the previous five years as a result of greater competition. The success of the sex industry, it seems, may disadvantage prostituted women.

One study explores the effect of prostitution on a woman's economic prospects over the life cycle. Linda DeRiviere examined, through eight case studies and 54 interviews, the economics of prostitution in the life experience of prostituted women in Canada. Her research subjects were overwhelmingly (90.3 per cent) indigenous women, and had worked in a variety of prostitution settings (DeRiviere 2006). In Canada, as she explains, indigenous women are hugely overrepresented in prostitution. She explains that 'Current literature in

North America is riddled with debate about whether prostitution is a profit-making and empowering venture of rational, utility-maximizing actors' (DeRiviere 2006: 367). 'Most' she says, 'propose that prostitution is financially lucrative', and equate 'the sex trade with entrepreneurial skills'. They represent the 'choice' to enter 'sex work' as a rational decision in which the individual 'weighs personal costs and benefits or the expected utility of engaging in this lifestyle'. DeRiviere, in contrast, looks at prostitution in Winnipeg, Canada, over the life cycle. It usually begins in adolescent years, with Canadian research showing that 96 per cent of women enter prostitution before 17 years, and thus leads to 'opportunity costs' such as the loss of education, skills, work experience and on-the-job training which could enable prostituted women to leave prostitution and move on to another occupation. It is a temporary situation for most but has a permanent effect on lifetime earnings and productive outcomes. The gross earnings of her respondents were $27,071 per annum, but the women did not receive this amount for their own use as 'transfers to pimps and dependent partners and escort agency owners' amounted to $10,068 annually or 37.2 per cent. Drugs and alcohol, which are necessary to enable the women to survive prostitution and disassociate from the abuse, accounted for $12,617 or 46.6 per cent. Lost earnings following violent incidents, etc amounted to $2,305, 8.5 per cent. Thus the net annual surplus funds after subtracting substantial costs are less than 8 per cent of gross earnings.

The women she studied also suffered reduced lifelong earnings, as a result of the physical and mental health issues which resulted from prostitution, the costs of which, in DeRiviere's estimation, far exceeded the benefits over the woman's lifetime. She concludes, from her eight case studies, 'that throughout the period of involvement in the sex trade, a small earnings premium is the only direct benefit of prostitution at a personal level. However, such benefits are short term relative to the individual's available working years, and the offsetting costs of prostitution are huge' (DeRiviere 2006: 379). The 'agency' of women entering prostitution in Canada, then, is likely to be exercised as a teenager. It is most likely to be exercised by women who are racially subordinated and poor. It may lead to continued poverty, serious health problems and unemployment over the life cycle. It is hard to see this as representing 'rational choice' on their part when the consequences are so serious. 'Choice' may be an inappropriate term when there are no alternatives to be 'chosen' from.

Radical Feminist Responses to the 'Agency' Approach

The neo-liberal approach to the industry of prostitution has been strongly challenged on many levels by radical feminist critics, who have been sharply critical of what they identify as the liberal individualism of scholars and activists who emphasize the importance of women's 'agency', and concentrate on the freedom of action of the individual prostituted woman in contradiction to the oppressive relations of power within which she acts (Miriam 2005;

Pateman 1988). The 'agency' approach is used in feminist theory in relation to other issues such as the veil, makeup and fashion, as well as prostitution. Rosalind Gill (2007) has addressed the problems involved in this approach to the politics of appearance. She explains that an approach which focuses on 'autonomous choices', 'remains complicit with, rather than critical of, postfeminist and neoliberal discourses that see individuals as entrepreneurial actors who are rational, calculating and self-regulating' (p. 74). Pro-sex work writers practice precisely this problematic approach in their interpretation of the experiences of trafficked women, 'The neoliberal subject is required to bear full responsibility for their life biography no matter how severe the constraints upon their action ... Just as neoliberalism requires individuals to narrate their life story as if it were the outcome of deliberative choices' (Gill 2007: 74). She asks why so much feminist theory has taken up choice language and suggests that it is because a postfeminist perspective no longer allows recognition of the oppression of women, 'Is there a subtext to this? A postfeminist subtext that no longer views women as oppressed?' (Gill 2007: 74).

Kathy Miriam addresses the way the 'agency' approach is employed in relation to trafficking in women in particular and characterizes well the problematic liberal individualism that underlies this approach (Miriam 2005). She argues that the sex work approach 'depends on a contractual, liberal model of agency that both conceals and presupposes the demand side of the institution of prostitution' and also conceals the power relations within which women are prostituted (Miriam 2005: 2). The radical feminist approach, on the other hand, 'radically *challenges* feminism to theorize power and agency *outside a liberal framework*' (Miriam 2005: 2, original emphasis). The power relations in which prostitution takes place are founded, she argues, using Pateman's development of this concept (1988), on the male sex right. Under male domination, she explains, 'men's right to be sexually serviced is non-negotiable whatever else women can negotiate' (p. 14).

It is the fact that the male sex right cannot be questioned, that creates the greatest challenge for feminists in the anti-prostitution struggle, 'this legitimized and entrenched relation defined by men's right to demand access to women is the central conception of male power at stake for the feminist movement to abolish prostitution' (Miriam 2005: 13). Under a political system in which this male demand is understood as simply ordinary sex drive, or sexual initiation, the whole idea of women being able to express 'sexual agency', an idea central to the pro sex work position, becomes problematic. They may only express 'agency' through answering men's demand for paid sex and allowing access to their bodies, no other possibility is open. But because the male sex drive is seen as a fact of life, the very demand for prostitution itself is unquestioned. The pro-sex-work lobby cannot recognize the importance of demand because 'male power is invisible to it as *domination* and only intelligible as *coercive force*' (Miriam 2005: 13). Miriam makes the crucial point that agency and oppression are not in contradiction to one another. Women exercise agency in order to survive the power relations and oppressive circumstances in which they find themselves.

The theoretical task, Miriam argues, is for radical feminist theory to 'theorize freedom in terms of women's collective political agency (power to): this task requires an understanding that freedom is not negotiating within a situation taken as inevitable, but rather, a capacity to radically transform and/or determine the situation itself' (Miriam 2005: 14). The very general acceptance within feminism of the sex work position represents an accommodation to the male dominant construction of men's sexual drive and men's right to commandeer the bodies of women in which to act it out. In that sense it is a defeat of the idea that feminism can recreate sex as eroticized equality (Jeffreys 1990), and release women from the tyranny of the male sex right.

Prostitution as a Harmful Cultural Practice

An understanding of prostitution as a harmful cultural practice is also useful in rebutting the 'agency', 'rational choice' or 'empowerment' approach. Prostitution fits well into the criteria created by the UN Special Rapporteur on violence against women for recognizing harmful cultural practices against women and girls (Jeffreys 2004). Since the 1970s there has been considerable development in the recognition of what are called in United Nations document 'Harmful traditional/ cultural practices'[1] (Jeffreys 2005), as a result of feminist campaigning. The definition of harmful traditional practices was extended in 1995 in a UN Fact Sheet No. 23 entitled *Harmful Traditional Practices Affecting the Health of Women and Children*. The criteria offered in the introduction apply to prostitution very well. They recognize such practices as gendered, 'performed for male benefit', and it would be hard to argue that prostitution was not to men's benefit considering that men constitute the vast majority of sex buyers (United Nations 1995: 3–4; Coy et al.: Chapter 7). Prostitution is a gendered practice, par excellence. Whilst boys and young men are prostituted by men, there is not a similar market amongst female buyers. Brothels are gentlemen's clubs, and women, girls and young men are bought by men, not women. Prostitution does not allow an equal opportunity to express this 'agency' because it is an institution constructed politically from male domination and women's subordination.

These practices are defined as being harmful to the health of women and girls. In relation to the first criterion, harm to health, the evidence is overwhelming and there is a wealth of accumulating evidence to indicate the severity of this harm (Farley 2004). The health of prostituted women and girls is harmed by abrasion of the vagina and anus, sexually transmitted diseases, unwanted pregnancy and abortion, beatings and rapes from male buyers, pimps and traffickers (Jeffreys 2010a). One argument for legalizing/decriminalizing the industry is that such harms will be reduced, but this does not necessarily follow. The occupational

---

1   The words traditional and cultural are used interchangeably in UN literature on this subject.

health and safety codes introduced in legalized environments, to advise prostituted women on their safety, in detailing the harms that require mitigation provide useful information as to their extent and severity, e.g. unwanted pregnancy, physical and sexual assault, sexually transmitted diseases (Sullivan 2007). Psychological harms include those associated with the disassociation of mind and body that are necessary for survival, and can lead to post-traumatic stress disorder (Farley 2003). The possibility of being murdered has to be taken into account in prostitution as it does not in other occupations. A respondent in a study by pro decriminalization of the sex industry advocate, Melissa Petro, shows how this possibility continues even in a legalized environment such as The Netherlands (Petro 2010). 'Valencia' says legalization in The Hague has made her feel safe, 'Everything you see is controlled. ... They keep the names of all the prostitutes so if somebody is killed they know who it is. It's a safe feeling here in Holland' (Petro 2010: 163). Workers in other industries, though their conditions may be hazardous in other ways, do not have to consider the possibility of being murdered as an occupational risk.

Traditional cultural practices are also said to 'reflect values and beliefs held by members of a community for periods often spanning generations' and are said to persist because they are not questioned and take on an aura of morality in the eyes of those practicing them (United Nations 1995: 3–4). Prostitution fits the criterion for recognizing a harmful cultural practice of being justified by tradition, as in the frequently uttered nostrum that it is the 'oldest profession'. Slavery is old too but seldom justified by its longevity. The feminist historian Gerda Lerner writes most usefully about the way in which brothel prostitution in the ancient Middle East originated in the enslavement of captives in warfare, as a way of tidily dealing with surplus women slaves (Lerner 1987). Though many values and beliefs of male dominance have been or are in the process of change in many societies, the idea that prostitution is a reasonable way to use women is institutionalized through the practice of legalization and the normalizing, commercial language that predominates in policy documents, such as the term 'sexual services'. Prostitution, like other harmful cultural practices, is a 'consequence' of 'the value placed on women and the girl child by society', and 'persists' 'in an environment where women and the girl child have unequal access to education, wealth, health and employment' (United Nations 1995: 3–4). The concept of harmful cultural practices enables the serious harm that women and girls suffer from being prostituted to be recognized. But the status of all women is harmed by the industry of prostitution.

The Status of Women

Concentration on the 'choice' and 'agency' of prostituted women excludes a consideration of the impact of the industry on non-prostituted women, who do not 'choose' to have their lives affected by the development of thriving prostitution industries. Prostitution affects streetscapes which contain legal or illegal brothels and strip clubs, sex industry advertising, and street prostitution. Women residents and others passing through such zones may not have the 'choice' to avoid these areas (AGSPAG 2002). They may not be able to avoid being solicited or catcalled, being stalked or having their girl children stalked, or just feeling miserably uncomfortable at the clear harm to women on display. They may suffer threats if they seek to intervene in violence by pimps and male buyers towards the women being prostituted on their doorsteps and in their yards. The 'agency' of non-prostituted women is reduced, as male buyers who have real power to make choices and exercise agency occupy areas of cities for their sexual exploitation of women.

The status of all women is affected by the construction by the sex industry of a model of sexuality that is deeply opposed to women's right to sexual pleasure and sexual equality (Barry 1995; Tyler: Chapter 5). As the industry of prostitution grows both in environments where it is legalized and those where it is not, the world of work for women is changed. At professional conferences and entertainments women workers may be expected to tolerate 'burlesque' or the fact that their male colleagues repair to strip clubs or brothels. Male executives entertain clients, make deals, and organize product launches in strip clubs (Jeffreys 2010b). Female executives are deprived of these business opportunities and of advancement. Certain forms of mainly female work face new burdens as nurses and carers are solicited by the men they look after to engage in acts of prostitution, and some academics in nursing studies tell them that this is a good way of expanding their roles (Jeffreys 2008).

As prostitution industries grow, their associated sexual values are adopted by sports, the music industry, fashion and affect how women and girls are expected to dress and are sexually objectified (Jeffreys 2005). A 'prostitution culture' is created. The normalization of the industry has led to the term 'pimp' becoming highly valued, for instance. Thus the search term 'pimp T-shirts' brings up more than 57,000 hits offering products with this logo in various forms. Zazzle.com offers T-shirts emblazoned with the logos, 'I'm a Pimp', 'Pimps don't fall in love', 'Guido the killer pimp', and a woman's T-shirt with the logo 'Pimp's Quarterly', 'Babies is pimps too', 'pimpin'', 'hookers on strike', 'president of Pimps International' and many, many more (Zazzle.com n.d.). The website Monster Baby offers a T-shirt for babies emblazoned with the logo, 'Pimp my Pram', which seems designed to appeal to fathers, with an image of a pram and the caption, 'Pimp My Pram for all the pimped out babies! Dad's love this print – especially if they make vroom-vroom noises while pushing said pram!' (Monster Baby n.d.). Neither women nor girls who are prostituted, or those who are not, can avoid living in the prostitution culture created by thriving prostitution markets. The communities, women and children, who suffer the harms that the industry of prostitution creates have their choices and agency reduced, through threats to their 'choice' of equal sexual relationships, the narrowing of opportunities in the workplace and the violation of their right to free movement by the takeover by the sex industry of streets and streetscapes. Arguments about prostitution that concentrate on the agency and choice of prostituted women divert attention from the way in which this harmful cultural practice harms the 'agency' of all women.

Conclusion

The language of 'choice', 'agency', entrepreneurship and empowerment in relation to prostitution individualizes the practice. It invisibilizes the material forces of male domination and the neo-liberal economics that underpin the expansion of the global sex industry, and create the gendered practices of prostitution. This makes it hard to see the forms of force that convey girls and women into prostitution, such as violence or psychological coercion by families, pimps/boyfriends, traffickers, and distracts attention from the violence used to season girls into prostitution. It obscures the degree of privation that underpins the 'choices' that women and girls who are prostituted make. These arguments make it hard to see the power of the global sex industry, and those who make the most serious profits. Industries of prostitution cannot grow without severely affecting the way girls, women and sex are understood. The language of choice and agency are not appropriate to an industry that stands in such stark contradiction to women's equality.

References

AGSPAG (2002) *Final Report*. Melbourne, Australia: Attorney General's Street Prostitution Advisory Group. Available at: http://www.sexploitation.biz/ attachments/AGSPAG.pdf [accessed: 10 November 2010].

American Psychological Association (2007) *Report of the APA Task Force on the Sexualization of Girls*. Washington, D.C.: American Psychological Association.

Barry, K. (1995) *The Prostitution of Sexuality*. New York: NYU Press.

Bradley-Engen, M.S. and Hobbs, C.M. (2010) 'To Love, Honor, and Strip: An Investigation of Exotic Dancer Romantic Relationships' in Melissa Ditmore, Antonia Levy, and A. Willman (eds), *Sex Work Matters. Exploring Money, Power and Intimacy in the Sex Industry*. London and New York: Zed Books, 67–84.

Coalition for the Removal of Pimping (n.d.). Available at: http://www.cropuk.org. uk/ [accessed: 8 August 2010].

Daley, S. (2001) 'New rights for Dutch prostitutes, but no gain'. *New York Times*, 12 August.

DeRiviere, L. (2006) 'A Human Capital Methodology for Estimating the Lifelong Personal Costs of Young Women Leaving the Sex Trade'. *Feminist Economics* 12(3): July, 367–402.

Doezema, J. (1998) 'Forced to Choose. Beyond the Voluntary v. Forced Prostitution Dichotomy' in K. Kempadoo and J. Doezema, *Global Sex Workers. Rights, Resistance, and Redefinition*. New York: Routledge, 34–50.

Farley, M. (ed.) (2003) *Prostitution, Trafficking, and Traumatic Stress*. Binghamton, New York: Haworth Maltreatment and Trauma Press.

Farley, M. (2004) '"Bad for the Body, Bad for the Heart": Prostitution Harms Women Even if Legalized or Decriminalised'. *Violence against Women* 10(10): October, 1087–125.

Farr, K. (2004) *Sex Trafficking. The Global Market in Women and Children*. New York: Worth Publishers.

Gill, R.C. (2007) 'Critical Respect: The Difficulties and Dilemmas of Agency and "Choice for Feminism." A Reply to Duits and van Zoonen'. *European Journal of Women's Studies* 14(1): 69–80.

Hurt, M. (2005) 'Sex business lives on despite crackdown'. *The Korea Herald*, 27 May.

IBISWorld (2007) *Sexual Services in Australia*. Q9528. IBISWorld Pty Ltd.

Jeffreys, S. (1990/91) *Anticlimax. A Feminist Perspective on the Sexual Revolution*. London: The Women's Press; New York: New York University Press.

Jeffreys, S. (1997) *The Idea of Prostitution*. Melbourne: Spinifex.

Jeffreys, S. (2004) 'Prostitution as a Harmful Cultural Practice' in C. Stark and R. Whisnant (eds), *Not For Sale. Feminists Resisting Prostitution and Pornography*. Melbourne: Spinifex, 386–99.

Jeffreys, S. (2008) 'Disability and the Male Sex Right'. *Women's Studies International Forum* 31(5): 327–35.

Jeffreys, S. (2010a) 'Brothels without Walls: The Escort Sector as a Problem for the Legalization of Prostitution'. *Social Politics* 17(2): 210–34.

Jeffreys, S. (2010b) 'The Sex Industry and Business Practice: An Obstacle to Women's Equality'. *Women's Studies International Forum* May–June 2010, 274–82.

Kapur, R. (2002) 'The Tragedy of Victimization Rhetoric: Resurrecting the "Native" Subject in International/Post-colonial Feminist Legal Politics'. *Harvard Human Rights Journal* 15: Spring, 1–37.

Kempadoo, K. and Doezema, J. (eds) (1998) *Global Sex Workers. Rights, Resistance, and Redefinition*. New York: Routledge.

Kempadoo, K. (2001) 'Freelancers, Temporary Wives, and Beach-Boys. Researching Sex Work in the Caribbean'. *Feminist Review* 67: Spring, 39–62.

Lim, L.L. (ed.) (1998) *The Sex Sector. The Economic and Social Bases of Prostitution in Southeast Asia*. Geneva: International Labour Office.

Mahmood, S. (2001) 'Feminist Theory, Embodiment, and the Docile Agent: Some Reflections on the Egyptian Islamic Revival'. *Cultural Anthropology* 16(2): 202–36.

McCurry, J. (2005) 'Red light for Tokyo's "entertainment" trap'. *The Irish Times*, 15 March.

Miriam, K. (2005) 'Stopping the Traffic in Women: Power, Agency and Abolition in Feminist Debates over Sex-Trafficking'. *Journal of Social Philosophy* 36(1): Spring, 1–17.

Monster Baby (n.d.). Available at: http://www.monsterbaby.com.au/index.php/londoncalling?page=shop.browse&category_id=116 [accessed: 10 November 2010].

Montgomery, H. (1998) 'Children, Prostitution and Identity: A Case Study from a Tourist Resort in Thailand' in K. Kempadoo and J. Doezema (eds), *Global Sex Workers. Rights, Resistance and Redefinition*. New York: Routledge, 139–150.

Montgomery, H. (2008) 'Buying Innocence: Child-sex Tourists in Thailand'. *Third World Quarterly* 29(5): 903–17.

Moon, K.S. (1997) *Sex Among Allies. Military Prostitution in U.S.-Korea Relations*. New York: Columbia University Press.

Moor, K. (2007) 'How crime gangs clean up'. *Herald Sun*, 17 April.

Monzini, P. (2005) *Sex Traffic: Prostitution, Crime, and Exploitation*. Translated by Patrick Camiller. London and New York: Zed Press.

Murphy, E. and Ringheim, K. (2001), 'An Interview with Jo Doezema of the Network of Sex Work Projects: Does Attention to Trafficking Adversely Affect Sex Workers' Rights?' *Reproductive Health and Rights*. Available at: http//www.walnet.org/csis/papers/RHR-Doezema [accessed: 14 June 2011].

Niemi, J. (2010) 'What We Talk About When We Talk About Buying Sex'. *Violence Against Women* 16(2): 159–72.

O'Connell Davidson, J. (2005) *Children in the Global Sex Trade*. Cambridge, UK: Polity Press.

Oriel, J. (2006) 'All Quiet on the Western Front!: The International Sexual Politics of HIV/AIDS'. PhD thesis. Melbourne: Department of Political Science, University of Melbourne.

Otto, D. (2007) 'Making Sense of Zero Tolerance Policies in Peacekeeping Sexual Economies' in Vanessa Munro and Carl Stychin (eds), *Sexuality and the Law: Feminist Engagements*. London: GlassHouse Press.

Pateman, C. (1988) *The Sexual Contract*. Cambridge, UK: Polity Press.

Pattaniak, B. (2002) 'Where Do We Go From Here?' in S. Thorbek and B. Pattanaik (eds), *Transnational Prostitution. Changing Global Patterns*. London and New York: Zed Press, 217–30.

Petro, M. (2010) 'Selling Sex: Women's Participation in the Sex Industry' in M. Ditmore, A. Levy and A. Willman (eds), *Sex Work Matters. Exploring Money, Power and Intimacy in the Sex Industry*. London and New York: Zed Books, 155–70.

Poulin, R. (2005) *La Mondialisation des Industries du Sexe*. Paris: Imago.

Queensland Government (2007). Office of Economic and Statistical Research. *Average Weekly Earnings*. Available at: http://www.oesr.qld.gov.au/products/tables/average-weekly-earnings-qld-aus/index.php [accessed: 14 June 2011].

Sexploitation in St. Kilda (2010). 'Residents Say NO to Street Prostitution'. Available at: http://www.sexploitation.biz/ [accessed: 10 November 2010].

Stark, C. and Whisnant, R. (eds) (2004). *Not For Sale. Feminists Resisting Prostitution and Pornography*. Melbourne: Spinifex.

Sullivan, M. (2007) *Making Sex Work: The Failed Experiment of Legalized Prostitution in Australia*. Melbourne: Spinifex.

Tambe, A. (2006) 'Brothels as Families. Reflections on the History of Bombay's Kothas'. *International Feminist Journal of Politics* 8(2): June, 219–42.

Tanaka, Y. (2002) *Japan's Comfort Women. Sexual Slavery and Prostitution during World War II and the US Occupation*. London and New York: Routledge.

Teng, Z. (2006). 'Chinese Migrant Sex Workers in Hong Kong'. *Research for Sex Work* 29–32.

United Nations (1995). *Harmful Traditional Practices Affecting the Health of Women and Children*. Fact Sheet No. 23. Geneva: United Nations.

Willman-Navarro, A. (2006). 'Money and Sex: What Economics Should Be Doing for Sex Work'. *Research for Sex Work 9. Sex Work and Money*, 18–21.

Wilson, K. (2007). 'Agency' in Georgina Blakeley and Valerie Bryson (eds), *The Impact of Feminism on Political Concepts and Debates*. Manchester, UK: Manchester University Press, 126–45.

Zazzle.com (n.d.). Available at: http://www.zazzle.com.au/pimp+tshirts [accessed: 10 November 2010].

Zhou, J. (2006) 'Chinese Prostitution: Consequences and Solutions in the Post-Mao Era'. *China: An International Journal* 4(2): 238–62.

Chapter 5

Theorizing Harm through the Sex of Prostitution

Meagan Tyler

The so-called 'sex wars' of the 1980s delivered a new wave of writing by those claiming the label feminist but championing prostitution or 'sex work' as either a matter of individual choice or sexual liberation. How women exercise agency through and within various segments of the sex industry became a primary focus of research and popular debate (see Jeffreys: Chapter 4). This shift in academic approaches to the sex industry has occurred alongside a significant expansion of the sex industry itself (Jeffreys 2009), mostly notably the very public rise of a burgeoning pornography industry that is becoming increasingly normalized and mainstreamed (Tyler 2011). These trends have seen a glamorized version of prostitution become prominent in both the academy and in popular culture (Coy et al.: Chapter 10; Tyler 2011). The 'sex work' position has also gained increasing traction in policy approaches to prostitution (Jenness 1990; Sullivan 2007) despite a growing literature available on the harms that women experience in systems of prostitution (e.g. Dalla 2000; Downe 2003; Farley et al. 2003; Jeal and Salisbury 2004; Kramer 2003; Nixon et al. 2002; Raphael and Shapiro 2002; Ross et al. 2003; Tutty and Nixon 2003). In this academic, popular and political environment, it has become increasingly difficult to bring the harms of prostitution into focus.

In contrast some feminists, most notably radical feminists, have continued to critique prostitution on the basis of harm. Radical feminist theorizing on prostitution emphasizes the range and pervasiveness of violence that prostituted women[1] suffer at the hands of johns[2] (and often pimps as well) but also the harm

---

1   In line with many other works that adopt an abolitionist position on prostitution, the terms 'prostituted woman' and 'prostituted women' are used throughout this chapter. These terms are thought to have originated among anti-prostitution activists in the Philippines as a way of conveying women's lack of choice in entering and remaining in systems of prostitution (Ditmore (ed.) 2006: xxvi, 6). The terms are also useful in that they bring 'the perpetrator into the picture: somebody must be doing something to the woman for her to be "prostituted"' (Jeffreys 1997: 5).

2   The term 'john' will be used throughout this chapter and is used interchangeably with 'buyer' instead of 'client' or 'customer'. This is useful, firstly, because it is a term specific to prostitution and, secondly, as Jeffreys (1997) and Farley (2003) note, because it

caused through the act of prostitution itself. That is to say, *acts of prostitution are seen as harmful in and of themselves* even if there is no additional act of physical or sexual violence. The sex required in systems and institutions of prostitution is seen as objectifying and dehumanizing (Barry 1995), as a violation of women's human rights and even as a form of violence against women (Farley et al. 2003; Jeffreys 1997; Raymond 1995). This chapter argues that these claims are supported by significant sociological evidence that can no longer be overlooked or dismissed.

While social science and medical literature on the harms of prostitution has traditionally focused on general social harms in relation to law and order or public health (Farley and Kelly, 2000), during the last decade there have been a number of sociological studies, conducted in varying contexts, which have begun to more thoroughly document the experiences of prostituted women and girls (Coy: Chapter 6; Dalla 2000; Downe 2003; Farley et al. 2003; Kramer 2003; Nixon et al. 2002; Raphael and Shapiro 2002; Ross et al. 2003; Tutty and Nixon 2003). There are three significant types of harms to women that become evident from these studies. First, is the significantly increased likelihood of experiencing physical and sexual violence. Second, are psychological harms (in particular post-traumatic stress and dissociation). Third, is the experience of harm associated with the sex of prostitution. But these forms of harm are not so easily separated. This chapter will therefore seek to link together sociological research and feminist theory regarding prostitution in order to explore not only the physical and psychological harms associated with prostitution, but also those enacted in what is conceptualized here as 'the sex of prostitution'. Focusing on the sex of prostitution may enable recognition of connections between harms and also why the act of prostitution itself may be seen as fundamentally harmful. Furthermore, this theorizing is supported by the empirical evidence presented by Coy (Chapter 6).

The Harms of Physical and Sexual Violence

A number of sociological and psychological studies have demonstrated the increased likelihood that women in prostitution will experience violence (Farley et al. 2003; Parriott 1994; Nixon et al. 2002; Vanwesenbeeck 1994). Violence at the hands of pimps and violence at the hands of johns are most often the focus of attention, but as Kendra Nixon et al. (2002) have suggested, women in prostitution also tend to become targets for 'other prostituted women, and intimate partners, as well as representatives from mainstream society and the police' (p. 1023). They also add that women in prostitution are more likely to experience suicidal ideation and self-harm. In contrast, the medical literature on prostitution, where there has also been investigation into risks, has been largely limited to sexual health and

---

helps to differentiate a critical approach to prostitution from those which seek to legitimize prostitution by presenting it as labour. The term 'john' is also used by Baldwin (2004), Monto (2004) and Parker (2004).

the transmission of disease (Farley and Kelly 2000). As Nixon et al. (2002) point out, however, while sexually transmitted diseases are certainly of serious concern, 'the risk of injury and death from violence is considerable, as was indicated by the retrospective accounts of women interviewed for the current study. Violence and abuse were dominant themes in the women's narratives …' (p. 1036). Indeed, the women they interviewed often spoke of the frequent experience of extreme violence, and noted how it eventually came to appear normal: '*If something bad happened, I wouldn't have known the difference. That to me would have just been normal*' (Nixon et al. 2002: 1024). Moreover, the experience of 'something bad' becomes so normalized that it is seen as almost inseparable from prostitution, it becomes impossible to tell the difference.

The women in the study by Nixon et al. (2002) consistently linked violence to their experience of prostitution, even when they were not directly asked about it. This is not surprising given the high incidence of physical and sexual assault which have been found in studies on the experiences of prostituted women. Ruth Parriotts' (1994) study of prostituted women in America found that 85 per cent of her respondents reported having been raped while in prostitution, 90 per cent reported being physically assaulted during their time in prostitution, and 50 per cent of the overall sample reported being beaten 'once a month or more often' (n.p.). Also in the United States, Mimi Silbert and Ayala Pines (1982) found that 70 per cent of their sample of women in street prostitution had been raped, and approximately two-thirds had been physically assaulted. Such findings, indicating extremely high rates of physical violence are further corroborated by the most comprehensive study on prostitution and violence to date, conducted by Farley and colleagues (2003). Farley and her research team surveyed 854 women, girls, men and transgendered people[3] in nine countries, on five continents, about their experiences in prostitution. They found that 73 per cent had been physically assaulted while in prostitution, and more than half of the overall sample (57 per cent) had been raped while in prostitution. Approximately a third of the overall sample reported having been raped more than five times while in prostitution (Farley et al. 2003: 43).

There are persistent claims from pro-prostitution organizations and scholars who frame prostitution as work that the violence experienced by women in prostitution is often a result of the fact that prostitution is illegal or socially stigmatized and that violence could be reduced or eradicated through a process of legalization (e.g. Kempadoo (ed.) 2005; Weitzer 2005, 2007). However, claims that legalized forms of prostitution are inherently safer for prostituted women are forcefully undermined by the work of Mary Sullivan in her in-depth tracking of the consequences of legalized prostitution in the state of Victoria, Australia (Sullivan 2007; Chapter 8). Sullivan's research demonstrates the ways in which women in legalized brothel prostitution are still likely to experience many of the risks

---

3   It should be noted that of the 854 people surveyed the vast majority (n=782) were women and girls (Farley et al. 2003: 37–9).

associated with illegal street prostitution, such as exposure to STIs and violence at the hands of johns and brothel owners/pimps (Sullivan 2007; Chapter 8). Her work also undermines arguments about the safety of 'indoor prostitution' promoted by those like Ronald Weitzer (2000, 2005, 2007) who assert that while street prostitution may be harmful, brothel prostitution (and indeed any form of indoor prostitution) is safer, if not virtually unproblematic.

It has also been argued that sociological studies on violence in prostitution focus too heavily on street prostitution and therefore over-state the experience of physical and sexual violence in other forms of prostitution, such as brothel and escort prostitution (Weitzer 2000, 2005, 2007). Weitzer (2005), for example, has criticized a number of feminists, including Melissa Farley, for focusing on street prostitution but extrapolating their findings to cover prostitution as a whole. Such criticisms clearly do not hold up against Farley's work, however, which does include women (and girls, men and transgendered people) in several forms of prostitution (Farley et al. 2003). Indeed, this extensive study revealed that experiences of rape while in prostitution did not substantially differ across various forms of prostitution, including brothel, street and strip-club prostitution (Farley et al. 2003: 49). As the final report concludes: 'Prostitution is multi-traumatic whether its location is in clubs, brothels, hotels/motels/john's homes (also called escort or high class call girl prostitution) motor vehicles or the streets' (p. 60). Discourses and debates that foreground agency and empowerment, however, can reduce the space available for these findings, not least as the picture of endemic violence and rape in prostitution is not one which fits well with the glamorized version of porn and prostitution chic which has become prominent in popular media (Coy et al.: Chapter 10).

Psychological Harms

Arguments that legalization or indoor prostitution reduce or eliminate harm also overlook an important part of radical feminist theorizing on prostitution, supported by psychological and sociological research with prostituted women, that is, the concept that harm may be intrinsic to prostitution acts. This enables a way to understand safety in a wider sense than protection from physical and sexual violence which is often the focus of attempts to address prostitution as a form of work. As Liz Kelly and colleagues suggest, with respect to domestic violence, 'safety is more than the absence of assault, it is a state of mind which replaces a guarded and anxiety laden daily life with a life context in which it is possible to flourish' (Kelly et al. 2008, cited in Coy and Kelly 2011: 61).

Again, the study by Farley et al. (2003) provides support for the contention that there is something about prostitution that is inherently harmful, particularly if the implications for psychological health are taken into account. One of the elements in the 2003 study was to assess the frequency of symptoms of Post-Traumatic Stress Disorder (PTSD) among people working in a variety of types of prostitution.

According to the most authoritative diagnostic text for mental disorders, *The Diagnostic and Statistical Manual of Mental Disorders* (*DSM*) produced by the American Psychiatric Association, PTSD can occur after exposure to:

> [E]xtreme traumatic stressors involving direct or indirect personal experience of an event that involves actual or threatened death or serious injury; threat to one's personal integrity; witnessing an event that involves death, injury or a threat to the physical integrity of another person; learning about unexpected violent death, serious harm, or threat of death or injury experienced by a family member or other close associate (quoted in Farley et al. 2003: 36).

Of the overall sample, 68 per cent met the *DSM* criteria for a diagnosis of PTSD (p. 47), a similar rate to that seen among combat veterans (p. 37). Given the high rates of violence experienced by prostituted women it is not surprising that high rates of PTSD were also found. However, as Farley et al. state: 'most prostitution, most of the time, includes these traumatic stressors' (Farley et al. 2003: 36). The psychological stress as well as the trauma that may be associated with the sex of prostitution itself, also need to be taken into account.

This finding also dispels the myth that street prostitution is violent and harmful *only* because it is street-based, while other forms of prostitution, particularly brothel prostitution reduce levels of harm (e.g. Weitzer 2005). The study, in particular the research carried out in Mexico, suggests that rates of PTSD are similar across various types of prostitution including street prostitution, brothel prostitution and stripping (p. 48–9). The authors suggest this is due to the intrinsically damaging nature of prostitution, and further support this claim by comparing their own research on women in street prostitution with research from William Pick, Mary Ross and Yasmin Dada (2002) on women street vendors in South Africa.

The research by Pick and colleagues (2002) focused on the reproductive and occupational health of women street vendors in Johannesburg. The study found that the majority of the several hundred women surveyed, reported being 'not comfortable' with their working environment. The two most common reasons given for this were 'lack of shelter and dirt' and 'noise' (Pick et al. 2002). Farley et al. (2003) then compare the research on the street vendors to their own study of women in prostitution in a similar neighbourhood of Johannesburg, and the results are revealing. The rate of physical violence was found to be more than 10 times greater for women in prostitution. While only 6 per cent of the street vendors reported having been physically assaulted, 66 per cent of women in prostitution reported physical abuse. While Pick et al. (2002) found that only 7 per cent of their street vendor respondents reported being sexually harassed, 56 per cent of women in street prostitution reported having been raped at least once (Farley et al. 2003). Farley and her colleagues conclude that:

> Since the poverty, proximity to drug dealers, experience of street life and civil war were the same for both the street vendors and prostitutes, the large

differences in their experiences of sexual and physical violence can be attributed
to *the nature of prostitution itself* (p. 62 [emphasis mine]).

Even if it possible to partially attribute this difference in experience to the specific
stigmatization of prostituted women that has long served as a justification for
violence, empirical findings from research (Coy: Chapter 6; Farley et al. 2003)
support the radical feminist contention that there is something inherently harmful
about prostitution. It also challenges the claims of writers like Weitzer (2005);
that it is only by virtue of being outdoors that street prostitution is harmful. To
recognize what is actually at the centre of making the prostitution exchange
harmful requires an understanding of what actually constitutes sex in prostitution
and this is where the concept of 'the sex of prostitution' is most useful.

The Sex of Prostitution: Making Connections

Due at least in part to the prevalence of 'sex work' discourse, prostitution
is increasingly understood at both a popular and policy level as the legitimate
sale of sexual services (Jenness 1990; O'Connell Davidson 1998) and the term
'commercial sex' is commonly used as a synonym for prostitution (e.g. Chapkis
1997; Shrage 1989; Spector 2006). This fits very well with most existing theory
on prostitution, which tends to be focused primarily on the element of *economic*
exchange. It is the *sale* of sex or sexual services, that is, the *commercial* aspect,
which is seen as defining prostitution. The problem is not the sex that is required
in prostitution but the fact that it is bought and sold. Even in liberal and socialist
work that is critical of prostitution, the focus still often remains on the potential
for prostitution to be *economically* exploitative (e.g. O'Connell Davidson 1995b;
Overall 1992). That is, the main problem with prostitution can appear to be that
poor women are likely to be exploited by wealthy men.

    While these economic inequalities are certainly important and should not be
overlooked, from a radical feminist perspective, these approaches are inadequate
in that they do not account for the possibility that prostitution is exploitative on
a level more fundamental than economics. As Barry argues in *Female Sexual
Slavery* (1979):

> Feminist analysis of sexual power is often modified to make it fit into an economic
> analysis which defines economic exploitation as the primary instrument of female
> oppression. Under that system of thought, institutionalised sexual slavery, such
> as is found in prostitution, is understood in terms of economic exploitation...
> Undoubtedly economic exploitation is an important factor in the oppression of
> women, but here we must be concerned with whether or not economic analysis
> reveals the more fundamental sexual domination of women (p. 10).

In other words, to focus primarily on the economic dimension of prostitution can obscure what is really at the centre of prostitution, which is sex. This is not to dismiss prostitution as 'just sex', in the way many have done, but to understand that prostitution involves *a particular kind of sex* premised on inequality and gendered hierarchy (Jeffreys 1997). It is not just the *exchange* of something for the sex that is at issue. The concern is rather *the type of sex* that is actually required, a type of sex that because of its roots in domination and inequality is fundamentally harmful to the women directly involved in performing it (Barry 1995). The different ways in which the sex of prostitution has been conceived as harmful will be explored in this final section of the chapter.

One reason that the harms of prostitution can be seen as intrinsic is that the acts performed in prostitution, often euphemistically referred to as 'sexual services', cannot be separated from the person, usually a woman, involved in performing them (Barry 1995; Farley et al. 2003; Hoigard and Finstad 1992; Miriam 2005; Pateman 1988). As a number of feminists have argued, prostitution is better conceived of as the purchase of sexual rights over another person (Barry 1995; Cahill 2011: 106–26; O'Connell Davidson 1998; Pateman 1988). Julia O'Connell Davidson (1998), in her sociological work on prostitution, has argued, for example, that 'although prostitution is popularly defined as the exchange of sex or sexual services for money and/or other material benefits, it is better conceptualized as an institution which allows certain powers of command over one person's body to be exercised by another' (p. 9). While this is a useful starting point, it ignores one crucial part of the radical feminist understanding of prostitution: the importance of gender. To understand prostitution fully, as Carole Pateman (1988) has argued, we must question why there is a demand from *men* which fuels the prostitution of *women*. It is thus more reflective of social reality to say that prostitution involves the purchase of rights to sexually use a *woman's* body (Pateman 1988).[4] In Andrea Dworkin's rather more blunt terms, prostitution 'is the use of a woman's body for sex by a man, he pays money, he does what he wants' (Dworkin 1992: n.p.). Indeed, Kathy Miriam (2005) points out that it is this *male demand* for sexual access to women's bodies through prostitution that so often goes unquestioned in post-modern, liberal and libertarian 'sex work' literature.

However, it is not just a woman's body that is used in acts of prostitution. The person or self cannot be separated from either the body or the sexual services performed in prostitution. As professor of law and philosophy, Anita Allen (1988) has noted, the argument that women simply contract out their bodies in

---

4   This is not to say that there are no prostituted men or boys (there are, of course). The existence of prostituted men and boys, however, does not disrupt the concept of prostitution as a system in which men buy women. Firstly, the buyers remain almost exclusively men, whether those prostituted are women, men or children. Secondly, within the institution of prostitution, and even within male supremacy more broadly, the buyer will always remain *socially male* and the prostituted person always *socially female* regardless of biological sex (MacKinnon 1989).

prostitution is deeply unsound, as women's relationship to their bodies is not one of ownership; the self and the body are not so easily separated. Pateman (1988) makes a similar argument in *The Sexual Contract*. She states: 'There is an integral relationship between the body and the self. The body and the self are not identical, but selves are inseparable from bodies' (Pateman 1988: 204). Sociologists Hoigard and Finstad (1992) also describe the intimate connection between a woman's body and her sense of self in their research on women's experiences of prostitution in Norway: 'We are in our bodies – all the time. We are our bodies. When a woman prostitutes herself, her relationship to her body changes …' (Hoigard and Finstad quoted in Jeffreys 1997: 271). Moreover, Coy's empirical research in this volume shows quite clearly how prostituted women themselves link physical acts of prostitution; anchored in the body, to processes of the mind, emotionality and a sense of self-hood.

Indeed, this connection between mind, body and self is borne out in the experiences of prostituted women, recounted in numerous sociological studies which have found that what is done to women's bodies in prostitution has severe emotional and psychological consequences including dissociation and PTSD (Ross et al. 2003; Kramer 2003; Nixon et al. 2002; Parriott 1994). Dissociation is used as a coping mechanism by women in various forms of prostitution, from outdoor street prostitution, to more socially acceptable forms of prostitution such as stripping and pornography (Farley et al. 2003; Ross et al. 2003). Dissociation can be understood as an attempt by prostituted women to separate what is happening to them in prostitution from their own concept of self (Ross et al. 2003). As Pateman explains: 'the integral connection between sexuality and sense of the self means that, for self-protection, a prostitute must distance herself from her sexual use' (Pateman 1988: 207).

It has also been found to be common for women to try and psychologically escape the violence and abuse which is done to them in prostitution by using drugs and alcohol (e.g. Kramer 2003; Parriott 1994; Ross et al. 2003). A study of prostituted women in Arizona, for example, found that 70 per cent of respondents self-reported using drugs and/or alcohol use in order to 'detach emotionally' while in prostitution (Kramer 2003). Approximately half the women in studies by Kramer (2003) and Parriott (1994) responded that being high was necessary while performing acts of prostitution. It is telling, however, that for many women these strategies are never fully successful; ultimately the acts can never fully be separated from the self. As Farley et al. (2003) note, neither dissociation nor substance abuse 'fully shield the traumatized person from despair, demoralization, and hopelessness' (p. 206).

Colin Ross and colleagues (2003) suggest that given how frequently violence is experienced by women in prostitution it seems logical that there are also high rates of dissociative disorders. However, as Barry (1995) has argued, the use of dissociation as a coping method can also be found in women who have not experienced brutal physical trauma. She notes that maintaining emotional distance and dissociating is similar to 'what female teenagers, lovers and wives report in the experience of objectified sex' (Barry 1995: 31). She posits that it is the nature of the sex itself that is harmful, and it is precisely the type of sex, which is inherent in prostitution, that forces women to dissociate in order to survive:

> Commodification is one of the more severe forms of objectification; in prostitution it separates sex from the human being ... Sexual objectification dissociates women from their bodies and therefore their selves (Barry 1995: 29).

Barry's suggestion is that sexual objectification not only defines prostitution but also constitutes one of its harms. She notes that the sex of prostitution is the 'reduction of oneself to sexual object' (Barry 1995: 61), and that this objectification can be seen as destroying human dignity (p. 33). Similarly, in *The Idea of Prostitution*, Jeffreys conceives of objectification as an integral part of prostitution, describing it as 'eroticized hierarchy and objectification' (Jeffreys 1997: 218). Anderson and Estes (1998) argue along the same lines, stating that the sex of prostitution 'delivers a woman-thing without the responsibility of dealing with a woman' (p. 155). Harm is unavoidably attached to this process of objectification or 'thing-ification'. As John Stoltenberg has argued: 'every act of objectifying occurs on a continuum of dehumanization that promises male violence at its far end' (quoted in Jeffreys 1997: 59).

To claim that objectification is harmful and born of inequality can seem almost passé in a climate where sexist and objectifying imagery of women in the media is often defended by advertisers and cultural commentators as "ironic" (Kappeler 1986; Whelehan 2000; Williamson 2003; McRobbie 2009). Furthermore, as Judith Williamson argues, common understandings of objectification and sexism have become so depoliticized in much academic and popular writing that they are sometimes described not only as harmless, but even fun; something that both women and men can now enjoy in an era where gender equality has supposedly been achieved and sexism has been overcome (Williamson 2003). What is missing within this perspective is an analysis of the position of 'object' and its relative powerlessness in relation to the position of 'subject'. Or as Susanne Kappeler (1986) describes, an analysis of how gender is culturally constructed to make women into objects and men into subjects. That is, masculinity entitles men to have their full self-hood and humanity recognized, whereas the social construction of femininity relegates women to be a reflection of male desire, a mere object. What is also missing here is the understanding that objectification is a process of dehumanization which robs women of their full self-hood and, as Barry (1995) argues, their fundamental human rights (see Jackie Turner's analysis of human rights approaches with respect to prostitution, Chapter 2).

Ann Cahill (2011) has developed a sophisticated critique of objectification discourse in regard to prostitution. She argues that the use of 'objectification' has led to 'a morass of contradictions and confusions' (p. 116) in literature on prostitution and furthermore that objectification is a limited and inaccurate way of conceptualizing how johns view prostituted women. Instead, Cahill suggests the notion of derivatization as this allows for a greater understanding of prostituted women's subjectivity. She states: 'sexual derivatization entails a rendering of a sexual partner as nothing more than a mirror of one's own desires' (p. 117) and argues that this process can certainly be harmful on the basis that it reduces a person to less than a full self; that women are required to fulfil a john's fantasies. Indeed, this is almost exactly how Barry (1995) has argued that prostitution operates with regard to objectification. The two concepts of objectification/ derivatization, therefore, overlap considerably with regard to understanding the harms of prostitution. Furthermore, these feminist concepts of objectification/ derivatization are important and necessary for creating an understanding that the sex of prostitution itself is harmful.

To put forward that prostitution must involve the objectification/derivatization of women in order to function also implies that there is a fundamental inequity involved in the sex of prostitution. The context of material gender inequality, albeit in variations across the globe, is the backdrop against which all prostitution occurs. Prostitution relies on the two parties – the buyer and the bought – being unequal (Barry 1995; Jeffreys 1997). Farley et al. (2003) mention this in the introduction to their research on prostitution:

> In prostitution there is always a power imbalance, where the john has the social and economic power to hire him/her to act as a sexualized puppet. Prostitution excludes any mutuality of privilege or pleasure: its goal is to ensure that one person does *not* use her personal desire to determine which sexual acts do and do not occur – while the other person acts on the basis of his personal desire (Farley et al. 2003: 34 [emphasis original]).

Therefore, the sex of prostitution involves objectification, as a means to allow the full sexual servicing of the (male) buyer. The woman's body is not only used by the buyer, she must service him as he desires. According to Julia O'Connell Davidson, she has no sexual autonomy within the prostitution encounter, indeed that is the very point: 'The essence of the prostitution contract is that the prostitute agrees, in exchange for money or another benefit, not to use her personal desire or erotic interests as the determining criteria for her sexual interaction' (O'Connell Davidson 2002 quoted in Monto 2004: 178). Again, this is similar to Cahill's (2011) concept of derivatization. It is the john's desires which determine the interaction. The prostituted woman must sexually service the john with no regard for her own sexual pleasure. Furthermore, the sex required in prostitution does not allow for the full acknowledgement of the prostituted woman as a person or subject, but rather is premised on the use of her as either a severely diminished subject (as Cahill argues) or a dehumanized object (as Barry and others argue). As Barry notes, in prostitution, sex 'is reduced to the act of male masturbation that has nothing to do with the woman as human being …' (Barry 1995: 34).

In instances where it is just a body that is required, the oppression of the sex of prostitution is rather obvious. The sex is, as Barry suggests, clearly reduced to an act of male masturbation in which the woman is both objectified and dehumanized. There are reports from women in prostitution that this 'object' for male masturbation is indeed sometimes what they provide (O'Connell Davidson 1998). For some buyers, this is precisely what they value (Coy et al.: Chapter 7). In which case, objectification does seem an apt concept. As O'Connell Davidson reasons, this means that there are 'some clients who take pleasure in passivity – perhaps because they find an erotic charge in the idea of a woman or child submitting to sexual acts they visibly do not want ...' (O'Connell Davidson 1998: 143). The power relations of domination and submission here are obvious, not least because of the clear similarity to rape. Knowing that the sex of prostitution has nothing to do with women's pleasure, but that prostituted women must submit to it anyway, can provide a sense of power for the buyer. The sexualization of hierarchy and inequality is clearly evident.

While it is possible to characterize the sex of prostitution as the sexual servicing of men by women, where women submit 'to sexual acts they visibly do not want' (O'Connell Davidson 1998: 143), it is important to understand that it is generally *more* than the use of a passive body which is required. In both feminist theorizing on prostitution (e.g. Barry 1995; Cahill 2011; Pateman 1988) and sociological studies of buyers (e.g. Monto 2004; O'Connell Davidson 1998), it is often noted that male buyers of prostituted women want a response that indicates some form of emotional intimacy or sexual desire. In one such study, O'Connell Davidson (1998) notes that while some men are content to almost completely objectify prostituted women and are even quite open in viewing them as sub-human, most men require at least a semblance of enjoyment from the women they use. In Martin Monto's overview of research on men who buy sex, he notes that while some try and justify or rationalize their use of women in prostitution as a legitimate market exchange, when the actual sex of prostitution is in question, 'there is also ample evidence that customers often seek to minimize or ignore the economic aspects of prostitution encounters' (Monto 2004: 173). He explains further:

> Many johns object to sexual encounters that seem like nothing more than impersonal exchanges, with qualitative accounts showing frustration or anger toward prostitutes who are nonchalant, indifferent, cold, hurried, or seemingly do not care (Monto 2004: 174).

It is clear from these studies that a significant portion of men require not just a body, but a body that 'performs as self' (Barry 1995: 34). Barry (1995) explains further: 'Western men, particularly more "liberal" ones, often require from Western women an *enactment* that is sexually active and responsive as well as emotionally engaged' (p. 34 [emphasis original]).This can sometimes make the oppression of prostitution more difficult to discern, as it can appear, on the surface level, as though these men have some interest in women's pleasure, or that this version of prostitution is better than the more clearly objectified version. That johns require this more engaged performance from women, however, can actually be seen as a particularly cruel aspect of the sex of prostitution. While it may appear to indicate a desire for a more 'real' sexual experience, it can be also be seen as an integral part of gaining further control and power over the prostituted woman.

O'Connell Davidson (1998) maintains that the need for buyers to see a believable reaction of pleasure in prostituted women is based in the need to control. She explains that if a prostituted woman does not put on the appropriate 'show' for a john, this may be read as disrespectful, 'a refusal to be completely "bought"/ controlled by his money/power' (p. 142). Pateman takes this analysis even further, and likens it to the relationship between master and slave:

> Women engaged in the trade have developed a variety of distancing strategies, or a professional approach, in dealing with their clients. Such distancing creates a problem for men, a problem which can be seen as another variant on the contradiction of mastery and slavery. The prostitution contract enables men to constitute themselves as civil masters for a time, and like other masters, they wish to obtain acknowledgment of their status (Pateman 1988: 207).

Women are expected to feign enjoyment, in a believable manner, in sex that is founded on both objectification and derivatization, and therefore dehumanization. That johns command the power to demand that women feign this enjoyment reinforces just how fundamentally unequal the parties must be in order for the sex of prostitution to function.

Conclusion

It has been argued in this chapter that there are four main elements which define the sex of prostitution: sexual service, inequality, objectification/derivatization, and the requirement of a body that performs as 'self'. The notion of sexual service is critical to the sex of prostitution, that is, one party (usually a man) must be able to have their desires determine the sexual interaction regardless of the other person (usually a woman). This process necessitates inequality. In order for sexual service to take place there must be a power imbalance. It has also been suggested that objectification/derivatization is a defining element of prostitution and that the sex of prostitution demands that prostituted women are seen as less than fully human. Finally, the expectation that prostituted women should actively meet men's sexual demands and 'perform as self' or feign enjoyment, can also be seen as a key element of the sex of prostitution, although not always an essential one. That is to say, the sex of prostitution is the sexual servicing of men by women, it is premised upon inequality and, by its very nature, requires objectification/derivatization. The sex of prostitution also often requires that women pretend to enjoy their subordination and exploitation. As a concept, the sex of prostitution is useful in connecting the various harms associated with prostitution. The continuing use of this concept may help to refocus research and theorizing on the harms of prostitution beyond a discussion of economic exploitation exchange and into a discussion of what lies at the heart of prostitution: a harmful model of sex.

References

Baldwin, M. (2004) 'Strategies of Connection: Prostitution and Feminist Politics' in C. Stark and R. Whisnant (eds), *Not For Sale: Feminists Resisting Prostitution and Pornography.* Melbourne, Australia: Spinifex, 295–305.

Barry, K. (1979) *Female Sexual Slavery.* New York: New York University Press.

Barry, K. (1995) *The Prostitution of Sexuality.* New York: New York University Press.

Bell, S. (1995) *Whore Carnival.* Brooklyn, NY: Autonomedia.

Cahill, A. (2011) *Overcoming Objectification: A Carnal Ethics.* New York: Routledge.

Chapkis, W. (1997) *Live Sex Acts: Women Performing Erotic Labor.* New York: Routledge.

Coy, M. and Kelly, L. (2011) *Islands in the Stream: An Evaluation of Independent Domestic Violence Advocacy Schemes.* London: Trust for London/Henry Smith Charity.

Dalla, R. (2000) 'Exposing the "Pretty Woman" Myth: A Qualitative Examination of the Lives of Street-walking Prostitutes. *Journal of Sex Research* 37(4): 344–53.

Ditmore, M. (2006) *Encyclopedia of Prostitution and Sex Work, Volume 1.* Westport, CT: Greenwood Publishing.

Downe, P. (2003) '"The People We Think We Are": The Social Identities of Girls Involved in Prostitution' in K. Gorkoff and J. Runner (eds), *Being Heard: The Experiences of Young Women in Prostitution.* Manitoba, Canada: Fernwood Publishing, 46–68.

Dworkin, A. (1992) 'Prostitution and Male Supremacy'. Speech delivered at *Prostitution: From Academia to Activism* at the University of Michigan Law School, Michigan USA, 31st October.

Farley, M. and Kelly, V. (2000) 'Prostitution: A Critical Review of the Medical and Social Sciences Literature'. *Women and Criminal Justice* 11(1): 29–64.

Farley, M. (ed.) (2003) *Prostitution, Trafficking, and Traumatic Stress.* New York: Harworth Press.

Farley, M., Cotton, A., Lynne, J., Zumbeck, S., Spiwak, F., Reyes, M., Alvarez, D. and Sezgin, U. (2003) 'Prostitution and Trafficking in Nine Countries: An Update on Violence and Post Traumatic Stress Disorder' in M. Farley (ed.), *Prostitution, Trafficking, and Traumatic Stress.* New York: Haworth Press, 33–75.

Hoigard, C. and Finstad, L. (1986) *Backstreets: Prostitution, Money, and Love.* University Park, PA: Pennsylvania State University Press.

Jeal, N. and Salisbury, C. (2004) 'A Health Needs Assessment of Street-based Prostitutes: Cross-sectional Survey'. *Journal of Public Health* 26(1) 147–51.

Jeffreys, S. (2009) *The Industrial Vagina: The Political Economy of the Global Sex Trade.* New York: Routledge.

Jeffreys, S. (1997) *The Idea of Prostitution.* Melbourne, Australia: Spinifex.

Jenness, V. (1990) 'From Sex as Sin to Sex as Work: COYOTE and the Reorganization of Prostitution as a Social Problem'. *Social Problems* 37(3): 403–20.

Kappeler, S. (1986) *The Pornography of Representation.* Minneapolis: University of Minnesota Press.

Kempadoo, K. (ed.) (2005) *Trafficking and Prostitution Reconsidered: New Perspectives on Migration, Sex Work and Human Rights.* Boulder, CO: Paradigm.

Kramer, L. (2003) 'Emotional Experiences of Performing Prostitution' in M. Farley (ed.), *Prostitution, Trafficking, and Traumatic Stress.* New York: Haworth Press, 187–99.

MacKinnon, C. (1989) *Toward a Feminist Theory of the State.* Cambridge, MA: Harvard University Press.

McRobbie, A. (2009) *The Aftermath of Feminism: Gender, Culture and Social Change.* London: Sage Publications.

Miriam, K. (2005) 'Stopping the Traffic in Women: Power, Agency and Abolition in Feminist Debates Over Sex-trafficking'. *Journal of Social Philosophy* 36(1): 1–17.

Monto, M. (2004) 'Female Prostitution, Customers and Violence'. *Violence against Women* 10(2): 160–88.

Nagle, J. (ed.) (1997) *Whores and Other Feminists.* New York: Routledge.

Nixon, K., Tutty, L., Downe, P., Gorkoff, K. and Ursel, J. (2002) '"The Everyday Occurrence": Violence in the Lives of Girls Exploited through Prostitution'. *Violence Against Women* 8(9): 1016–43.

O'Connell Davidson, J. (1998) *Prostitution, Power and Freedom.* Cambridge: Polity.

Overall, C. (1992) 'What's Wrong with Prostitution? Evaluating Sex Work'. *Signs* 17(4): 705–24.

Paglia, C. (1994) *Vamps and Tramps: New Essays.* New York: Vintage Books.

Parker, J. (2004) 'How Prostitution Works' in C. Stark and R. Whisnant (eds), *Not For Sale: Feminists Resisting Prostitution and Pornography.* Melbourne, Australia: Spinifex, 3–14.

Parriott, R. (1994) *Health Experiences of Twin Cities Women Used in Prostitution: Survey Findings and Recommendations.* Minneapolis: WHISPER. Available at: http://www.angelfire.com/mn/fjc/healthex2.html [accessed: 20 November 2007].

Pateman, C. (1988) *The Sexual Contract.* Cambridge: Polity Press.

Pick, W., Ross, M. and Dada, Y. (2002) 'The Reproductive and Occupational Health of Women Street Vendors in Johannesburg, South Africa'. *Social Science and Medicine* 54(2): 193–204.

Raphael, J. and Shapiro, D. (2002) *Sisters Speak Out: The Lives and Needs of Prostituted Women in Chicago*. Chicago: Center for Impact Research.

Raymond, J. (1995) *Report to the Special Rapporteur on Violence Against Women. Coalition Against Trafficking in Women*. Available at: http://www.iswface.org/coalitionagainsttraffick.html [accessed: 11 January 2008].

Ross, C., Farley, M. and Schwartz, H. (2003) 'Dissociation Among Women in Prostitution' in M. Farley (ed.), *Prostitution, Trafficking, and Traumatic Stress*. New York: Harworth Press, 199–212.

Satz, D. (2006) 'Markets in Women's Sexual Labor' in J. Spector (ed.), *Prostitution and Pornography: Philosophical Debate about the Sex Industry*. Stanford, CA: Stanford University Press, 394–418.

Shrage, L. (1989) 'Should Feminists Oppose Prostitution?' *Ethics* 99(2): 347–61.

Silbert, M. and Pines, A. (1984) 'Victimization of Street Prostitutes'. *Victimology* 7(1): 122–33.

Spector, J. (2006) 'Obscene Division: Feminist Liberal Assessments of Prostitution versus Feminist Liberal Defenses of Pornography' in J. Spector (ed.), *Prostitution and Pornography: Philosophical Debate about the Sex Industry*. Stanford, CA: Stanford University Press, 419–45.

Sullivan, M. (2007) *Making Sex Work: A Failed Experiment with Legal Prostitution*. Melbourne, Australia: Spinifex.

Tutty, L. and Nixon, K. (2003) '"Selling Sex? It's Really Like Selling Your Soul": Vulnerability to the Experience of Exploitation through Child Prostitution' in K. Gorkoff and J. Runner (eds), *Being Heard: The Experiences of Young Women in Prostitution*. Manitoba, Canada: Fernwood Publishing, 29–45.

Tyler, M. (2011) *Selling Sex Short: The Pornographic and Sexological Construction of Women's Sexuality in the West*. Newcastle, UK: Cambridge Scholars Press.

Vanwesenbeeck I. (1994) *Prostitutes' Well-Being and Risk*. Amsterdam: VU University Press.

Weitzer, R. (2000) 'Why We Need More Research on Sex Work' in R. Weitzer (ed.), *Sex for Sale: Prostitution, Pornography and the Sex Industry*. New York: Routledge, 1–17.

Weitzer, R. (2005) 'Rehashing Tired Claims about Prostitution'. *Violence against Women* 11(7): 971–7.

Weitzer, R. (2007) 'Prostitution as a Form of Work'. *Sociology Compass* 1(1): 143–55.

Chapter 6

'I Am a Person Too':
Women's Accounts and Images about
Body and Self in Prostitution

Maddy Coy

This chapter explores impacts of prostitution on women's relationship with the body, drawing on key themes from life story interviews with a small sample of women from the UK, and images created with women on the theme of body and self. The focus is on how women who participated in the research experienced and expressed disruption to their embodied sense of self. The chapter also reflects on methodological approaches involving participatory arts, pioneered by Maggie O'Neill (2001, 2008, 2010; O'Neill et al. 2002) and used in this research to explore and (re)present women's experiences.

Psychosocial Harms and Prostitution

Harms associated with prostitution include: sexual and physical violence (Church et al. 2001; Farley et al. 2003; O'Neill 2001; Nixon et al. 2002; Phoenix 1999; Raphael and Shapiro 2004) increased likelihood of murder (Potterat et al. 2004); and multiple negative consequences for sexual, mental and physical health (Farley et al. 2003; Farley 2004; Jeal et al. 2008). Studies have also explored how women manage living with risk, threats and the actuality of violence (Hoigard and Finstad 1992; O'Neill 2001; Phoenix 1999; Plumridge 2001; Sanders 2004); and how substance misuse serves as a psychological survival tactic (Epele 2001; Jeal et al. 2008; Kramer 2003). This rich existing knowledge base reveals the complexity of women's lived experience of prostitution, encompassing vulnerability and victimization as well as a sense of autonomy for some.

As Meagan Tyler (Chapter 5) discusses in more detail, a trauma model is increasingly used to research impacts of prostitution on emotional and psychological wellbeing (see Choi et al. 2009; Farley et al. 2003; Roxburgh et al. 2006). Findings from these studies, conducted across many countries, demonstrate that significant proportions of women in prostitution meet the criteria for a diagnosis of Post Traumatic Stress Disorder (PTSD), including those in indoor prostitution. Yet drawing on a trauma model is mired in debate. The language of trauma, with etymological roots in the Greek for 'wound', has become part of everyday vocabulary, and provides a benchmark for establishing seriousness of harm. Feminists have long argued that models such as PTSD, used to measure the harms of combat for men, should acknowledge the seriousness of the legacies of violence and abuse (Burstow 2003). Trauma framings also have pragmatic uses in specific socio-economic contexts where diagnoses of PTSD are required for health insurance companies to pay for therapeutic support, including counselling. At the same time, the concept of trauma has been argued to be inherently individualist, with medicalized notions of recovery eclipsing social contexts (Burstow 2003).

So, while trauma models offer one means to capture harms in and associated with prostitution, there are also wider dimensions of 'emotional diminishment' (Hoigard and Finstad 1992; see also Farley 2003, 2004; Hedin and Mansson 2003) that have been explored and documented. In one US study involving 119 women in street and escort prostitution, three quarters (76 per cent) experienced selling access to their bodies as emotionally painful, with the same proportion reporting a decrease in self-esteem (Kramer 2003). When asked to describe the emotions associated with prostitution, women reported feeling: sad; detached; resentful; dirty; unattractive; fearful; and anxious. Almost all emotional responses (90 per cent) were negative. Another recurrent theme in women's accounts of prostitution is feeling 'depersonalized' (Farley 2004; Hoigard and Finstad 1992; Vanwesenbeeck 2005). This has been described as 'social death'; that even where women experience degrees of control or autonomy, the required minimization of self is such that 'there is a sense in which prostitutes are socially dead within each transaction' (O'Connell Davidson 1998: 134).

The theme of depersonalization cuts across women's experiences in this chapter, explored and expressed through the lived experience of the body. Contexts in which women are engaged in prostitution, individual life histories including social and economic resources, and legal and policy frameworks shape experiential realities of prostitution. Yet as access to the body for sexual purposes is at its core (O'Connell Davidson 1998; Pateman 1988), exploring relationships with the body is critical. In recognition that even acts that do not involve penetration of the body still require touch and contact, and perhaps additional visual stimulation such as exposure of breasts, the female body that is bought and sold in prostitution has been subject to much empirical enquiry and conceptual analysis. Julia O'Connell Davidson (1998) suggests that men who buy sex are afforded a 'power of command' over women's bodies that is not just physical but also symbolic; that what is purchased is not simply specific functions which require the use of the body, but also a transfer of control. Drawing on this, the focus here is to explore psychosocial meanings of prostitution, specifically relationships with the body and how women expressed a sense of depersonalization.

Reflections on Methodology: Interviews and Participatory Arts Work

The research that forms the basis of this chapter comprised two overlapping layers of data collection: life story interviews with young women who had backgrounds of state care and involvement in prostitution; and participatory arts workshops on the theme of the body and self. The arts workshops were a collaborative project with a local youth arts team and a highly skilled and experienced arts worker, following methodology developed by Maggie O'Neill (2001, 2008, 2010; O'Neill et al. 2002) and consisted of group and one-to-one sessions exploring women's sense of self and bodily autonomy. Some women who participated in the life story interviews were involved in the early stages of the arts project and contributed to the development of ideas and themes, although none of those interviewed ultimately also created one of the final images. There is, however, considerable overlap in experiential terms between how women in both strands of the research described the self and the body. Both methods also endorse what Maggie O'Neill (2001) terms a 'politics of feeling', privileging emotions that women attach to lived experience.

The Interviews

Life story interviews provided ways to explore how women attached meaning to lived experience, by offering maximum control over the direction of the dialogue. For women in prostitution, this approach avoids focussing only on sexual activities, contextualizing involvement in the sex industry with a fuller focus on women's lives (O'Neill 2001). Participants were accessed through my daily outreach contact with women in street and indoor prostitution. The dual role of researcher and outreach worker required an ongoing negotiation of ethical dilemmas, while granting privileged access into women's lives (Coy 2006). The development of themes from the interviews was thus informed by daily contact with women, an ethnographic engagement which enabled a deeper understanding of women's lived experience.

Fourteen women aged between 17–33 years old participated in life story interviews. Twelve identified as white and two as mixed race. As the focus of the research was to explore connections between local authority (state) care and routes into prostitution, all women who participated had spent time in care, ranging from 18 months to 16 years. Ten women disclosed experiences of sexual abuse; all had histories of neglect, abandonment and instability within care placements. Ages of entry into prostitution varied from 11 to 16 years, and routes in were characterized by combinations of poverty, peer introduction, stigmatization and coercion, with emotional vulnerability as significant as material need. All were initially involved in street prostitution, but at the time of the interviews three women had moved to indoor prostitution. Only two women cited a need to pay for drugs as their entry route, yet the cycle of entrapment once women were engaged in both was clear (Cusick et al. 2003; Jeal et al. 2008; Kramer 2003) and all reported use of illegal drugs at some point. This was a qualitative study with a small sample of women who were among the most vulnerable, and not representative of all women in the sex industry. As most of the women who participated in the life story interviews (and indeed the arts work) had experienced historic and current sexual and physical violence, and many were coerced into prostitution, relationships with the body may be inflected differently than for women without similar histories (Coy 2008). Yet abuse, coercion and emotional isolation are well-documented in women's routes into prostitution, as are multiple forms of violence within it (Cusick et al. 2003; Farley et al. 2003; Nixon et al. 2002; O'Neill 2001), and accounts here may thus have wider resonance.

Transcripts were analysed using a version of 'Voice Centred Relational Ontology' developed by Natasha Mauthner and Andrea Doucet (1998), a method which advocates several readings of the text in order to situate accounts within women's relationships and social contexts. While analysis here and elsewhere is 'my story of their stories' (Birch 1998: 182), as already noted, ongoing involvement in the social relationships in which the narratives were told was integral to the development of interpretative frameworks. For instance, observation of women's 'bodily deterioration' and 'estrangement' (Epele 2001) through everyday ethnography enabled insights into women's relationships with their selves and bodies. Themes of self and body also emerged from the life story interviews with women as significant to their introduction into, and lived experience of, prostitution. The arts workshops were developed to explore this in more depth.

The 'MyBody MySelf' Arts Workshops

The use of participatory arts workshops as a social research methodology was pioneered by Maggie O'Neill, who over a decade of research with women in the sex industry and refugees developed an approach she defines as 'ethno-mimesis', combining participatory action research and participatory arts, making participation and (re)presentation accessible beyond the academic arena (O'Neill 2001, 2008, 2010; O'Neill et al. 2002; www.safetysoapbox.co.uk). She suggests that artistic representation is potentially transformative by offering a more authentic voice of participants' lived experience, and 'can transgress conventional or traditional ways of analyzing and representing research data' (O'Neill et al. 2002: 29). For exploring women's relationships with the body, the use of art enables experience to be visible from multiple points of view; visual data designed by participants supplement verbal data by revealing thoughts and emotions not always consciously understood or even recognized (Newell-Walker 2002). In this research, to borrow from Stanley and Wise (1983: 146), arts work provided another means to explore and represent 'language[s] of experience'. The images are women's stories about lived experiences of prostitution that cannot be so easily elicited by conversation alone.

The arts workshops were developed with the voluntary sector community based arts team[1] who had led on Maggie O'Neill and Rosie Campbell's (2001) previous participatory action research and arts project in the same area (see also O'Neill 2008; www.safetysoapbox.co.uk). The same artist, Kate Green, was engaged for *MyBody MySelf*; she had a thorough understanding of the issues and sensitivities of working with women in transient social and emotional locations, and a keen awareness of the ethical dimensions of research and arts-based work. Conducting the arts workshops was itself an ethnographic process over 18 months, where both Kate and I spent considerable time with women discussing and exploring if and how prostitution, and aspects connected to it (drug use, self harm), had an impact on their relationship with the body. Over 40 women with differing degrees of involvement in the sex industry participated during this time, including those in street and indoor prostitution and young women at risk of sexual exploitation.

During daily outreach to street and indoor prostitution sites, initial discussions engaged women to participate in the arts workshops, and were important to build trust and rapport with Kate. However, mobile outreach with women in street prostitution proved to be a difficult environment to talk about relationships with bodies beyond superficial discussions. An alternative approach was developed: individual sessions with women in both street and indoor prostitution, and group sessions arranged by a local voluntary sector project that provided support to young women at risk of sexual exploitation. The intense work to create the images took place in computer studios at a specialized youth arts project. For many women who participated, communicating experience using visual arts was a new concept.[2] Kate's role was therefore to introduce the idea of making artwork about themselves, their body and life experiences; to identify the significant issues, and what women wanted to express through the artwork. The collaborative process of co-authoring the images between women and Kate as an artist was central; this involved 'visual conversations' exploring what women wanted to communicate and experimentation to explore how images can convey meaning. Women's involvement in directing the photography was crucial for generating the ingredients for their piece. Kate then worked with women to devise and create

---

1   The arts workshops were funded by grants from the National Youth Agency and Awards for All, enabling both the engagement of Kate Green and Mark Webster, a freelance arts consultant who led the strategic and financial direction of the project, as well as the final display of the images in light boxes as an exhibition ('*MyBody MySelf: Getting Under the Skin*') that ran in the Midlands in early 2004. A steering group of local experts on the relevant issues was also formed, to provide advice throughout the arts workshops process. '*MyBody MySelf*' would not have not have been possible without all these contributions, as well as support and guidance from Maggie O'Neill throughout.

2   Some women who had participated in *Safety Soapbox* were eager to participate in further arts workshops and created, or contributed to, some of the final images in both projects.

a multi-layered piece incorporating image, text and graphics, using what image women wanted to represent their thoughts and feelings, what colours related to their message and what or how much text to include. These verbal commentaries were superimposed over the photographs using Adobe Photoshop, and reflected the meanings attached to the image.

The final 11 photographic images (re)presented women's experiences of '*MyBody MySelf*', including rape, childhood sexual abuse, drug use, self-harm, and the ontology of selling access to the body. Through creating visual representations of emotions and experience, the arts workshops moved beyond recording of knowledge to actually creating *new* knowledge (O'Neill 2001; O'Neill et al. 2002), here about women's relationships with their bodies. Some of the images reflect feeling and ideas that several women expressed, and their contributions are visible in the final products; they enriched understanding of how women managed emotional and psychosocial dimensions of prostitution.

One question that was explored within the arts project was if, or how, disruption to the relationship with the body varied by context of prostitution. Studies demonstrate that women in street prostitution report higher levels of violence, drug use, homelessness, ill health, and stigma associated with criminalization (Jeal and Salisbury 2007; McKeganey and Barnard 1997; Phoenix 1999; O'Neill 2001). This raises the possibility that women who sell sex on the street might have had qualitatively different experiences of the body. Nuances did emerge – women involved solely in street prostitution more commonly expressed deeper disconnection from the body, evident in images about drug use and self harm. However, one of the difficulties of drawing such vivid lines between street and indoor prostitution in terms of harm is the mobility between sectors, as some women who participated were involved in combinations of street, indoor and escort prostitution (also noted by Kramer 2003). Overall women's accounts and the images reveal that disruption to self and body cut across different prostitution contexts and individual biographies.

The chapter now turns to the key interlinked themes of women's lived experience of the body that emerged from both interviews and arts work: sexual objectification (Coy 2008); disconnection from the body leading to disembodiment (Coy 2009a); and parallels between violation in prostitution and sexual violence (Coy 2009b). These themes have been discussed in depth elsewhere, and are introduced here to contextualize some of the images from '*MyBody MySelf*'[3] that are presented in subsequent sections.

---

3   Images that feature full-length photographs of women, although non-identifiable, are not reproduced here.

Women's Experiential Relationship with the Body: Key Themes

Women's experience of sexual objectification in prostitution has been well documented (Farley 2004; Hoigard and Finstad 1992; McKeganey and Barnard 1997; O'Neill 2001; Phoenix 1999). In Chapter 5, Meagan Tyler identifies four characteristics of the 'sex of prostitution', as she defines it as 'a harmful model of sex'. One of these is objectification.[4] Martha Nussbaum (1995) also provides an elaborate conceptual framework for objectification, defined as 'seven ways to treat a person as a thing' (p. 256). Two of these – fungibility (being interchangeable with others of the same type, a process of commodification) – and denial of subjectivity (experiences and feelings of 'object' not recognized) have been applied to prostitution by Marshall (1999). Elsewhere I have drawn on these and added a third of Nussbaum's elements to explore the experiences of men who buy sex and women who sell sex – instrumentality (where objectifiers treat the object as a tool of their purpose) (Nussbaum 1995: 257, cited in Coy 2008). Together these elements enable an understanding of the dynamics of objectification in prostitution that rests on women's sense of self being absent or minimized, and women's bodies used as a means to fulfil men's sexual desires and requests without mutuality (see also O'Connell Davidson 1998; Pateman 1988). Accounts from men who pay for sex demonstrate that what some value is the ability to view women as interchangeable instruments for satisfying their sexual requirements (Coy et al.: Chapter 7; Mansson 2004; see also Raphael: Chapter 3 with respect to men who paid for sex in Chicago). In a recent British study, this was explicitly articulated by one as 'there is no obligation put on me to have a relationship with a person, they're available, therefore at your disposal' (cited in Coy 2008: 188).

Although, as the images will illustrate, the theme of objectification was evident throughout women's accounts, there was also no one story of how women managed this. The status of being an object was evident primarily through the lens of interchangeable instrumentality, expressed by Jackie[5] and Tammy that men sought 'a hole' where women's own sense of self was irrelevant. Distancing strategies were here described by women as necessary to negotiate this designation of their bodies as interchangeable instruments. This can be understood as enacting objectification in ways that reflect how they are viewed and constituted by sex buyers (Coy 2008). Thus supporting existing literature (e.g. Farley 2004; Hoigard and Finstad 1992; Sanders 2004; Vanwesenbeeck 2005), a strong feature of women's accounts was the need to separate the thinking, feeling self from the physical body – 'switching off' to avoid feeling 'degraded'; 'pretending I wasn't there'; feigning enjoyment as a distraction; using substances to alter mood and dull sensation. Dissociation can become so fully integrated into the lived

---

4   Meagan also draws on Ann Cahill's (2011) notion of derivization to extend conceptualization and analysis of objectification (see Chapter 5).

5   All names are pseudonyms, chosen by the women who participated.

knowledge of the body that it segues into disembodiment, becoming 'a profound alienation from the life of the body' (Scott 2001: 177).

For many women who participated in the interviews, practices of dissociation began with sexual abuse in childhood and were fundamental to a relationship with the body in prostitution. Experiences of the body that involve violation of its boundaries – sexual violence – create a template for a relationship with the body (Coy 2009a), a process that phenomenologist Merleau Ponty (1962) conceptualized as a 'habit body'. This concept captures how knowledge of the world is embodied, developed via a 'corporeal schema' that is derived from and shaped by lived experience. Feminist theorists have drawn on Merleau-Ponty's work to illustrate how the 'habit body' (corporeal schema) is experienced as gendered and informed by experiences of abuse, harassment and violation. Wendy Parkins (2000), for example, suggests that experiential, embodied knowledge 'give[s] us resources for acting meaningfully in the world through the 'expressive space' that is our body' (p. 60). Stacey (25) constructed a narrative where significant experiential events centred on multiple sexually abusive experiences in childhood and adolescence. Subsequently coerced into prostitution, she said that 'after a couple of weeks I'd just got used to it' and described prostitution as 'what she [knew] best'. Her habit body was characterized by violation of its boundaries. For Becky, sexually abused in adolescence and subsequently sexually exploited through a process of being 'groomed' by an older man posing as her boyfriend (see also Raphael: Chapter 3), violation and 'feeling dirty' also became normalized.

> The prostitution, it just feels normal. That feels even more normal than the drugs. I always felt dirty though (Becky, 17).

How templates of disembodiment are relevant to entry into prostitution is not simply that invasions of the body become normalized, but also about more complex negotiations about the value and function of the body (Hoigard and Finstad 1992; Wesely 2002). For instance, engagement in prostitution enabled some women to reclaim, reframe and re-establish a sexualized sense of self in ways they perceived as positive and offering personal power (see Coy 2009a). Women's accounts revealed, however, that this was based on objectifying the body as a commodity (Coy 2008).

The third key theme of women's narratives and images thus builds on objectification and disembodiment, and addresses the ways in which women experienced prostitution as violating in similar terms to sexual violence. While 'the sex of prostitution' (Tyler: Chapter 5) conceptually captures the ways in which women are required to be objects to facilitate men's sexual entitlement to release within, or in relation to, a woman's body, prostitution is also made up of different interactions and even moments within them, and some may be more experienced as intrusive/violating than others. It is, therefore, revealing that in both interviews and arts workshops, parallels between experiences of sexual violence and prostitution were expressed in terms of a sense of invasion, dissociation, and for some women, a sense that they no longer belonged in their body or had control over violation of its boundaries (Coy 2009b). Emotions associated with prostitution in the life story interviews and '*MyBody MySelf*' arts workshops were, for the most part, identical to those used by women to describe the legacies of sexual abuse and violence: shame, guilt, hating the body, blame and alienation from the self. In Lynn's image about rape, part of the text was 'I felt dirty and ashamed' and in Wendy's image about childhood sexual abuse 'I hate my body'. That these words also resonated throughout many women's accounts of prostitution itself points to the sex of prostitution in various manifestations and practices disrupting women's relationship with the body.

Images about '*MyBody Myself*'

Drawing on these key themes as they appear to varying degrees and in combination with each other, the images are presented here as heuristic devices to illustrate harmful psychosocial impacts on relationship with the body and sense of self for women who participated.

The image below, created with Jessica, places her face, as symbol of her self, at the centre. The nightmares described in the image began to plague her when she stopped using drugs, which in turn she had used to 'block out the work I'm doing'.

> Thinking it's real... hearing... breathing... getting in a car... dreaming of men's faces... on top... menacing... too scared to sleep... crying...men's faces... men's faces... dreaming... nightmares... drowning...crying... men's faces... bad dreams... drowning... breathing in a pool of blood... bad dreams... IT WILL STICK IN YOUR MIND FOREVER

This image and text as reflections of '*MyBody MySelf*' are revealing, as they connect 'getting in the car' (with men who pay for sex) to nightmares, menace, and 'men's faces'. This visual (re)presentation echoes legacies of sexual violence – flashbacks of the sounds and sensations of abusive experiences, powerlessness, fear and a sense of metaphorical and literal death (Kelly 1998; Scott 2001). Nightmares about drowning in pools of blood and 'men on top' speak powerfully of losing her sense of bodily autonomy. These harms expose a superficiality of empowerment discourses for Jessica; while she talked about prostitution as financially rewarding, its psychosocial and emotional legacies are shown in the invasive thoughts that she feared would last 'forever'. Another image created by Jessica, not reproduced here, showed her arms dotted with vivid sores from drug use; yet scars and wounds on the skin were the external signs of an internal turmoil. In choosing the text for this image – 'scars reminding me ... not just physical, it's mental too' – Jessica wanted to convey the message to other young women that prostitution had been, for her, emotionally painful.

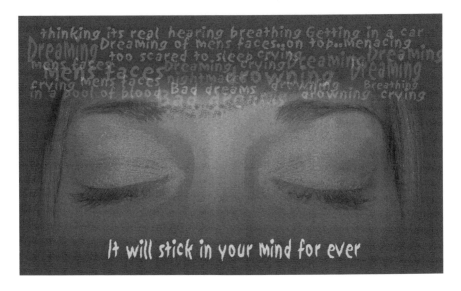

Figure 6.1   'It will stick in your mind forever'
Source: © Kate Green and women in prostitution in Midtown.

Here Jessica also highlights the complexity of association between prostitution and drug use; while connections are evident, for some women entry into prostitution is a means to pay for a drug habit, for others drug use is a dissociative mechanism that begins as an emotional survival strategy (Epele 2001; Farley 2004; O'Neill 2001). In an interview, Jackie described using vodka and cocaine 'just to get me through the night ... every day to keep my mind off what I was doing'. Similarly for Becky, heroin and crack cocaine enabled her to manage a sense of invasion and 'feeling dirty'; 'when I was working it made me feel dirty, but the gear stopped that, and stopped me thinking about the abuse'. Research with women in prostitution in the US similarly suggested that use of substances to heighten/dull sensation frequently began as an attempt to manage and manipulate the body and mind, yet led to cycles of craving which in turn led to the body becoming 'an "alien" entity that clamour[ed] to be comforted' (Epele 2001: 170). Jane echoed this; 'it [heroin and crack] becomes an everyday thing you've got to do'.

In the arts project, drug use emerged as a central theme of women's relationship with the body, particularly for women involved in street prostitution. The following image is a stark representation of how Gemma perceived that use of heroin, crack cocaine and alcohol diminished both her sense of self and autonomy/control over her body.

Drugs eating away at my body and soul ... making me less

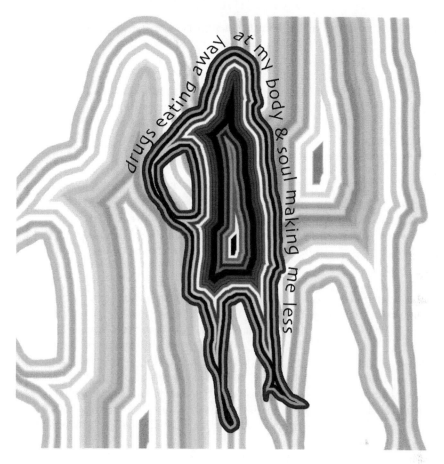

Figure 6.2   'Drugs eating away at my body and soul'
Source: © Kate Green and women in prostitution in Midtown.

Gemma had been involved in street, indoor and escort prostitution for over a decade. The image is at one level a literal statement about how drug use and the accompanying neglect of her basic bodily needs rendered Gemma thin and frail. There was also a deeper impact on her bodily autonomy, as physiological cravings and dependency led to her body drifting away from her control, just as her sense of self became similarly detached; 'eating away at my soul'. In another image about the way she used self-harm (cutting) to manage emotional distress, she described 'slicing herself up like a joint of beef ... You can't love yourself when you can cut yourself like that'. Gemma's experience of her body and self was that harmful impacts of prostitution were direct and indirect, central and peripheral, visible and hidden.

Another image (not reproduced here), created with Tammy, revealed how objectification through 'the sex of prostitution' led to her disembodied 'habit body'. Tammy had been working in indoor prostitution for many years, framed this as economic entrepreneurship and had a strong personal support network. That her lived experience of her body was characterized by negativity, disconnection and alienation is a starting point to explore a continuum of harm (Kelly 1988) experienced by women involved in prostitution under different personal circumstances. In the image, a photograph of Tammy was framed by text which reveals the words she used to describe how she feels about prostitution, herself, and her body.

> Men come to the flat and pay to have sex ... I won't kiss men, it's too intimate ... I think that I'm unattractive, I hate my body ... I don't have sex with my husband anymore ... I hate myself ... Sometimes I feel I am just a hole for men to use ...

Elements of objectification are evident in how Tammy perceived that her (dis)embodied self was an interchangeable instrument; 'sometimes I feel I am just a hole for men to use'. Tammy also revealed the inefficacy of preserving areas of her body, such as her mouth, for intimacy as a means to sustain a sense of bodily autonomy. Strategies such as bodily zoning and retaining certain sexual acts for intimate relationships are well documented in women's accounts of prostitution (Farley 2004; Sanders 2002; Vanwesenbeeck 2005). For Tammy, these strategies were unsuccessful as she felt unable to have 'have sex with [her] husband anymore' (also noted by Hoigard and Finstad 1992; Kramer 2003). As a statement about her lived experience of 'hating' her body and self and being 'just a hole', Tammy's account echoes Kathleen Barry's (1995) observation about the parcelling into pieces of the body in prostitution.

> when the human being is reduced to a body, objectified to sexually service another, whether or not there is consent, violation has taken place ... some body parts, some physical acts cannot be relegated for sale while others are protected (pp. 23/32).

This was not the experience of all women who participated in the arts work. In text for another image (not reproduced here), Julie and Helen reported that:

> When the men come into the brothel you see them as £ signs. On an average shift you might see five men. I have strong limits and boundaries – it's my body and I'm in control. Never without a condom ... At home it's real, at work it's just acting ... Some days you feel guilty ...

The image comprised a series of photographs of both women, rooms in the brothel and accessories such as costumes, shoes and lubricants. These props demonstrate the performative dimension of prostitution required to create and re-create men's fantasies, described by Julia O'Connell Davidson (1998) as:

> The prostitute's skill and art lies in her ability to completely conceal all genuine feelings, beliefs, desires, preferences and personality (in short, her self) and appear as nothing more than the living embodiment of the client's fantasies (p. 190).

For Julie and Helen, the use of costumes and performance to become 'the living embodiment of men's fantasies', and strategies such as condom use (Sanders 2002) enabled a division of self between 'real me' and 'work me' (Hoigard and Finstad 1992). Both had been involved in prostitution for several years, motivated by limited opportunities for economic independence. The reference to men as currency also featured in a small number of the interviews, and is an example of how, at the level of everyday interaction, capitalizing on use of the body can afford individual women power. If analysed at the level of structural gender orders (Connell 2009; see Coy: Introduction), however, power is exercised by those who have capital to buy rather than those driven to sell by economic 'compulsion' (see also O'Connell Davidson 1998: 17). In terms of '*MyBody MySelf*', Julie and Helen were clear that they maintained 'strong limits and boundaries', demonstrating that dissociative practices and processes of compartmentalization were successful since 'at home it's real, at work it's just acting'. This protection of subjectivity and bodily autonomy – 'it's my body and I'm in control' – was not, however, entirely without ambiguity; 'some days you feel guilty'. While Julie and Helen's account indicates that there is no one story of how women manage lived experiences of prostitution, it was also an exception to the recurrent theme of depersonalization, objectification and disembodiment that women reported in both interviews and arts work.

The final image presented here was therefore inspired by and draws on ideas expressed by many women who participated in the arts workshops – objectification and depersonalization in prostitution, and attempts to resist this, to reassert a sense of personhood. Reflecting that 'conversations may invoke images' (Pink 2001: 17), this piece depicts an egg being shattered in several stages by a human hand, accompanied by the words:

> I am fragile, I am a person too, when you touch me it hurts, I am breakable

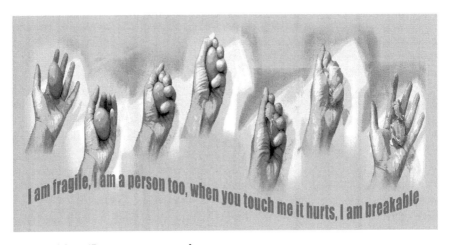

Figure 6.3   'I am a person too'
Source: © Kate Green and women in prostitution in Midtown.

The message communicated through this image is multi-layered. First, it reiterates how women's ability to retain a sense of personhood is minimized during encounters with men who are buying sexual release in or in relation to their bodies; that women are required to be 'substantively present but subjectively absent' (Coy 2008: 187). This depersonalization meant that most women who participated expressed their experience of prostitution as being 'forced to see themselves as objects ... reinforcing and reminding women of their inferior status' (Wesely 2002: 1183). The image speaks of how women absorbed a sense of being disposable and devalued through the actions of men who seek instrumental release without the requirement to interact with a person; suggesting that 'othering' is not simply about social stigmatization but also the ways that women are constituted as 'worth less' (Kelly et al. 2003) in the prostitution transaction (Coy 2008; O'Connell Davidson 1998). In addition, the image highlights that physical and emotional pain and diminishment is a consequence not just of violence, but also in the very touch of strangers who are paying for access to women's bodies – 'I am fragile, when you touch me it hurts'. The text thus comments on a common thread of discussion at all stages of the arts workshops; a sense of invasion through touch. In interviews too, references to how women talked about disembodiment and the 'power of command' (O'Connell Davidson 1998) carried a motif of touch. For Hannah (21), that her body did 'not belong to me anymore, [was] not special anymore' had developed 'since everybody got their fingers on it' and for Dee (26): 'you're lying there naked so you're totally exposed to this person ... they touch you in a sensitive way and it'll just make you feel sick'. Physiological responses to withdrawal that propelled women back to prostitution to make money accentuated feelings of bodily invasion.

I've had to work before rattling [withdrawing], so I could get some money so I could score, and it's horrible. When you're rattling you can't bear anyone to touch you, but you just have to (Lisa, 21).

This image crystallizes many of the themes of women's accounts; that exercises of dissociation or bodily zoning, the use of substances to numb the mind and dull sensation, did not entirely erase a sense of invasion and trespass. In short, the image is both illustration of depersonalizing experiences of the sex of prostitution (Tyler: Chapter 5) and a challenge to the notion of women as instrumental orifices, stigmatized as less than human, through the powerful assertion 'I am a person too'.

Conclusion

In this research, autobiographical narratives and images reveal that for women who participated, a significant thread of lived experience of prostitution was violation and a disrupted relationship with the body. Psychosocial harms of prostitution can therefore be multiple and include disconnection from the body and self. Women conveyed, both verbally and visually, hatred of their body, feeling that it was no longer a part of them, while also hating themselves. While Kari Kesler (2002: 229) rightly challenges feminists to consider that 'prostitutes are not simply "bodies"', one of the key findings from both life story interviews and the arts workshops is that many women perceived that they were reduced to a body, a body which was then experienced as outside of their control and autonomy. Parallels between violation in prostitution and sexual violence were also evident in terms of habit bodies based on dissociation and expressed as emotional legacies that included 'feeling dirty' and 'not belonging' in the body.

As a creative methodology, participatory arts methods offered a deeper route to explore lived experience (O'Neill 2001, 2008, 2010; O'Neill et al. 2002), here related to women's ontological relationship with the body, and enabled women to visually (re)present compelling reminders of their struggles to maintain embodied selfhood while involved in prostitution. The images 'illustrate *at a feeling level* the issues that women selling sex are experiencing' (O'Neill 2008: 88, emphasis mine). Most significantly, the process of co-authoring the images facilitated exploration of emotional diminishment and resilience; the reflective space of participatory arts made it possible to both explore harmful impacts of prostitution and recognize women's myriad practices of coping, resistance and survival.

References

Barry, K. (1995) *The Prostitution of Sexuality.* New York: Basic Books.

Birch, M. (1998). 'Re/constructing Research Narratives: Self and Sociological Identity in Alternative Settings' in J. Ribbens and R. Edwards (eds), *Feminist Dilemmas in Qualitative Research.* London: Sage.

Bourdieu, P. (1977) *Outline of a Theory of Practice.* Cambridge: University Press.

Burstow, B. (2003) 'Toward a Radical Understanding of Trauma and Trauma Work'. *Violence against Women* 9(11): 1293–317.

Choi, H., Klein, C., Shin, M.-S. and Lee, H.-J. (2009) 'Posttraumatic Stress Disorder (PTSD) and Disorders of Extreme Stress (DESNOS) Symptoms Following Prostitution and Childhood Abuse'. *Violence against Women* 15(9): 933–51.

Church, S., Henderson, M., Barnard, M. and Hart, G. (2001) *Violence by Clients towards Female Prostitutes in Different Work Settings; Questionnaire Survey.* BMJ, 322: 554–5.

Coy, M. (2006) 'This Morning I'm a Researcher, This Afternoon I'm an Outreach Worker: Ethical Dilemmas in Practitioner Research'. *International Journal of Social Research Methodology Theory and Practice* 9(5): 419–31.

Coy, M., Horvath, M.A.H. and Kelly, L. (2007) *It's Just Like Going to the Supermarket: Men Buying Sex in East London.* London: Child Woman Abuse Studies Unit, London Metropolitan University.

Coy, M. (2008) 'The Consumer, the Consumed and the Commodity: Women and Sex Buyers Talk about Objectification in Prostitution' in V. Munro and M. Della Giusta (eds), *Demanding Sex: Critical Reflections on the Regulation of Prostitution.* Aldershot: Ashgate.

Coy, M. (2009a) 'This Body Which is Not Mine: The Notion of the Habit Body, Prostitution and Dis(embodiment)'. *Feminist Theory* 10(1): 61–75.

Coy, M. (2009b) 'Invaded Spaces and Feeling Dirty: Women's Narratives of Violation in Prostitution and Sexual Violence' in M.A.H. Horvath and J. Brown (eds), *Rape: Challenging Contemporary Thinking.* Cullompton: Willan.

Cusick, L., Martin, A. and May, T. (2003) *Vulnerability and Involvement in Drug Use and Sex Work.* Home Office Research Study 268 London: Home Office.

Epele, M. (2001) 'Excess, Scarcity and Desire among Drug-Using Sex Workers'. *Body & Society* 7(2/3): 161–79.

Farley, M. (2003) 'Prostitution and the Invisibility of Harm'. *Women & Therapy* 26(3/4): 247–80.

Farley, M. (2004) '"Bad for the Body, Bad for the Heart": Prostitution Harms Women Even if Legalized or Decriminalized'. *Violence against Women* 10(10): 1087–125.

Farley, M., Cotton, A., Lynne, J., Zumbeck, S., Spiwak, F., Reyes, M., Alvarez, D. and Sezgin, U. (2003) 'Prostitution & Trafficking in Nine Countries: An Update on Violence and Post-Traumatic Stress Disorder' in M. Farley (ed.), *Prostitution, Trafficking, and Traumatic Stress.* Binghamton: Haworth Press.

Hedin, U.-C. and Mansson, S.A. (2003) 'The Importance of Supportive Relationships among Women Leaving Prostitution'. *Journal of Trauma Practice* 2(3–4): 223–37.

Hoigard, C. and Finstad, L. (1992) *Backstreets: Prostitution, Money and Love.* Cambridge: Polity Press.

Jeal, N. and Salisbury, C. (2007) 'Health Needs and Service Use of Parlour-based Prostitutes Compared with Street-based Prostitutes: A Cross-sectional Survey'. *BJOG: An International Journal of Obstetrics and Gynaecology* 114(7): 875–81.

Jeal, N., Salisbury, C. and Turner, K. (2008) 'The Multiplicity and Interdependency of Factors Influencing the Health of Street-based Sex Workers: A Qualitative Study'. *Sexually Transmitted Infections* 84: 381–5.

Kelly, L. (1988) *Surviving Sexual Violence.* Cambridge: Polity Press.

Kelly, L., Wingfield, R. and Balding, V. (2003) *Worth Less or Worth More? An Evaluation of the MAZE Marigold Project.* London: Child and Woman Abuse Studies Unit.

Kesler, K. (2002) 'Is a Feminist Stance in Support of Prostitution Possible? An Exploration of Current Trends'. *Sexualities* 5(2): 219–35.

Kramer, L. (2003) 'Emotional Experiences of Performing Prostitution' in M. Farley (ed.), *Prostitution, Trafficking, and Traumatic Stress.* Binghamton: Haworth Press.

Mansson, S. (2004) 'Men's Practices in Prostitution and Their Implications for Social Work' in S. Månsson and C. Proveyer (eds), *Social Work in Cuba and Sweden: Achievements and Prospects.* Göteborg/Havanna: Department of Social Work/Department of Sociology.

Marshall, S.E. (1999) 'Bodyshopping: The Case of Prostitution'. *Journal of Applied Philosophy* 16(2): 139–50.

Mauthner, N.S. and Doucet, A. (1998) 'Reflections on a Voice Centred Relational Method of Data Analysis: Analysing Maternal and Domestic Voices' in J. Ribbens and R. Edwards (eds), *Feminist Dilemmas in Qualitative Research: Private Lives and Public Texts.* London: Sage.

McKeganey, N. and Barnard, M. (1996) *Sex Work on the Streets.* Buckingham, UK: Open University Press.

Merleau-Ponty, M. (1962) *Phenomenology of Perception.* London: Routledge.

Newell-Walker, U. (2002) 'Getting a Picture of the Client's World View: Art Making and Subjectivity as Evidence'. *Journal of Social Work Practice* 16(1): 43–54.

Nixon, K., Tutty, L., Downe, P., Gorkoff, K. and Ursel, J. (2002) '"The Everyday Occurrence": Violence in the Lives of Girls Exploited through Prostitution'. *Violence against Women* 8(9): 1016–43.

Nussbaum, M. (1995) 'Objectification'. *Philosophy and Public Affairs* 24(4): 249–91.

O'Connell Davidson, J. (1998) *Prostitution, Power and Freedom.* Cambridge: Polity Press.

O'Neill, M. (2001) *Prostitution and Feminism: Towards a Politics of Feeling.* Cambridge: Polity Press.

O'Neill, M. (2008) 'Sex, Violence and Work: Services to Sex Workers and Public Policy Reform' in G. Letherby, K. Williams, P. Birch and M. Cain (eds), *Sex as Crime?* Cullompton: Willan.

O'Neill, M. (2010) *Asylum, Migration and Community.* Bristol: Policy Press.

O'Neill, M. and Campbell, R. (2001) *Working Together to Create Change: Community Consultation Research on Prostitution.* Available at: www. safetysoapbox.co.uk [accessed: 10 March 2011].

O'Neill, M. with Giddens, S., Breatnach, P., Bagley, C., Bourne, D. and Judge, T. (2002) 'Renewed Methodologies for Social Research: Ethno-mimesis as Performative Praxis'. *The Sociological Review* 50: 69–88.

Parkins, W. (2000) 'Protesting Like a Girl: Embodiment, Dissent, and Feminist Agency'. *Feminist Theory* 1(1): 59–78.

Pateman, C. (1998) *The Sexual Contract.* Cambridge: Polity Press.

Phoenix, J. (1999) *Making Sense of Prostitution.* Cambridge: Polity Press.

Pink, S. (2001) *Doing Visual Ethnography.* London: Sage.

Plumridge, L. (2001) 'Rhetoric, Reality and Risk Outcomes in Sex Work'. *Health, Risk & Society* 3(2): 199–215.

Potterat, J.J., Brewer, D.D., Muth, S.Q., Rothenberg, R.B., Woodhouse, D.E., Muth, J.B., Stites, H.K. and Brody, S. (2004) 'Mortality in a Long-term Open Cohort of Prostitute Women'. *American Journal of Epidemiology* 159(8): 778–85.

Raphael, J. and Shapiro, D.L. (2004) 'Violence in Indoor and Outdoor Prostitution Venues'. *Violence against Women* 10(2): 126–39.

Roxburgh, A., Degenhardt, L. and Copeland, J. (2006) 'Posttraumatic Stress Disorder among Female Street-based Sex Workers in the Greater Sydney Area, Australia'. *BMC Psychiatry* 2006 (6).

Sanders, T. (2002) 'The Condom as Psychological Barrier: Female Sex Workers and Emotional Management'. *Feminism & Psychology* 12: 561–6.

Sanders, T. (2004) 'A Continuum of Risk? The Management of Health, Physical and Emotional Risks by Female Sex Workers'. *Sociology of Health & Illness* 26(5): 557–74.

Stanley, L. and Wise, S. (1983) *Breaking Out: Feminist Epistemology and Ontology.* London: Routledge.

Vanwesenbeeck, I. (2005) 'Burnout among Female Indoor Sex Workers'. *Archives of Sexual Behavior* 34(6): 627–39.

Wesely, J. (2002) 'Growing up Sexualized: Issues of Power and Violence in the Lives of Female Exotic Dancers'. *Violence against Women* 8(10): 1128–207.

Chapter 7

Troubling Notions of Male Entitlement: Men Consuming, Boasting and Confessing about Paying for Sex

Maddy Coy, Miranda A.H. Horvath and Liz Kelly

Despite the proliferation of scholarship on prostitution, men who buy sex have been largely unseen – they are in many ways the 'shadow partner' of the sex industry (Keeler and Jyrkinen 1999). For decades this disinterest reflected heteronormative constructions of masculinity; 'a man who buys sex is viewed simply as a "man" doing what "men" do, and therefore there is nothing unique or interesting enough about his behaviour to justify research' (Ben-Israel and Levenkron 2005: 13). There is, however, a more recent tilt of the analytic gaze, in both research and policy, towards exploring and addressing the role of demand, seeking to make visible not only the characteristics of the men who buy sex but also the contexts in which they do it and their motivations (Coy, Horvath and Kelly 2007; Durchslag and Goswami 2008; Earle and Sharp 2007, 2008; Farley, Macleod, Anderson and Golding 2011; Marttila 2008; Sanders 2008). This chapter presents findings from research in London, UK, with a large sample of men who paid for sex. At the time the research was conducted (the end of 2006), the evidence base on men's accounts of buying sex was mostly limited to: samples of men in contact with statutory agencies such as sexual health clinics or law enforcement (Groom and Nandwani 2005; Hester and Westmarland 2005; Monto and McRee 2005; Ward et al. 2005); small studies exploring specific national contexts (e.g. Chen 2003) and ethnographic research with women in prostitution that also briefly shone a light on buyers (McKeganey and Barnard 1997; O'Connell Davidson 1998). Here we draw on the London research findings, locating them in what has since become a more developed knowledge base, to explore notions of male entitlement, including how some men are troubled by buying sex.

Profiles of Men Who Buy Sex

Attempts to gauge the prevalence of buying sex are beset by the difficulties of identifying and contacting men to participate in research, and limited by the stigma and illegality that surrounds prostitution related activities (Chen 2003; Soothill and Sanders 2005). Whilst prevalence estimates vary widely, surveys suggest that the proportions of men paying for sex in a number of countries remain a minority (for more details, see Coy et al. 2007; Farley et al. 2011).

The demographic profiles of men who buy sex are broadly similar across the international research base. In Scotland, a recent study of 110 sex buyers found an average age of 37 years, with almost half aged between 18–35 (Farley et al. 2011); in other studies in England, the average age was 35 years old (Hester and Westmarland 2005) or 38 years old (Farley, Bindel and Golding 2009). U.S. research revealed the age of men attending education programmes for kerbcrawlers to be 38 years old (Monto and McRee 2005). This suggests that paying for sex is primarily, although by no means exclusively, associated with men in their twenties and thirties (Coy et al. 2007). Farley et al. (2011) confirm this; almost three-quarters of men they interviewed (74 per cent) had paid for sex by the time they were 25 years of age. In a sample of men from London, UK, almost half (44 per cent) reported first buying sex before their 21st birthdays (Farley et al. 2009). Similarly, in Chicago, the average age of the 113 men interviewed by Durchslag and Goswami (2008) when they first bought sex was 21 years old.

Patterns are also found in terms of other demographic markers. Several studies report around half of participants being currently in relationships or married: (Coy et al. 2007; Farley et al. 2011; Groom and Nandwani 2005; Hester and Westmarland 2005). Most are also in regular employment with no previous criminal convictions (ibid). The congruence between profiles of sex buyers and general populations challenges the caricature of men who buy sex as 'deviant' or without sexual partners, suggesting we need to delve deeper into why, where and how they do it.

Settings and Contexts: Where Men Buy Sex

Part of the stereotypical notion of the sexually deviant sex buyer is the association of prostitution with the street. Studies that focus on men arrested for kerbcrawling, while providing valuable insights into demographics and motivations in a context widely recognized as most harmful and dangerous for women, do not capture how prostitution settings might be perceived differently. Recent shifts in the social organization of the sex industry, with law enforcement diminishing street sex markets and increases in the numbers of massage parlours, saunas and brothels evident at least in urban areas of Western countries (Hubbard et al. 2008), also has an impact on buying behaviours, not least because indoor commercial sex establishments increasingly position themselves in mainstream consumer markets. As Brents and Hausbeck (2007: 432) note with reference to brothels in the US, domestic sex industries use similar marketing strategies as 'mainstream business forms ... trying to appeal to broader audiences'. A key technique is to offer men a luxury 'experience' which redefines buying sex as a 'service' with expectations of professionalism (ibid).

Research indicates that the majority of men paying for sex in the UK do so indoors (Coy et al. 2007; Farley et al. 2011). For many, this preference appears to be linked to fears of disease, robbery and general illegality surrounding street prostitution, with the belief that women selling sex indoors are cleaner and more 'professional' (Coy et al. 2007). Another possible insight into the preference for indoor settings is that men posting reviews on a website for sex buyers value locations which have 'the maintenance of order' (Soothill 2004). Both of these explanations support the contention that the marketing and packaging of commercial sex premises as socially legitimate leisure and entertainment venues influences men's behaviours.

What Men Say: Motivations for Buying Sex

Although motivations provided by male sex buyers are multiple and varied (Elliot et al. 2002; Mansson 2004; O'Neill 2001), at the core, they draw on notions of biological imperative and/or the rights of purchasers. These are typically articulated through a male 'sexual drive/need' discourse (Hollway 1984); more colloquially expressed as a physical 'need' for release/relaxation; and/or that paying means they can choose which woman and what kinds of sex without responsibility.

This consumerist discourse provides both easy legitimation and a means of obscuring analyses of prostitution as a practice of gender inequality. Clearly, if paying for sex is framed by the buyers as 'not resorting to commercial sex but as a conscious, consumer choice' (Marttila 2003: 6), then other more complex motivations and contextual factors become increasingly hidden. The gendered nature of the 'prostitution contract' is apparent in the economic power of men to purchase women for the purposes of fulfilling fantasies and desires, and the power over women's bodies, however temporary, that is inherent in the transaction itself (O'Connell Davidson 1998). Research indicates that for many men, this sense of male entitlement (Coy et al. 2007) or privilege (Durchslag and Goswami 2008) is precisely what they value about paying for sex and also one way in which they justify it. International data on men who pay for sex suggests that they are likely to be using other aspects of the sex industry such as pornography and lap dancing clubs (Farley et al. 2011; Lammi-Taskula 1999; Monto and McRee 2005) and have had higher numbers of sexual partners than other men (Farley et al. 2011; Ward et al. 2005). Findings are mixed as to whether men who buy sex are more likely to endorse rape myths, with some studies suggesting low levels (Busch et al. 2002; Klein et al. 2008; Monto and Hotaling 2001) and others high (Farley et al. 2011).

Men's accounts also suggest that buying sex is not regarded as a direct substitute for 'free' sex or that within relationships (Bernstein 2001; Della Giusta et al. 2008). Instead, the parameters of the commercial sex exchange itself fulfil a perceived biological imperative without the emotional entanglements of intimate sexual relationships. What many sex buyers value is the 'clarifying effect of payment' (Bernstein 2001: 399). This reveals important elements of paying for sex noted across several studies: the underpinning sense of male entitlement for sexual release in/on a woman's body (Coy et al. 2007); the appeal of sexual engagement without emotional responsibility (Coy 2008; Coy et al. 2007; Durchslag and Goswami 2008; Farley et al. 2011; Mckeganey and Barnard 1997) and the construction of an account of mutual and equitable exchange where a buyer's sexual needs are met while women benefit financially (Coy et al. 2007; O'Connell Davidson 1998).

Some studies identify ways in which men seek emotional company and comfort in the commercial sex transaction. Both Chen (2003) and Sanders (2008) found a desire for intimacy to be a significant theme of men's narratives. However as Chen (2003) also suggests, where men require this level of intimacy, additional emotional labour is required of women to meet the expectations of talking, flirtation and performing the transaction as a quasi-date. As Maggie O'Neill suggests, 'women have to be good at "gentling" men, at flattering, counselling and consoling the male ego, while at the same time providing his ideal fantasy woman, even though he may make her "feel sick"' (O'Neill 2001: 142–3). Earle and Sharp (2008: 69), in their study of sex buyers' accounts posted on the 'Punternet' website, find men often expect a 'courtship script[s] similar to that of non-commercial heterosex' – reciprocity of sexual pleasure and rituals such as music, wine and preamble. Even where the encounter is valued by some buyers for resembling 'girlfriend sex', men's sexual satisfaction is the principal concern, and many sex buyers' evaluations 'focus on a woman's willingness to please' (ibid: 72) – most importantly that he got exactly what he wanted and has paid for.

Conducive Contexts: The Sexualization of Popular Culture

The motivations offered by men who pay for sex demonstrate a relationship between the sexualization of everyday lived experience and demand for commercial sex that is under-explored by researchers (Agustin 2005; Bernstein 2001). It is important to 'situate sexual consumption within the context of an expanded and normalized field of commercial sexual practices' (Bernstein 2001: 397). The increase in reported rates of paying for sex over the last decade has occurred contemporaneously with what is referred to as 'sexualization' of popular culture (Gill 2007), 'pornification' (Paul 2005), and McSexualization (Jyrkinen: Chapter 1) featuring sexual consumerism as a recreational activity (Brewis and Linstead 2000; Coy et al.: Chapter 10; Mansson 2006). The internet and globalization have played their part, providing ease of transport for the purposes of buying sex and easy access to information about sex markets and pornography closer to home, not only creating more opportunities for buying sex, but also extending the sex industry through lap dancing and pole dancing clubs – now features of most urban spaces – and the mainstreaming of sexualized imagery of women in 'lads mags', advertising and music videos (Gill 2008). As commercial sex premises (including large chain lap dancing clubs) develop an increased presence in urban spaces (Hubbard et al. 2008), questions arise about how this seeps into psycho-social landscapes, implicitly supporting and normalizing the purchase of 'sexual services' as a legitimate form of leisure and entertainment. The glamorization of prostitution in popular culture, evident in the increasing mainstreaming of pimp and ho chic, reflects and reproduces this framing (see Coy et al.: Chapter 10).

Simultaneously commercial sex has become even more associated with everyday collective male events such as stag nights and sporting events, potentially tempering social stigma through such normalization. Thus where sex industries are growing and becoming integrated into leisure and entertainment, definitions of gendered respectability shift. While stigma continues to be attributed to women who sell sex, for men buying sex appears to be viewed as increasingly acceptable in certain contexts and settings (Coy et al. 2007). Internet fora that enable men to evaluate women's bodies and their 'sexual services' for the purpose of making recommendations to others further enhance a sense of collective consumerism (Sharp and Earle 2007, 2008; Jyrkinen: Chapter 1).

Exploring how men draw on available discursive vocabularies to articulate their motivations for buying sex, and contextualizing these accounts in socio-cultural constructions of prostitution was a key aim of the research that is reported on here. The remainder of the chapter presents findings and analysis.

The London Research

This exploratory study was designed to extend the limited knowledge base on men who pay for sex on the street.[1] Originally we intended to target those men identified as actual or potential buyers through police kerb crawling operations. However, very low numbers of men agreed to take part through this route so the methodology was adapted. Subsequently, men were recruited through advertisements in London based newspapers, selected for local relevance and/or wide availability and readership. The advertisements invited men to take part in a telephone interview. In response to the first round of advertisements, 105 interviews were completed. The majority (73.3 per cent) of the first 105 respondents reported buying sex solely in off street commercial sex locations. As one aim of the study was to explore the decision making processes of men who buy sex on the street, a second round of adverts were placed. Despite the explicit mention of street prostitution in these

---

1   The research was commissioned by Safe Exit at Toynbee Hall to explore the decision-making processes of men who pay for sex in the borough of Tower Hamlets and was funded by the Tower Hamlets Partnership.

advertisements, of the 32 respondents, three reported only buying on street, 12 said they only bought off street and 16 bought both on and off street (one respondent did not answer the question). Whilst the criminalization and stigma attached to street prostitution makes men less likely to volunteer to participate in research, another possible explanation is that the sex industry is increasingly privatized.

The telephone interviews asked about the material circumstances in which the men bought sex: the area they live and work in; area they buy sex; setting in which they buy sex and making contact with women in prostitution. Subsequent sections explored: beliefs about, and experiences of, buying sex; which sexual acts they paid for; preferences; motivations and gains; what if anything would deter them; opinions about women who sell sex; basic demographic data such as age, ethnicity, marital/relationship status, sexuality and employment status (See Coy et al. 2007 for the full guide). A coding dictionary was developed using content based coding and some questions were re-coded for more detailed analysis. In order to ensure consistency of the data coding and entry 10 per cent (n=14) were selected randomly and two other researchers checked the data. No major problems were identified. All quantitative data was analysed using descriptive statistics. All discursive responses were transcribed and analysed using a grounded theory approach (Glaser and Strauss 1967) to identify key themes and coded into emergent patterns. Particular attention was paid to how the men construct their accounts of paying for sex.

The Men Who Participated

The respondents ranged from 19–64 years, with a mean age of 32. The majority were aged between 20 and 49, with the largest group aged 20–29 (40 per cent). Whilst this might reflect the readership of the newspapers, it also echoes findings from international and UK studies detailed earlier. Just over a third reported being in a relationship (35.7 per cent) and a further 16.1 per cent were married. The majority (88.4 per cent) were in paid employment, and over a fifth (22.3 per cent) had children. Interestingly, one in five (19 per cent) did not define themselves as heterosexual, with the alternatives ranging through refusing to answer (6.3 per cent), to bi-sexual (8 per cent) and 'other' (4.5 per cent). This last category included answers such as 'I think I'm gay but I can't accept it', 'Open-minded, I have dabbled with men but don't seek them out' and 'I have fantasies about men but I have never been with a man'.

Revealing Engagements

For some men, participation was a confessional process, which they appeared to be using for cathartic reasons. Acknowledging either a personal sense of shame and guilt or an awareness of the social stigma attached to buying sex was important for these men. They may have decided to participate in the research in order to 'renegotiate meaning' attached to their experiences of paying for sex (Grenz 2005: 2111).

> It's been quite beneficial for me to talk to about it, it's given me a chance to reflect on it (Q105).

> There's a big element of guilt on me, that's why I thought I would volunteer to call and talk to you (Q8).

Some men even sought reassurance that their experiences and opinions were 'usual' and 'typical' responses, perhaps in order to re-affirm their own sense of normative masculinity.

Some men explicitly eroticized the conversation, and in doing so sexualized the female interviewers (see also Chen 2003; Grenz 2005). This ranged from referring to the interviewer as 'love', asking personal questions about appearance or relationship status, to more explicit statements about sexual prowess (e.g. having 'a big cock'), and or requests to say 'something sexy'. One in 10 men answered the question about how they defined their sexuality (intended to elicit information such as heterosexual, bisexual or gay) with responses such as 'very very excessive', 'very erotic', 'excited', 'good in bed' or 'extremely hot'.

Some respondents evidenced a sense of male entitlement through the ease and candour with which they talked about the sexual acts that they purchased (Grenz 2005). For example, the questions concerning the decision making processes such as areas that they go to pay for sex, where they find adverts for commercial sex premises, what would deter them (possibly all questions guided at developing intervention or regulatory mechanisms) did not interest these respondents. Yet questions regarding what types of sexual acts they pay for, preferences in women, and their motivations, resulted in some offering considerable detail. In contrast, those who reported shame and guilt were reluctant to specify or describe the actual acts that they paid for. For others, their accounts juxtaposed elements of personal shame and a gendered sense of entitlement, and they clearly struggled to reconcile this contradiction. It was through paying close attention to how men engaged with the research process and questions that the conceptual framework and analysis were in part developed. We paid attention not only to what men said, but how they said it and the responses they sought from us as female interviewers.

Buying Sex: Decisions and Choices

Debates around choice and agency are almost always focussed on women in prostitution rather than the men who pay for sex. Men's capacity to choose and act is rarely the subject of critical scrutiny. In order to contextualize the meanings that men attached to buying sex, we sought information about their activities and decision-making processes.

The overwhelming majority reported paying for sex in off street premises. This finding is significant; as noted earlier, the commercial sex transaction is different depending on the setting – indoors, the encounter is more easily constructed as a 'date' that can simulate intimacy, whilst also being impersonal. In contrast, street paid sex is 'business', occurs as quickly as possible in cars, alleys, whatever the weather, constrained by constant vigilance for the possibility of attack and police surveillance. A very small number of men reported buying sex on the street (6.6 per cent) but four times as many bought sex in both street and off street locations (25.5 per cent). Thus just under a third (32.1 per cent) had bought sex on the street. Half (n = 69) stated that their preferred type of premises was a private flat (see also Farley et al. 2011). This may indicate that the unlicensed, clandestine nature of private flats holds an appeal for sex buyers that 'legitimate' and/or licensed massage parlours and saunas do not.

Frequency of purchase was one area where clear distinctions in behaviours could be made. International research has presented typologies of first time/ occasional/regular customers (Mansson 2004; Monto and Mcree 2005). In our study, the largest group of men, constituting a fifth overall (20.4 per cent) had only paid for sex on one/two/three occasions, followed by those who buy sex on a monthly basis (16.8 per cent). Taking 'regular' sex buyers to include all those paying for sex once a month or more, a total of 57 per cent can be classified as regulars.

That almost three quarters (73 per cent) refer only to vaginal and/or oral sex reveals the mundanity of commercial sex, and raises some uncertainty that claims – from men and researchers – that prostitution provides access to wider repertoires. That most were paying for conventional heterosexual practices also raises a question about how men view the instrumental purpose of sexual intercourse and women's bodies both within and outside of commercial sex (Coy 2008).

Whilst the majority had not told anyone that they had paid for sex, almost two-fifths had (39.3 per cent). Mostly those who knew were friends, and few had told family members or partners. Despite increasing sociocultural legitimacy and association with celebrity, paying for sex remains a clandestine activity, hidden from all but male peer groups. For some of the respondents, buying sex was associated with the culmination of an evening out with a group of male friends, linking contemporary sexual consumerism with peer cultures and male bonding practices that collectively support buying sex as a group activity that is embedded in normative constructions of masculinity (see Jyrkinen: Chapter 1).

> It was with a couple of friends and we'd been on a night out and we were all a bit horny and we just thought it would be a bit of a laugh really (Q53).

While some men referred to buying sex as an extension of collective sexual consumerism such as visiting sexualized dance clubs, one talked of choosing not to visit strip clubs, since being unable to have sex with the women in the clubs frustrated him. His account also illustrates the sense of entitlement that many men's consumerist responses contained.

> Now any red-blooded male goes to these strip clubs, it's waving it in his face, so he's going to leave there and he's going to feel turned on ... It's all very well having a gorgeous woman dancing on the stage, but that man in the back of his mind is thinking he wants to have sex with her but he can't. And he has to put money in the jar or money in her garter or whatever, if that's what goes on, but he's got to look but he cannot touch. And that is a frustration. That's why I've never been to one and I'll never ever go to one. If I go to a brothel or a massage parlour and I see a gorgeous woman, I can have her for twenty minutes or thirty minutes, and that's it, and I've got personal satisfaction there (Q76).

The deterministic language is revealing here; the paragraph is replete with 'has to', 'got to', 'going to', an implicit version of the biological urge/imperative which serves to bury any notion of conscious choice or agency in men's actions.

Clearly for some men strip and lap-dancing clubs are considered preludes to paying for sex, demonstrating connections across a spectrum of sexual consumerism. Where there are clubs in which women perform sexualized dance in order to titillate men, nearby premises offering sexual services may potentially benefit. However, for this respondent, the sense of entitlement to sexual access means that being able to look but not touch is of no interest to him; purchasing sexual acts gives him the chance not only to admire women but also to 'have' them.

One way of exploring how demand might be decreased was to ask directly about any reservations or nervousness and what, if anything might stop men from buying sex. Just over half of the respondents (56.3 per cent) stated that they sometimes felt uneasy or nervous when paying for sex. A larger proportion (75 per cent) reported that something might stop them. Some men interpreted this question as referring only to a specific occasion ('woman unattractive', 'if woman coerced') whereas others were thinking more generally ('regular sexual partner', 'being found out'). Fear of disease was the most common preventative factor, closely followed by having a regular sexual partner. This clearly connects to powerful constructions of women in prostitution as reservoirs of infection who pose a public health threat not only to men who pay for sex but also the wider community.

Only a minority mentioned criminal sanctions as a deterrent; however this may be a methodological artifact, since men were asked an open question. As the majority were buying sex indoors, and therefore not committing a crime under local law at the time of the research,[2] it is unlikely that the possibility of

---

2   In April 2010, Section 14 of the Policing and Crime Act 2009 introduced a new strict liability criminal offence of paying for sex with someone who is subject to exploitative conduct.

criminalization was factored into their decision-making. In another study where legal sanctions were offered in a range of possible options, three-quarters of men identified imprisonment or criminal penalties as deterrents (Farley et al. 2011). Moreover, that men were more positive about buying sex where it was legal or decriminalized strongly suggests that legal and policy frameworks influence men's practices and perceptions (Coy et al. 2007). For instance, almost a third (n = 43, 31.4 per cent) had paid for sex overseas. The most popular destinations were the Netherlands, Spain and Germany, and while not all stereotypical sexualized tourist spaces, all have prostitution policy regimes (Kelly et al. 2009) of legalization or decriminalization. Buying sex was viewed more positively where it was legal, which resulted in descriptions such as 'a better service', 'friendlier', 'girls [are] better quality' and 'cheaper'.

Consuming, Boasting and Confessing

Analysis of the reasons men offered for buying sex reflected an underlying theme of male entitlement, bolstered by normalization; that men paying for sex is to be expected and accepted, with frequent justificatory references to history and pre history.

> I think it's just normal, I mean this is probably what's gone on since the beginning of humanity, when women probably tried to deal with men somehow, through the marriages ... So it's just normal really (Q 34).

Men's narratives also revealed more complex attitudinal patterns that have been analysed along three dimensions: Consuming; Boasting; Confessing. The distribution of these patterns is shown in Figure 7.1. The fact that they were not mutually exclusive in men's accounts meant a typology of 'boasters', 'consumers' and 'confessors' would not only have been inaccurate, but missed the overlaps that were apparent for a third of the sample. We present this typology, therefore, as kinds of behaviours rather than kinds of people. Each can be summarized as follows:

> **Consuming** – paying for sex is framed as a leisure activity that is based on fulfilling a sexual 'need' and/or where women's bodies and sexual services are regarded as commodities that are purchased in a similar fashion to other goods.

> **Boasting** – characterized by an equation of masculinity with sexual prowess and women's sexual availability.

Confessing – characterized by guilt, ambivalence and negative feelings, including for some recognition of harm and exploitation within the sex industry.

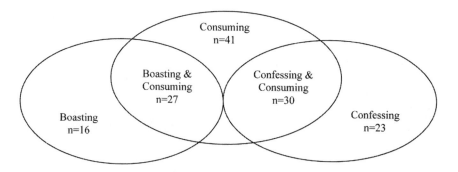

Figure 7.1   Distribution of confessing, consuming, boasting

Clearly consuming is the most common theme, present for more than two-thirds (n = 98) of the men interviewed. Each of the three themes is explored in more depth below.

Consuming

The key elements of the consumption theme centre on conceptualizing commercial sex as 'just a job'; a profession and occupation. Within this discourse, men focused on the quality of service, ease and convenience, locating commercial sex in the market economy. They often invoked a rhetoric of mutual exchange and frequently mentioned the relative cost of buying sex. Another key manifestation of the consumerist discourse was the prominence of 'choice' in the transaction. While some men described themselves as 'indifferent' or indiscriminate' when choosing women, for others this was an essential element of their consumerist privilege. In either case there is a process of commodifying women's bodies involved (Coy 2008).

> I confirm with them the kind of services that they offer, whether they are offering the kind of services that I want (Q37).

> It depends on the situation, when I've seen a girl I can decide which one to take (Q64).

Some men made a straightforward equation between buying sex and other lifestyle commodities, suggesting that paid sex was an equivalent form of indulgent relaxation to a takeaway or decent bottle of wine, or a luxury that in the words of one buyer was 'like paying for cab instead of walking'. A number of men explicitly acknowledged that the mainstreaming of the sex industry into popular culture formed the backdrop for this sexualized consumerism.

> I just think it's like we live in a consumer society, do you know what I mean? And I think that's become a bit of a commodity now, the whole sex thing. I think, because the internet's there and magazines are there and you've got images all the time (Q101).

> For a man, he knows that as long as he's got £50 in his wallet, he can get it (Q76).

One buyer succinctly captured the framing of commercial sex as a touristic experience (Brents and Hausbeck 2007) in his account of buying sex overseas as a 'holiday treat'.

> I went on a spontaneous holiday to Europe, like that evening, so that was all just part of one massive pointless binge of spending money having sex and I suppose in a way enjoying myself (Q119).

That he says 'in a way' he was enjoying himself, however, also suggests ambivalence, possibly either that buying sex does not really constitute a form of enjoyment, or that it is way of achieving pleasure of which he is not particularly proud.

Men also referred frequently to market forces influencing their decision making processes. For some this centred on quality of service and ensuring that contractual obligations were fulfilled, drawing on norms and conventions of the 'institutional field of consumerism', expectations that become part of people's worldview and accordingly shape how they act (Storper 2000). The most transparent expression of this in men's accounts was 'getting value for money', comparing the relative cost of paying for sex to heterosexual dating:

> To go out looking for a girl, it's a lot of expense, it can be a very expensive night … paying for sex, it's an agreement between you and the girl, you pay your money and then that's done with (Q90).

> It's easier than meeting a girl and having loads of aggro and then spending about £100 and then not getting nothing (Q113).

Interestingly a study in Australia reports virtually the same account from one sex buyer 'I could spend 100 bucks a night taking some bird out, you could do that 3 or 4 times you know before you're anywhere … I'd rather come here every now and again and then, pay my money and you know, that's that' (cited in Plumridge et al. 1997: 172). Similar sentiments were also noted in diary accounts of sex tourists to Thailand – where buying sex is viewed as buying a product, with quality related to cost and economic value (Bishop and Robinson 2002). The sovereignty of consumer rights enabled some sex buyers to draw on paying for sex in these terms; 'conceptualizing prostitution as a consumer service shifts the emphasis from the interpersonal interaction to the benefits for seller and buyer in a similar way to other market economic transactions' (Coy 2008: 190).

Boasting

The key elements in the boasting accounts were: using explicit sexual detail; a professed love of sex; focus on own sexual prowess and the size of their penis; a belief that all women want sex and gain pleasure from selling sex. All the men who were categorized as boasting also reported that nothing made them nervous about buying sex. The themes of excitement, having no partner and sex as 'no hassle' featured strongly here.

> It's not just the sexual thing, it's more the excitement of going in, of maybe walking up to a door and knowing that five minutes later you might be having sex with somebody that you've never met before, never had any connection with, I quite like the excitement of that. Obviously the sexual part is – is certainly an aspect but there's other reasons as well, the excitement and the adrenalin (Q28).

The desire for sexual variety was offered by 11 men as a motivating factor and for an additional two, as the ultimate outcome.

> Sexually I like a lot of variety, and I've got quite a high sex drive anyway, but my drive's only high with a lot of variation, I mean even if I went to a place that was really nice and the girl was really nice, I'd never go back to see the same girl, I'd always try something – something different (Q28).

Here the biological imperative of male sexuality is invoked in a somewhat different way, linked to multiple sexual partners. The frequency with which men mentioned variety suggests that this group view it as something they are entitled to – paying for sex enables them to exercise this prerogative.

The entitlement to sex was nowhere more obvious than for the 67 respondents (48 per cent) who reported that they were currently single or not in a relationship. Less than half of this group referred to their singlehood as a motivation for paying for sex, but for the majority a strong biological need argument that has been termed the 'male sex drive discourse' (Hollway 1984) was evident. The requirement for sex was presented as taken for granted reality, illustrated by the recurrent use of the words 'need' and 'urge'.

> I'm a single person, I have no partner. I'm not getting it elsewhere so I need to pay for it (Q70).

Whilst some acknowledged that masturbation offered a way to ease frustration, the availability of commercial sex made this a less attractive option.

> When I get the urge, I want to relieve the tension ... Instead of masturbating myself I get relieved (Q6).

This suggests, as Chen (2003: 5) has noted about male sex buyers in Taiwan, that 'physical sexual needs are not the first concern; instead it is how to have sex in masculine ways that makes seeking prostitutes desirable'. The 'ease and convenience' of paying for sex to meet these unquestioned 'needs' enabled some men to argue that this entitled them to a prompt sexual transaction which required little other than cash on their part (Mansson 2004).

> Sometimes I'm busy and just want to go in quick (Q99).

To maintain heteronormative masculinity for this group requires not just sexual relief, but that this happens in relation to, and within, a female body. A theme found in previous research on sex buyers is the desire for sex without any emotional connections (Chen 2003; Kinnell 2006). This 'no strings' or 'no hassle' story was also evident in the boasting accounts.

> There's no ties, really, you know what I mean, it's just like – it's more or less a business, I mean we pay for it and we get what we want, and at the end of the day there's no strings attached (Q29).

The absence of negotiation, emotional responsibility and even respect are strong attractions for some men.

Questions about how men viewed women in prostitution elicited a wide range of responses, including 'sympathy', acknowledgement of women's 'desperation', and for some, the invocation of the free/forced dichotomy.

> They come in two categories, those that are very positive about the environment, doing it, if you will; and those who almost feel like victims ... the ones that feel like victims, it's dire. That's horrible. I don't like that. But the ones that are confident with what they're doing, that's a really positive experience, I enjoy that (Q133).

A minority reported taking time in order to make sure women were 'free' to choose, while others simply presumed that so long as there was no incontrovertible, visible evidence of force, women were on an equal footing with them. In this sample it was a very small minority who developed emotional relationships with women they paid for sex. For these men, the emotional element was as important as the sexual encounter. But they too, like their more detached counterparts choose to ignore that women were paid to act in this way. In a similar way boasting that emphasized how they gave women sexual pleasure involves a choice to forget that they paid women to simulate sexual enjoyment. Men enjoyed being able to treat women in the commercial sex encounter in ways that they would not or were not able to treat women with whom they had ongoing relationships, and in this process undoubtedly constructed women who sell sex as 'other' (Coy 2008; O'Connell Davidson 1998).

> I don't have to ask or think 'No, is that too dirty for her?' or – like I don't really have to be as respectful as if it was my girlfriend or my wife or partner (Q48).

References to a distinction between women with whom they would form an intimate relationship and the women that they paid were common, suggesting that a double standard – the twenty-first-century re-working of the virgin/whore dualism – persists in men's views of women who do and do not sell sex.

Confessing

We define as confessing those accounts that contained descriptions of ambivalence, guilt and shame and where men chose to expose negative feelings as a consequence of paying for sex. These ranged through disappointment to self-hatred, for some reflected in the confessional process of participation in the research. This finding was the most unexpected, having not featured in previous research, and provides a route to explore the nuances of male entitlement.

Some men drew on notions that commercial sex was wrong, including for some a recognition of their implication in harm and exploitation although only a very small minority (n = 6) demonstrated awareness of coercion and trafficking. Some also reported conflict with their religious or moral framework. Almost half of those classified as confessing (22 of 53) had only paid for sex on one/two/three occasions and stated that they were unlikely to buy sex again. All reported feeling nervous during the process and often afterwards.

> At the time I get temporary relief from negative feelings, but actually it fed the negative feelings so it's not productive (Q11).

This raises questions about some of the glib ways in which men and prostitution have been written about recently, about both why men do it and what it actually delivers at emotional and social levels. For some, lack of fulfillment was rooted in the emotional vacuum of commercial sex transactions that others valued.

> [I didn't get] as much as I thought. No comfort, so not the best experience. It made me realize I need the comfort you get from a girlfriend (Q23).

A few accounts were suggestive of something which is close to addictive behaviour, but had relatively little insight into why they were driven in this way.

> For me it's a constant battle to not go more regularly ... it's something I think about quite a lot, but I'm trying to limit it to once every two or three months now for more the quality rather than quantity experience, but it is a bit of a battle for me and a few of my friends are the same, who go regularly ... if you are sexually intense and you like experimentation it's difficult to keep it under wraps sometimes (Q28).

> I think if I was going to be brutally honest, I'd say [I have] a slightly damaged self-esteem and a really ridiculously high sex drive (Q119).

There are few places where men are able or encouraged to express this level of ambivalence. Monitoring of websites such as Punternet suggests that men who express uncertainty are censored and discouraged from becoming regular posters (Earle and Sharp 2007). The normative rules for such online communities are clear; defend entitlement at all costs.

Undertaking this study, somewhat surprisingly, led us to thinking that there is considerable scope to engage with men about the gap between their expectations and the reality and outcomes of paying for sex. Exploring men's own uncertainties may be a more fruitful route for alternative ways of thinking to develop, offering the potential for change to emerge in the intersection between cultures of masculinity and men's conflicting personal experiences – to engage with men about how they negotiate the landscapes of McSexualization (Jyrkinen: Chapter 1).[3]

Is the Market All?

Where the overlap was boasting and consuming, accounts were characterized by a form of hedonistic excitement in which the subjectivity of the women was absent – 'I never think about them' being a common response. For these men, paying for sex is pleasurable, the women gain pleasure and for some men, the thought and the process of finding women and the negotiation are part of the pleasure. Some described paying for sex as a mutually beneficial exchange between buyer and seller. This was framed primarily as an economic transaction where men paid to satisfy their sexual needs and met women's financial needs. For some, however, the notion of a mutual exchange rested on the sexual enjoyment that they presumed they were giving women. Julia O'Connell Davidson (1998) suggests that this 'fiction of mutuality' is one way in which men justify buying sex: if women are enjoying paid sex and apparently benefiting then there can be nothing wrong with the idea or the practice.

---

3   Maria Garner, London Metropolitan University, is currently undertaking doctoral research exploring how men negotiate sexualized popular culture (Garner forthcoming).

I've got a need and they've got a need, so we're both taking care of each other's needs (Q29).

Where confessing and consuming overlapped, tensions were evident between the perceived social normalization of commercial sex and their emotional experience of buying sex. Consumerist normalization reassuringly offered a way to justify or explain their behaviour in terms that minimized moral censure.

I think it's wrong, in a way, but I suppose it's just life really, innit? It's just the way it is. I do think it's wrong (Q80).

Another respondent reflected on the negative consequences of his own participation in local sex markets.

The more I go, the more the industry is going to be growing, isn't it? If I can stay away, then probably it will make it better (Q8).

Conclusion

International research and findings from the study reported here show both that men who pay for sex are demographically similar. Socio-cultural contexts of masculinity and legal frameworks appear to influence sex buyers' perceptions and decisions. Interrogating men's accounts of buying sex also highlights how gendered cultural practices are influenced by increasing commodification of intimacy and sexualization (Brents and Hausbeck 2007). Furthermore these reveal that many perceived buying sex in the same commodity bracket as takeaway food or expensive wine. In other words, paying for sex is an act of consumerism within which women in their bodies are commodities to be evaluated like any other (Coy 2008; Mansson 2006). Our research indicates that while consuming sex is (re)presented as an epistemological mode of masculinity (Altman 2001), many men have rejected this construction since most do not buy sex. Still others find their engagement in it disquieting. The unease amongst some men who have paid for sex offers a potential route for intervention, beginning with contrasting the normalization message of much contemporary popular culture, and developing resources that explore the guilt, shame and ambivalence that they report.

References

Altman, D. (2001) *Global Sex.* Chicago: University of Chicago Press.

Bernstein, E. (2001) 'The Meaning of the Purchase: Desire, Demand and Commercial Sex'. *Ethnography* 2(3): 389–420.

Chen, M.H. (2003) *Contradictory Male Sexual Desires: Masculinity, Lifestyles and Sexuality Among Prostitutes' Clients in Taiwan.* Paper presented at British Sociological Association Annual Conference University of York, 14th April 2003.

Coy, M., Horvath, M.A.H. and Kelly, L. (2007) *'It's Just Like Going to the Supermarket': Men Buying Sex in East London.* London: Child and Woman Abuse Studies Unit. Available at: www.cwasu.org [accessed: 1 June 2010].

Durchslag, R. and Goswami, S. (2008) *Deconstructing the Demand for Prostitution: Preliminary Insights with Chicago Men who Purchase Sex.* Chicago Alliance Against Sexual Exploitation. Available at: http://www.chicagohomeless.org/files/images/Deconstructing_the_Demand_For_Prostitution.pdf [accessed: 20 December 2008].

Earle, S. and Sharp, K. (2007) *Sex in Cyberspace: Men Who Pay for Sex.* Aldershot: Ashgate.

Earle, S. and Sharp, K (2008) 'Intimacy, Pleasure and the Men Who Pay for Sex' in G. Letherby, K. Williams, P. Birch and M. Cain (eds), *Sex as Crime?* Cullompton: Willan.

Elliott, K., Eland, H. and McGaw, J. (2002) 'Kerb Crawling in Middlesbrough: An Analysis of Kerb Crawler's Opinions'. Safer Middlesbrough Partnership Unpublished report.

Farley, M., Bindel, J. and Golding, J. (2009) *Men Who Buy Sex: Who They Are and What They Know.* London: Eaves.

Farley, M., Macleod, J., Anderson, L. and Golding, J.M. (2011, March 28) 'Attitudes and Social Characteristics of Men Who Buy Sex in Scotland'. *Psychological Trauma: Theory, Research, Practice, and Policy.* Advance online publication. doi: 10.1037/a0022645'.

Farley, M., Baral, I., Kiremire, M. and Sezgin, U. (1998) 'Prostitution in Five Countries: Violence and Post-traumatic Stress Disorder'. *Feminism and Psychology* 8(4): 405–26.

Garner, M. (forthcoming) 'The Missing Link? The Sexualisation of Culture and Men'. *Gender and Education.*

Groom, T.M. and Nandwani, R. (2005) 'Characteristics of Men Who Pay for Sex: A UK Sexual Health Clinic Survey. *Sexually Transmitted Infections* 82: 364–7.

Hester, M. and Westmarland, N. (2004) 'Tackling Street Prostitution: Towards an Holistic Approach'. *Home Office Research Study* 279. London, Home Office.

Hollway, W. (1984) 'Gender Difference and the Production of Subjectivity' in J. Henriques, W. Hollway, C. Urwing, C. Venn and V. Walkerdine (eds), *Changing the Subject.* London: Methuen.

Keeler, L. and Jyrkinen, M. (1999) 'On the Invisibility of Sex Buyers in the Sex Trade' in L. Keeler and M. Jyrkinen (eds), *Who's Buying?: The Clients of Prostitution.* Helsinki: Council for Equality Ministry of Social Affairs and Health.

Kinnell, H. (2006) 'Clients of Female Sex Workers' in R. Campbell and M. O'Neill (eds), *Sex Work Now.* Cullompton: Willan.

Lammi-Taskula, J. (1999) 'Clients of the Sex Industry in Finland: The Habitus Study' in L. Keeler and M. Jyrkinen (eds), *Who's Buying? The Clients of Prostitution.* Helsinki, Finland. Council for Equality. Ministry of Social Affairs and Health.

Mansson, S. (2004) 'Men's Practices in Prostitution and their Implications for Social Work' in S. Månsson and C. Proveyer (eds), *Social Work in Cuba and Sweden: Achievements and Prospects.* Göteborg/Havanna: Department of Social Work/Department of Sociology.

Mansson, S. (2006) 'Men's Demand for Prostitutes Pourquoi les hommes recherchent-ils des prostituées?' *Sexologies* 15(2): 87–92.

Marttila, A. (2003) *Consuming Sex – Finnish Male Clients and Russian and Baltic Prostitution.* Paper presented at Gender and Power in the New Europe, the 5th European Feminist Research Conference, Lund University, Sweden, 20–24 August, 2003.

Marttila, A. (2008) 'Desiring the "Other": Prostitution Clients on a Transnational Red-Light District in the Border Area of Finland, Estonia and Russia'. *Gender Technology and Development* 12(1): 31–51.

McKeganey, N. and Barnard, M. (1997) *Sex Work on the Streets.* Buckingham, UK: Open University Press.

Monto, M. and Mcree, M. (2005) A Comparison of the Male Customers of Female Street Prostitutes with National Samples'. *International Journal of Offender Therapy and Comparative Criminology* 49: 505–29.

O'Connell Davidson, J. (1998) *Prostitution, Power and Freedom.* Cambridge: Polity Press.

O'Neill, M. (2001) *Prostitution and Feminism: Towards a Politics of Feeling.* Cambridge: Polity Press.

Paul, P. (2005) *Pornified: How Pornography is Transforming Our Lives, Our Relationships, and Our Families.* New York: Times Books.

Policing and Crime Act (2009). Available at: http://www.legislation.gov.uk/ukpga/2009/26/notes/contents [accessed: 17 June 2011].

Soothill, K. (2004) 'Parlour Games: The Value of an Internet Site Providing Punters' Views of Massage Parlours'. *Police Journal* 77(1): 43–53.

Soothill, K. and Sanders, T. (2005) 'The Geographical Mobility, Preferences and Pleasures of Prolific Punters: A Demonstration Study of the Activities of Prostitutes' Clients'. *Sociological Research Online* 10(1).

Ward, H., Mercer, C.H., Wellings, K., Fenton, K., Erens, B., Copas, A. and
Johnson, A.M. (2005) 'Who Pays for Sex? An Analysis of the Increasing
Prevalence of Female Commercial Sex Contacts among Men in Britain'.
Sexually Transmitted Infections 81: 467–71.

Chapter 8
Legitimizing Prostitution: Critical Reflections on Policies in Australia

Mary Lucille Sullivan

Introduction

Australia, a nation ostensibly committed to women's rights to equality, has been in the forefront of legally recognizing prostitution as work. Six of the eight states and territories have introduced laws which allow some forms of prostitution to be treated as a legitimate commercial activity and where occupational health and safety standards apply.[1] Kelly et al. (2009) note that no Australian state can claim to have 'fully legalized prostitution' (p. 17), and policy regimes across states vary, from a highly regulated approach that operates in the State of Victoria to a decriminalization approach that exists in the State of New South Wales. In the former, licensed brothel, prostitution and escort prostitution are permitted, while unlicensed brothel prostitution and street prostitution remain illegal. Under New South Wales' decriminalized model all forms of adult prostitution are allowed; the only restrictions being that brothels must comply with local planning laws and street prostitution must occur in zoned areas.[2]

A key rationale for acceptance of prostitution within these states is harm minimization, based on the myth that prostitution is inevitable (Sullivan 2007). In this context, the role of state and territory prostitution legislation is to bring the industry into a regulatory framework in order to minimize the potential dangers and health risks associated with prostitution and reduce associated harms, on

---

1   The states and territories are New South Wales, Queensland, Victoria and Tasmania and the Australian Capital Territory and the Northern Territory. Currently in South Australia and Western Australia while prostitution itself is not illegal associated activities such as brothel keeping and street prostitution remain illegal.

2   I understand legalization as it operates in Australia to mean that some forms of prostitution (e.g. brothel prostitution) are lawful while other continue to be included in the criminal code (e.g. street prostitution). Like other legitimate businesses legal prostitution comes under the authority of state public health and local planning bodies, and some form of licensing usually is required. Decriminalization means that a government completely removes prostitution and prostitution related activities from the criminal code and it is regarded in no way to be different from other commercial practices. In practice in Australia, some restrictions still apply such as where a brothel or street prostitution may operate only in specified areas.

the basis that these are caused by the legal environment in which such practices take place. This is a wide-reaching goal as state and territory governments intend legislation to minimize harms not just to people in prostitution, but to the buyers and the community as well. Taken together, Australia's liberalizing prostitution laws were intended to contain highly visible and expanding brothel and street prostitution trade; lessen the impact of prostitution on communities; prevent any criminal involvement; protect against sex trafficking; protect against sexual exploitation of children and protect the sexual health of people in prostitution and buyers; and prevent violence.[3] These reflect two core aims to 'address the "nuisance" aspects of prostitution' and enhance the rights and welfare of women involved in prostitution (Bindel and Kelly 2003: 12). Thus one of the more compelling claims for treating prostitution as work was the theory that this would protect those within the industry from exploitation and violence. Victoria's legal prostitution system notionally provides the most optimal conditions for creating a safe place and system of work by placing prostitution within an industrial rights framework (Sullivan 2007).

In this chapter, the intention is to compare the aims underpinning Australia's current prostitution legislation against what actually occurs in a society where prostitution is legally acceptable. While reference is made to other states, particularly Queensland where brothels are licensed and regulated, the primary focus is the state of Victoria where trade in women and girls in systems of prostitution has now been legalized for over two decades. The state thus offers a case study for determining whether any government legislation that treats prostitution as an acceptable commercial transaction can alleviate problems associated with the sex industry. My primary critique of legalization and decriminalization approaches is that they do not take account of prostitution as cause and consequence of gender inequality. The reality is that legitimizing prostitution enables profiteers and buyers to regard women and girls[4] as commodities they can buy and sell like any other marketable product in a neoliberal marketplace, and confirms men's entitlement to women's bodies. Simultaneously, the law accepts brothel owners as business operators and places minimal restrictions on their promoting prostitution as a professional, profitable business enterprise. This obscures the intrinsic violence of prostitution. It also raises serious questions about what it means for the civil status of all women for prostitution to be normalized.

---

3   Clear evidence of unifying principles across the relevant Australian states and territories are contained either in the preamble to the authorizing Act or in the Second Reading speeches utilized by government to introduce the corresponding bill to Parliament. The state recognizes these readings as a legitimate source to give a clear and proper meaning to the Act. For example, in Victoria the stated objectives are found in the preface to the *Prostitution Control Act 1994* (Part 1, s.4).

4   I use the term women and girls as these make up the vast majority of those in prostitution and/or trafficked in Australia. My analysis, however, relates to all those in this system of sexual exploitation.

I start with a discussion of how the sex industry in Australia has expanded, and turn to: economic vulnerability that underpins women's entry into prostitution; illegal sectors; organized crime and sex trafficking; street prostitution; limitations of occupational health and safety standards.

Expansion and Profits: Who Benefits?

Legalization and decriminalization has in all states and territories resulted in expansion of a highly profitable sex trade that operates both inside and outside of the law. A recent study on health service delivery in Melbourne, Sydney and Perth, respectively the capital cities of Victoria (legalized prostitution), New South Wales (decriminalized prostitution) and Western Australia (illegal prostitution), concluded that each of these cities 'had a thriving, brothel, escort, and private (call girl) sex industry, plus a small street-based sex industry' (Harcourt et al. 2010: 484). Australian based economic business monitor, IBIS Business Information, reported that towards the end of the twentieth century 'decriminalization of prostitution and relaxed police enforcement of prostitution laws created a culture where prostitution thrived' (IBISWorld 2010: 35).[5] By 2005 IBIS found that in Australia 'sexual services' (of which prostitution – brothel prostitution, escort service and street prostitution – makes up the vast majority) ranks highest of all personal services in terms of revenue (IBISWorld 2005: 3).[6] When in 2003 Australia hosted the world's first stock market-listed brothel, the Daily Planet, it demonstrated that it is now economically viable and publicly respectable (at least in the corporate field) to profit from the prostitution of women. Fuelling such profits is men's demand. Research that surveyed 10,000 men in Australia found that one in six (15.6 per cent) had paid for sex (Rissel et al. 2003), and 'consistent with the international literature, older Australian men were more likely than younger men to have ever paid for sex, but younger men were more likely to have done so recently' (ibid: 196; see also Coy et al.: Chapter 7). This suggests possible normalization of buying sex among younger men.

Legalization and decriminalization have led the prostitution industry to become increasingly accepted and relied upon (and in some cases promoted) as a source of state revenue. In addition to the tax benefits for governments in bringing the prostitution industry into the legitimate economic sector, for governments there are, for example, returns from the states' prostitution licensing system. When we view states and territories comparatively, the impact of legislation becomes starkly apparent. On a per capita basis, in South Australia that criminalizes prostitution,

---

5   IBISWorld is made available by Australian universities and state governments for research purposes.

6   Strippers and exotic dancers (such as table top and pole dancers) make up the rest. The data does not include 'adult' Internet services (such as dating and display of pornography), telephone sex chat lines and the making and retailing of pornography.

the number of prostitution businesses appears to be significantly below other states. This is also the case in Tasmania, which has the most stringent form of legal prostitution (IBISWorld 2010).

The Victorian experience brings into focus the relationship between legislation and the expansion of prostitution. In practice, successive state governments, by allowing prostitution businesses to be recognized as a legal land use under local planning laws, have ensured that every municipality is open to organizers of the brothel industry (Sullivan 2007). Local communities and their representatives have no authority to restrict brothels if their operators hold a valid license from the Victorian Business Licensing Authority.

The growing importance of prostitution to Victoria's tourism and hospitality industries was made explicit in IBIS Business Information's (2006) report on *Sexual Services in Australia*. IBIS maintained that 'a significant contributor to the prostitution industry revenue growth was the hosting of the Commonwealth Games in Melbourne. The Games were followed immediately by the Formula 1 Grand Prix. Over this period, clubs have effectively marketed themselves to a wide audience – companies tend to hire drive-around advertisement hoardings – which have helped normalize sexual services in the eyes of many (especially the young males they seek to attract)' (IBISWorld 2007: 26). In 2010, this link continued with the busiest times at brothels in Melbourne coinciding with major sporting events such as the AFL Grand Final and the Spring Racing Carnival, events that attract groups of males who frequent bars, clubs and brothels in the area (IBISWorld 2010; see also Jyrkinen: Chapter 1). Business spending on prostitution for international clients visiting Australia is predicted to remain a buoyant segment of the industry (IBISWorld 2010).

While the recent economic downturn has led to a more modest growth in overall revenue for Australia's prostitution businesses (IBISWorld 2010) this has primarily affected legal brothel prostitution. Australia-wide, the number of prostitution businesses was estimated to be growing (IBISWorld 2010) via an expanding illegal sector which successive government legislation has failed to curtail.[7] Contours of economic recessions may also have an impact here; IBIS found that 'clients who lose their income or jobs may be disinclined to stop patronizing sex workers and as such, may simply shift to lower-cost operations [for example, unlicensed brothels] depriving the legal industry of revenue, without lowering patronage' (IBISWorld 2010: 6). Buyers are simply choosing 'cheaper' and 'unrestricted' prostitution rather than abandoning the practice of paying for sex. A 2009 report on the State's brothel sector had a similar view. It disclosed that 'many small licensed operators felt they were in direct competition with these unlicensed brothels and attributed significant revenue downturns to the growth of such operations' (Pickering et al. 2009: 40). I discuss the implications of this growth for aims to address harms of prostitution through legalization and

---

7   Victoria, for example, has had to date 33 pieces of prostitution legislation.

decriminalization, as well as the expansion of illegal sectors, but first briefly focus on women's routes into prostitution in Australia.

Routes into Prostitution: Social and Economic Marginalization

Expansion and normalization of prostitution have correspondingly provided the major rationale for the mobilization of a female 'workforce' to supply the trade. There are minimal official figures kept on the numbers of women who work in the legal industry, as in most states and territories prostituted women are not required to register.[8] However, just subsequent to Victoria's legalization of prostitution in 1984, a principal government inquiry on the State's prostitution trade – the Neave Inquiry (1985) – determined that there were around 3,000 people in prostitution. This covered both the legal massage parlour trade (a pseudonym for brothels) and the illegal sectors (illegal brothels, escort agencies, private workers and street prostitution). By 2000 the number of women in the legal prostitution industry alone was estimated to be as high as 4,500.[9] Queensland's experience similarly indicates increases post-legalization. Research revealed that 'over half the respondents working in legal brothels had started work in that sector, suggesting that the introduction of legal brothels may have allowed a significant number of women to enter the sex industry' (Woodward et al. 2004: 56–7).

Under Australia's legalized/decriminalized models prostitution is taken to be a consensual act between parties where the prostituted woman 'consents' to be used sexually by the male buyer. This legal interpretation takes for granted that the social conditions under which men participate in the prostitution transaction are the same as those for women. Legalization and decriminalization do not alter the reality that gender inequality in the form of economic vulnerability, which extends to homelessness, remains prime reasons why women 'choose' and remain in prostitution. For instance, the Melbourne-based Legal Centre and the Advocacy Program for Women in Prison have made the point that:

> Women, simply by being women, are automatically employable as prostitutes. This makes prostitution among the most accessible jobs for economically disadvantaged women who do not have a level of social security that allows

---

8   The exception is the Northern Territory. Under the *Prostitution Regulation Act* 2001 private workers must be registered with the Licensing Commission (Part 3 d7 ss41, 42 [2]). It is vital to note that the requirement for individuals to register is opposed by specialist organizations working with those in prostitution because of stigma, and concern over privacy of the information (Crime and Misconduct Commission 2004).

9   This estimate was taken from *The Age Insight Series* (1999) by Australian investigative journalist Mark Forbes. His findings were referenced in Victorian parliamentary debates (see for example, Victoria (1999) Parliamentary Debates, Council 1 June (1999): p. 967 and Victoria, Parliamentary Debates, *Assembly* 25 May (1999: 1193, 1195) http://tex. parliament.vic.gov.au/bin/texhtmlt?form=VicHansard.adv.

them to consistently and effectively acquire and maintain skills in order to be
more widely employable (Fallon et al. 2003: 8).

Various state and territory studies on why women enter and remain in prostitution
in Australia have highlighted economic and social vulnerability as the most
common motivations. A report from the Queensland Prostitution Licensing
Authority found that women's primary reason for entering prostitution was
'I needed the money' – 90 per cent for women in legal brothels; 79.3 per cent for
women involved in private prostitution and 63.6 per cent for street prostitution
(Woodward et al. 2004: 31). Moreover, over three-quarters of the participants
had taken short breaks, with most only returning because of financial reasons
(ibid: 33). The recent Consumer Affairs of Victoria (CAV) report into the
Victorian brothel sector also highlighted that the major driver for women to
enter and remain in prostitution is 'financial need' (Pickering et al. 2009). The
combination of financial reward and flexibility meant that prostitution was found
to be 'particularly attractive to mothers raising children alone, to students and
other workers whose opportunities for work were limited by lack of skills or
training/and or language barriers. Older workers reported facing struggles to
maintain earnings' (ibid: v). There are also indications of an increasing number
of students, many international, who take up prostitution. Currently estimates
of people involved in brothel prostitution in Australia who are students range
from 10–25 per cent (Pickering et al. 2009). International students have particular
difficulty in accessing economically viable work because of restrictions to their
student visas (Lantz 2005; Pickering et al. 2009). Research has also found that
young indigenous women are particularly vulnerable to prostitution (Holmes
and McRae-Williams 2008; Roxburgh et al. 2006). Supporting international
evidence, Australian research also documents high prevalence of sexual violence
in childhood and adulthood amongst women in prostitution and identifies this
as a pathway into the sex industry (Crime and Misconduct Commission 2004;
Woodward et al. 2004). These are the experiences, constraints and limited options
for economic independence or survival which influence many women's entry into
prostitution.

Illegal Prostitution under Australia's Model Regimes

The one legal avenue for women within the Victorian context to become self-
employed is to operate an exempt brothel where one or two women can control a
prostitution business without going through the normal license and probity checks
required of larger prostitution operations. However, competition with established
players and zoning restrictions, which prevent women from operating in residential
areas, means that few achieve this aim. Of the 2,083 women who registered
as 'exempt' prostitution service providers in 2007, for example, only three ran
their own prostitution businesses (State of Victoria 2007). In 2009 there were

1,700 women registered as exempt service providers (Pickering et al. 2009), suggesting that fewer women view exempt prostitution as viable. One finding from research is that the illegal prostitution sector can offer potentially higher earnings since women do not have to give business owners a percentage (Pickering et al. 2009; State of Victoria 2007).

Given its clandestine nature, it is inherently difficult to determine the extent of the illegal sex industry. However, indications are that it is significantly larger than the regulated sector. The illegal industry in Victoria is estimated to earn around $A52 million per annum (IBISWorld 2010). Queensland's (2004) Crime and Misconduct Commission prostitution law review confirmed that 'only about 10 per cent of all prostitution services available in Queensland are currently operating within the legal brothel system' (p. xii). Moreover, 'According to all informants to the review, including the PETF [Prostitution Enforcement Task Force], illegal prostitution activities in Queensland have continued unabated since the implementation of the Prostitution Act, despite the increase in policing activities illustrated by the official statistics' (p. 80).

One of the major myths of legalized/decriminalized prostitution systems is that there is a clear demarcation between the legal and illegal/unregulated sectors. Consumer Affairs Victoria has indicated that 'operators previously clustered in the unlicensed sector are now moving into the licensed sector' a trend which according to respondents affects the 'probity of the licensed sector' (Pickering et al. 2009: 47). Moreover, some commented that 'the granting of a license did not result in the abandonment of the illegal sector, but rather in the development of new connections between the licensed and unlicensed sectors' (Pickering et al. 2009: 47). Despite the aims of legislation to suppress the illegal sector, women move between licensed and unlicensed brothels and/or street/escort prostitution:

> Worker employment patterns were characterized by movement between licensed and unlicensed premises, and into and out of private and/or escort work. Approximately half of the workers had worked in at least three sectors ... [and a] number of workers had worked in premises offering add-on sexual services without a license, often in conjunction with, or as a break from, brothel work (Pickering et al. 2009: v).

Queensland's earlier 2004 inquiry on the State's 1999 *Prostitution Act* likewise determined that 'many of the respondents indicated that they work in several environments at the same time, including legal and illegal establishments' (Crime and Misconduct Commission 2004: 48). Evidence also suggests ongoing illegal activity in prostitution that operates in contravention of the various state and territory prostitution legislations. The 2009 report on Victoria's brothels found evidence of alleged illegal activity that included 'larger scale organized networks of illegal brothels' (Pickering et al. 2009: vii). Additionally there were alleged 'breaches in the license conditions or holdings such as licensees selling or trading licenses; unregistered escort agencies; and independent workers offering sexual services without being registered for exemption, or in breach of the conditions for exemption' (ibid). There was further evidence of 'connections between the licensed and unlicensed sectors ... evidenced by the movement of licenses and licensees, the movement of managers and licensees, and the provision of workers by "brokers" or agents' (ibid: vi). Thus many women remain marginalized and subject to lack of redress to at least the health and safety regulations of the legal/ decriminalized sector, despite legal reforms.

Organized Crime: Myth or Reality

A major rationale for the legalization or decriminalization of prostitution is that it would eliminate organized crime from involvement in prostitution. Within Victoria, the State Police have spoken about a continuing criminal connection. In his evidence to the ACC's inquiry into organized crime in Melbourne in May 2007, Detective Superintendent Mark Porter from the Victorian Police Intelligence Division stated that 'Serious and organized crime is well entrenched in [Victoria's] regulated industries such as prostitution and gaming' (Joint Committee on the Australian Crime Commission, 1st May 2007). He pointed out that while 'regulation has gone some way to legitimizing the industries by preventing direct ownership of legitimate venues by criminals ... it has not removed the underlying criminal attraction to the industries. The attraction still results in direct ownership of illegitimate venues, criminal associations and activities that are related to serious and organized crime' (ibid). Further, an examination of nine prostitution policy regimes noted the rationale in Victoria and the Netherlands to restrict criminal activity and address violence and exploitation through legalization/decriminalization, and found that 'Neither of these aims have been achieved, with organized crime, including trafficking, flourishing in both localities, and the illegal layers of the industry continuing to accommodate women who are funding drug addiction' (Kelly et al. 2009: 61).

Sex Trafficking: Importing Women for Profit

Australia's anti-trafficking legislation, the Criminal Code Amendment (Slavery and Sexual Servitude Act) 1999, prohibits slavery, sexual servitude and deceptive recruitment. Establishing the scale of trafficking is extremely difficult, and available statistics often take no account of women and girls who are trafficked domestically, that is between states and territories, as this is largely undetected. In 2004, Project Respect uncovered nearly 300 cases of trafficking for sexual exploitation in a six-week period, recruited through deception and/or coercion, with an estimated extrapolation of 1,000 victims per year (cited in Fergus 2005). This continuing importation of women for prostitution including trafficking is perhaps one of the more overt demonstrations that violence and exploitation against women in prostitution has not been reduced under legalized/decriminalized systems. Victoria's Drugs and Crimes Convention Committee in its (2010) inquiry into sex trafficking noted concerns 'that the illicit trade in women for sexual purposes is increasing in Victoria ... Evidence also suggests that Melbourne is second only to Sydney as a destination for sex trafficking' (p. 3). The United States Trafficking in Persons (2004–10) reports have consistently identified Australia as a destination country for women and children trafficked for prostitution although with 'modest' numbers reported proportionate to population (US Department of State 2010b). Australia is also ranked high as a destination country in the United Nations Office on Drugs and Crime citation index (UNODC 2006).

According to the United States 2010 Trafficking in Persons Report most often traffickers implicated in the Australian trade 'are part of small but highly sophisticated organized crime networks that frequently involve family and business connections between Australians and overseas contacts' (US Department of State 2010b: 66). The majority of the victims detected so far have come from Southeast Asia. However, source countries are constantly changing as those importing women can tap into a worldwide market of women whose economic and social disadvantage make them vulnerable.

Jackie Turner (Chapter 2) discusses the limitations of approaches to tackle trafficking that focus only on the 'means of delivery' rather than also on the sex industries into which women are delivered. Thus one of the most crucial factors in understanding the link between prostitution and the importation of women from abroad is the existence of a legal market. Women brought in to work in prostitution from abroad (including victims of trafficking) are also brought into Australia's legalized/decriminalized markets. Prostitution businesses where these women and girls are prostituted are generally the same operations as where Australian women are prostituted. In 2010, Victoria's Drugs and Crimes Prevention Committee concluded that 'there is a clear and close connection between sex trafficking and the legal and unregulated sex industry' (Drugs and Crime Prevention Committee 2010: v). That this has been an ongoing problem is evident in statements by Detective Senior Sergeant Ivan McKinney, from the Asian Squad of the Victorian Police, to the 2004 Parliamentary Joint Committee on trafficking for sexual servitude. He made the point that sex traffickers in Australia had no boundaries. According to evidence given to this committee, on an operational basis, a split between the legal sector and the illegal sector is ineffective when dealing with sex trafficking (Commonwealth of Australia 2003). It is possible that legal and social acceptance of prostitution in most states and territories makes Australia an attractive option for traffickers. The difficulty in combating sex trafficking might also be aggravated by the growth in demand for prostitution services that accompanied decriminalization and legalization.

Another question is whether legalization assists in the discovery or care of victims, or if it can hamper policing of legal brothels if law enforcement assumes criminal activity, including sex trafficking is associated with the illegal brothel trade. As a legal entity, brothels are mainly considered a planning issue and police have minimal rights to enter the premises (Sullivan 2007). Efforts to provide support for those who have been trafficked have been viewed positively since the introduction of new measures in 2009 (US Department of State 2010a) and the government is classified as in full compliance with international minimum standards (US Department of State 2010b). In recognition of the ongoing importation of women into the state, recommendations by the Victoria Drugs and Crime Prevention Committee (2010) included: extra resources for specialist NGOs to support victims of trafficking, including exit programmes; the establishment of a cross-government unit policy to monitor trafficking; greater flexibility for police and support services to enter brothels in order to identify potential victims. A welcome focus on men who pay for sex was also included, in the form of education campaigns and a recommendation to criminalize 'intentionally, knowingly or recklessly' buying sex from trafficked women (ibid: 10). This shift in focus is in line with international obligations under the UN Protocol (ibid). It is, however, a limited approach which does not challenge the male sex right (Pateman 1988; Jeffreys 1997) which fuels the sex industries into which women are trafficked, and which legalization policies normalize.

Street Prostitution: Ongoing Harm to Women and Communities

The ongoing existence of women and girls in street-based prostitution post-legalization/decriminalization further demonstrates that government legitimization of the trade cannot solve the problems associated with the industry. In all jurisdictions when prostitution legislation was introduced, street prostitution was recognized as undesirable and dangerous and measures introduced to deal with the 'nuisance' it caused to local communities.[10] The various state and territory governments have adopted different approaches to dealing with the harms and abuses of women and girls prostituted on the street. Under legalized models such as those that operate in Victoria and Queensland, soliciting and street prostitution remain illegal. The aim here was to curtail the street trade by targeting male demand as well as street prostitution, with women ideally moving into the regulated industry. In contrast, under the New South Wales decriminalized system, street prostitution is permitted to operate except in areas near or in view of a house, school, church, hospital or public place. The rationale for this approach is that targeting women on the streets is discriminatory on both a class and gender basis, and penalizes women and not men. In practice, neither system has diminished either the presence of, nor the harms associated with, street prostitution. This results in street prostitution becoming what has been termed a 'third tier' in regimes of legalization/decriminalization (Kelly et al. 2009: 16) where the most vulnerable women continue to be marginalized.

---

10   See for example, New South Wales, 'Parliamentary Papers', *Questions Without Notice* 16 September (1992): p. 5754 and Victoria, 'Parliamentary Papers', *Assembly* 21 October (1994): p. 1547.

Evidence of Victoria's ongoing street prostitution emerged in 2000 when the then Attorney-General Robert Hulls established an advisory group on street prostitution. The Attorney-General Street Prostitution Advisory Group (AGSPAG) (2001) admitted that the trade was invasive and had become significantly more prevalent with increases in the number of women on the streets in parallel with increased violence and rape. Moreover, both prostituted women and residents were subjected 'to violence, abuse and harassment, [with] serious damage being caused to traders and the local amenity' (ibid: 8). Reiterating the concerns of the AGSPAG some years later, Residents Inc. (2010) describe how street prostitution still 'occurs 24 hours a day, seven days a week'. In this context, the Victorian Government's introduction of stronger laws to curtail the State's street-prostitution trade (Consumer Affairs Victoria 2010) demonstrates a continuing failure of Victoria's legalized model to lessen the impact of street prostitution on communities.[11]

The AGSPAG's (2002) proposals for addressing street prostitution in the State included the introduction of 'tolerance areas' and 'street worker centres' or 'safe houses'. Yet the Queensland Crime and Misconduct Commission (2004) rejected the introduction of safe houses and safety zones in the state, claiming that similar programs in Sydney and the Netherlands had not proved successful. However, the most critical limitation of both the safe house model and tolerance zones is its failure to address the reality that street prostituted women may have minimal power to negotiate safe sex practices with buyers. The report *Selling Sex in Queensland 2003* found with regard to street prostitution that 'many authors have found links between drug use and inconsistent condom use, decreased ability to negotiate with clients and increased risk of violence' (Woodward et al. 2004: 56), and noted in their sample poor mental health and use of legal and illegal drugs (ibid). Women in street prostitution experience higher rates of violence than women in other forms of prostitution (Quadara 2008).

The failure of Australia's harm minimization approach to effectively find solutions to harms of street prostitution is inevitable. Legitimizing prostitution as work does nothing to alter the social and economic conditions of inequality that make some women and girls extremely vulnerable to involvement in the street trade.

Limitations of Occupational Health and Safety

One of the strongest arguments for legalization/decriminalization is that regulated brothels provide optimal conditions for women involved in prostitution because occupational health and safety (OHS) standards are applicable.[12] Guidance for women has been developed by several specialist support organizations covering

---

11   The new laws give police the authority to ban cars from specified areas for 72 hours if found cruising the streets for soliciting purposes.

12   The Victorian 1999 Prostitution Control (Amendment) Act, for example, extended the objects of the original 1994 Act, to specifically include the promotion of 'the welfare and occupational health and safety of prostitutes' and 'to ensure that brothels are accessible

safety strategies, acknowledging the prevalence and likelihood of violence (see Edler 2000). Women interviewed in studies in Victoria and Queensland report higher levels of safety in licensed sectors, although with varying awareness of rights under legislation (Pickering et al. 2009; Woodward et al. 2004). These improvements are however limited to legal/licensed sectors, which as noted earlier form a minority of prostitution businesses. In addition, inconsistent implementation of OHS guidelines is commonly noted (Quadara 2008). Australia's OHS strategies for prostitution businesses, in any event, are unambiguously focused on containing the spread of sexually transmitted infections (STIs), particularly in brothels (Sullivan 2007; Quadara 2008). But even in this limited capacity OHS fails to protect women. Compulsory testing for prostituted women is implied under most Australian prostitution legislation,[13] and some business owners insist on medical certificates (State of Victoria 2007). However, this is a relatively inaccurate means of determining whether a woman should continue to 'work' as there is a three-month dormancy window for the various STIs (Banach and Metzenrath 2000). Furthermore, critiques of mandatory testing have exposed the inadequacy of targeting women. HIV, for example, is overwhelmingly transmitted by men, via male-to-female vaginal and anal intercourse, not vice versa (Farley and Kelly 2000). By ignoring the male buyer, governments not only discriminate against women, but also help create the perception that they are the purveyors of disease. Mandatory testing is an outdated historical anachronism. In the mid-1800s, feminists such as Josephine Butler campaigned against the Contagious Diseases Acts that allowed compulsory examination of women suspected of prostitution. Feminists argued against the double standard of sexual morality that enforced such abuse of women in order to protect men's health (Jeffreys 1985). Yet now some licensees report that they welcome testing since it protects them from being sued by buyers because they have contracted an infection (State of Victoria 2007). This onus of responsibility is clear: to protect men from women as purveyors of disease.

While any measures that may minimize, or at least decrease, the harms of prostitution are beneficial for those who are involved in it, what other categories of workers have to accept STIs as an 'inevitable', rather than an accidental, consequence of just going to work? Research indicates that levels of sexually transmitted infections are low and condom use high, yet Consumer Affairs Victoria in its 2009 report on the State's brothels exposed that 'workers *in both the licensed and unlicensed sector* would offer unsafe sex for the right price' and some reported that demand was rising for sexual activity without condoms (Pickering et al. 2009: 20, emphasis original). More significantly, OHS strategies

---

to inspectors, law enforcement officers, health workers and service providers'. *Prostitution Control Act 1994*, s.4[g] amended by No. 44/1999, s. 6[2].

13   For example, mandatory testing of prostituted women for STIs is assumed within the 1994 *Prostitution Control Act*. Women found working with an STI are penalised together with the brothel management and the only reliable defence is proof that the infected woman has undergone regular health checks (*Prostitution Control Act 1994* ss. 19 and 20).

for women in prostitution assume that women are always able to negotiate safe sex, despite the power imbalance inherent in the prostitution transaction. This power inequity between a prostituted woman and the buyer is starkly evident in the risk prevention strategies prostituted women require to simply survive where violence is 'is an inherent risk of the job' (Crime and Misconduct Commission 2004: 21). These include panic buttons, video surveillance to screen clients and, when these fail, self-defence courses and expertise in negotiation skills and hostage skills. The harm inherent in prostitution 'work' practices and the prostitution 'work' environment is perhaps best illustrated by the fact that OHS guidelines list STIs, unwanted pregnancies, sexual harassment, physical violence, abuse and rape as specific health risks whether prostitution is legal or illegal (see Edler 2000).

One recent Australian review of research on sexual assault in the prostitution industry views implementation and monitoring of occupational health and safety by management as a primary issue of concern for women in prostitution. The author quotes research on the Victorian legal industry (Murray 2001) that

> showed that workers were entering into highly problematic 'contracts' or agreements with management about the extent of their duties to the point that they have little room to refuse a client. Sex worker safety ends up depending on the benevolence of the manager rather than any consistent framework (Quadara 2008: 19).

Significantly, the Melbourne-based legal advocacy group for women in prison drew attention to the fact that, 'Despite claims that brothels provide safer working environments, many women report ... that they prefer to risk violence at the hands of clients than be subjected to violence by both clients and brothel staff and security' (Fallon et al. 2003: 8). Research in Victoria also confirmed that 'workers in the licensed environment may still face coercion by employers which may compromise their safety and ability to regulate their own work' (Pickering et al. 2009: 3). The pro-legalization position becomes unstuck when the health and safety of prostituted women is not protected even where prostitution operates under supposedly optimal conditions.

Ultimately OHS strategies to eliminate harmful 'work' practices or the 'work' environment will prove ineffectual as prostitution is like no other form of work. It involves the use of a woman's body by the buyer for his sexual gratification. No other workplace has to cover the range of health and safety issues that ensue from this sexual and economic exchange. The proposition for legalization is based on a flawed premise that legal prostitution businesses have the capacity to create safe and healthy 'work' practices and 'work' environments. Where prostitution is viewed as a form of violence against women, as it is here, in that it involves the use of (mostly women's) bodies for (mostly men's) sexual gratification, then questions of health and safety are more than simply occupational health practices. Legitimizing prostitution does not keep women safe from what it is an intrinsic violence. The harms of prostitution extend beyond physical safety to psychological wellbeing, evident in research that shows that some women across many forms of prostitution, initiate or increase drug or alcohol use to anaesthetize the pain of physical injuries and verbal abuse inflicted on them in prostitution (Farley et al. 2003). Moreover, the short and long term emotional effects of prostitution where sexual violence is common remain similar irrespective of whether prostitution has been legalized or decriminalized (Farley 2004, 2005). These include depression, fear, anxiety, lack of trust, withdrawal, shame, self-blame, guilt, humiliation, anger or rage headaches, muscle tension, gastro-intestinal upset and genital or urinary complaints, suicidal actions, anorexia, alcohol and drug addiction, isolation, eating disorders, sleeping problems, phobias or nightmares (Farley et al. 2003; Farley 2004). These psychological and emotional issues are often overlooked by a focus on physical safety (Farley 2005), and suggest that the potential harms to women in prostitution from normalizing the practice as work are extensive.

It is also telling that stigmatization of women in prostitution also continues to be documented in studies (Pickering et al. 2009; State of Victoria 2007), suggesting that benefits of legalization do not extend to dissolving such negative perceptions. Although reducing stigma is a primary driver of legalization/ decriminalization approaches (Farley 2004), Quadara (2008) comments 'even where sex work is either decriminalized or legalized through licensing mechanisms (as it is in Victoria), sex workers' social position remains one of illegality and deviance' (p. 24). Policy documents acknowledge that women's ability to move out of prostitution is restricted the longer they stay in the industry partly due to this stigma (State of Victoria 2007). Victoria's 1994 Prostitution Act stipulated that the States' specialist Prostitution Control Board set up exit programs which brothel and escort agencies' licensing fees were to finance (Parliamentary Debates 1994). Supporting women to leave prostitution is complex, and time and resource intensive. However, after over two decades of legalized prostitution there are minimal services to support women leaving (Kelly et al. 2009), and sufficient government funding has not been provided despite multiple recommendations (Sullivan 2007; State of Victoria 2007). It seems unlikely that any government will make a strong commitment to exit programs where prostitution is increasingly normalized as 'just work' and a valid 'career option'.

Conclusion

Governments' acceptance of prostitution as a legitimate commercial practice, a job just like any other, holds the alluring promise that prostitution can be regulated and it can be made safe. The experiences within Australian states where regimes of legalization/decriminalization have been introduced demonstrate what happens when prostitution is normalized and protected by the State. Decriminalizing women in prostitution is an essential step forward, but this does not have to entail legitimizing the sex industry and thus men's demand for prostituted women (as the model of legislation in Sweden shows; see Erikson: Chapter 9).

Legitimizing prostitution as work produces an increased demand for prostitution services and a large expansion of the brothel trade (both legal and illegal). Over the last three decades, more and more women in Australia have been drawn into the industry. Most women still resort to prostitution because of financial hardship, since prostitution occurs against a backdrop of social and economic gender inequality. They experience violence at the hands of buyers and brothels owners, persistent stigma, low pay and for some, drug addiction. Moreover, street prostitution persists unabated. The 'work' of prostitution (including an absence of qualifications/training, and skills that are not recognized as transferable by mainstream employers) ensures that many women are not in a position to develop skills that would make them more widely employable, despite policy recommendations to increase programs to enable women to leave prostitution for other employment options (State of Victoria 2007).

It is also evident that the vast majority of the sex industry in Victoria and other states operates either on the margins of the legal sector or in a totally illegal environment. Victoria's approach has not eliminated exploitation, not least because of what many have recognized as the emergence of a 'two-tier' system between the legal and illegal sectors (Kelly et al. 2009). Thus a significant proportion of prostituted women continue to be involved in illegal prostitution. Many women operate across all sectors of the prostitution industry – licensed and unlicensed brothels, escort or private work. Research indicates that women in licensed/legal prostitution sectors report improved health and safety (Pickering et al. 2009; Woodward et al. 2004), but the same claims cannot be made in respect of women in the larger illegal sectors which continue to flourish. Safety also has deeper implications from a perspective that views prostitution itself as a form of violence.

Australia's lawmakers are confronted with the challenge of regulating an industry whose boundaries are constantly changing and expanding. This is an inherent weakness of a system that legalizes certain prostitution acts, under certain conditions, hoping that other forms of sexual exploitation will simply disappear. Moreover, taken together, evidence suggests that the boundaries between the legal and clandestine market are often illusory in terms of exploitation of women, and criminal ownership and practices. In the face of ongoing evidence that legalization or decriminalization fails to achieve its objectives, most Australian governments remain committed to a policy that accepts the inevitability of prostitution. Such policies primarily benefit prostitution businesses and governments alike. Male buyers, of course, are the major victors. They now have a ready supply of women and girls at their disposal for sex, intensifying the commodification of women and girls for sex and profit, a confirmation of a male entitlement to women's bodies. So while questions remain about how successful relevant states and territories have been in eliminating violence and exploitation, there are also significant questions about what it means for states to tolerate or endorse the commodification of women's bodies.

References

Attorney-General's Street Prostitution Advisory Group (2001) *Interim Report.* Melbourne: Victorian Department of Justice and Legal Policy.

Attorney-General's Street Prostitution Advisory Group (2002) *Final Report.* Melbourne: Victorian Department of Justice and Legal Policy.

Australian Bureau of Statistics (2010) *Average Weekly Earnings.* Available at: http://www.abs.gov.au catalogue number 6302 [accessed: 16 November 2010].

Banach, L. and Metzenrath, S. (2000) *Principles for Model Sex Industry Legislation.* Sydney: A Joint Project of the Scarlet Alliance and the Australian Federation of AIDS Organisations.

Bindel, J. and Kelly, L. (2003) *A Critical Examination of Responses to Prostitution in Four Countries: Victoria, Australia; Ireland; the Netherlands; and Sweden.* London: CWASU.

Commonwealth of Australia (2003) *Trafficking in Women for Sexual Servitude.* Melbourne: Joint Committee on the Australian Crime Commission, 18 November 2003.

Commonwealth of Australia (2007) *Future Impact of Serious and Organized Crime on Australian Society.* Canberra: Joint Committee on the Australian Crime Commission, 6 July 2007.

Consumer Affairs Victoria (2010) *New Laws Crack Down on St Kilda Kerb-Crawlers Media Release.* 10 August 2010.

Crime and Misconduct Commission (2004) *Regulating Prostitution: An Evaluation of the Prostitution Act 1999.* Queensland: Crime and Misconduct Commission.

Department of Victorian Communities (2005) *Safe at Work? Women's Experience of Violence in the Workplace.* Summary Report of Research. Melbourne: Office of Women's Policy.

Drugs and Crimes Convention Committee (2010) *Inquiry into People Trafficking for Sex Work: Final Report.* Melbourne: Parliament of Victoria.

Edler, D. (2000) *A Guide to Best Practice Occupational Health and Safety in the Australian Sex Industry.* Sydney: Scarlet Alliance and the Australian Federation of Aids Organisations.

Fallon, A., Hanna, J., Heyward, S. and Vidyasagar, A. (2003) *Joint Submission of Darebin Legal Centre and Advocacy Program for Women in Prison to the Senate Community Affairs References Committee Inquiry into Poverty in Australia.* Melbourne: Darebin Legal Centre.

Farley, M. and Kelly, V. (2000) 'Prostitution: A Critical Review of the Social Sciences Literature'. *Women and Criminal Justice* 11(4): 29–64.

Farley, M., Cotton, A., Lynne, J., Zumbeck, S., Spiwak, F., Reyes, M., Alvarez, D. and Sezgin, U. (2003) 'Prostitution & Trafficking in Nine Countries: An Update on Violence and Post-Traumatic Stress Disorder' in M. Farley. (ed.), *Prostitution, Trafficking, and Traumatic Stress.* Binghamton: Haworth Press.

Farley, M. (2004) '"Bad for the Body, Bad for the Heart": Prostitution Harms Women Even if Legalized or Decriminalized'. *Violence against Women* 10(10): 1087–125.

Farley, M. (2005) 'Prostitution Harms Women Even if Indoors: Reply to Weitzer'. *Violence against Women* 11(7): 950–64.

Fergus, L. (2005) *Trafficking in Women for Sexual Exploitation.* Melbourne: Australian Centre for the Study of Sexual Assault: Briefing no. 5. Available at: http://www.childtrafficking.com/Docs/austria_1_15.pdf [accessed: 2 March 2011].

Harcourt, C., O'Connor, J., Egger, S., Fairley, C.K., Wand, H., Chen, M.Y., Marshall, L., Kaldor, J.M. and Donovan, B. (2010) 'The Decriminalisation of Prostitution is Associated with Better Coverage of Health Promotion Programs for Sex Workers', *Australian and New Zealand Journal of Public Health* 34(5): 482–6.

Holmes, C. and McRae-Williams, E. (2008) *An Investigation into the Influx of Indigenous 'Visitors' to Darwin's Long Grass from Remote NT Communities – Phase 2.* Tasmania: National Drug Law Enforcement Research Fund.

IBISWorld (2005) *Personal Services in Australia.* Q9529 IBISWorld Pty Ltd.

IBISWorld (2006) *Sexual Services in Australia.* Q9528 IBISWorld Pty Ltd.

IBISWorld (2007) *Sexual Services in Australia.* Q9528 IBISWorld Pty Ltd.

IBISWorld (2010) *Sexual Service in Australia.* Q9528 IBISWorld Pty Ltd.

Jeffreys, S. (1985) *The Spinster and Her Enemies: Feminism and Sexuality 1830–1930.* Melbourne: Spinifex Press.

Jeffreys, S. (1997) *The Idea of Prostitution.* Melbourne: Spinifex Press.

Joint Committee on the Australian Crime Commission (2007) *Future Impact of Serious and Organised Crime on Australian Society Inquiry.* 1st May 2007. Melbourne: ACC 28.

Kelly, L., Coy, M. and Davenport, R. (2009) *Shifting Sands: A Comparison of Prostitution Regimes across Nine Countries.* London: CWASU.

Lantz, S. (2005) 'Students Working in the Melbourne Sex Industry: Education, Human Capital and the Changing Patterns of the Youth Labour Market'. *Journal of Youth Studies* 8(4): 385–401.

Neave, M. (1985) *Victoria, Inquiry into Prostitution: Final Report.* Melbourne: Government Printer.

Parliamentary Debates (1994) *Assembly.* 16 November, p. 1874. Victoria.

Pickering, S., Maher, J.M. and Gerard, A. (2009) *Working in Victorian Brothels: An Independent Report Commissioned by Consumer Affairs Victoria into the Victorian Brothel Sector.* Victorian Government: Melbourne.

Prostitution Control Act, State of Victoria, No. 102 (1994).

Prostitution Control Act, State of Victoria, No. 102 (1994) Version incorporating amendments as of June 19, 2000.

Quadara, A. (2008) *Sex Work and Sexual Assault in Australia: Prevalence, Risk and Safety.* Melbourne: Australian Centre for the Study of Sexual Assault.

Pateman, C. (1988) *The Sexual Contract.* California: Stanford University Press.

Residents First Inc (2010) 'Residents Say No to Prostitution'. *Sexploitation in St Kilda.* Melbourne.

Rissel, C.E., Richters, J., Grulich, A.E., de Visser, R.O. and Smith, A.M. (2003) 'Sex in Australia: Experiences of Commercial Sex in a Representative Sample of Adults'. *Australian and New Zealand Journal of Public Health* 27(2): 191–7.

Roxburgh, A., Degenhardt, L. and Copeland, J. (2006) 'Posttraumatic Stress Disorder among Female Street-based Sex Workers in the Greater Sydney Area, Australia. *BMC Psychiatry* 2006(6): 24.

Royal Melbourne Institute of Technology University Union (2004) *'Students and Sex Work', Your Rights as Workers.* Melbourne: RMIT.

State of Victoria (2007) *Improving the Regulation of the Sex Industry and Supporting Sex Workers Who Want to Move On.* Melbourne: Consumer Affairs Victoria.

Sullivan, B. (1992) 'Feminist Approaches to the Sex Industry' in S. Gerull and B. Halstead (eds), *Sex Industry and Public Policy: Proceedings of Conference Australian Institute of Criminology 6–8 May 1991.* Canberra: Australian Institute of Criminology.

Sullivan, M.L. (2007) *Making Sex Work: A Failed Experiment in Legalised Prostitution.* Melbourne: Spinifex.

United Nations Office on Drugs and Crime (UNODC) *Trafficking in Persons: Global Patterns.* New York: UN.

United States Department of State (2010a) *Trafficking in Persons Report 2010 – Australia*, 14 June 2010. Available at: http://www.unhcr.org/refworld/docid/4c18840cc.html [accessed: 5 January 2011].

United States Department of State (2010b) *Trafficking in Persons Report – 10th edition.* US: Office to Monitor and Combat Trafficking in Persons.

Woodward, C., Fischer, J., Naijman, J.M. and Dunne, M. (2004) *Selling Sex in Queensland.* Brisbane: Prostitution Licensing Authority.

Chapter 9

The Various 'Problems' of Prostitution –
A Dynamic Frame Analysis of
Swedish Prostitution Policy

Josefina Erikson

Introduction

What is the problem of prostitution? The answer to this question depends on
how it is framed. There is disagreement about how to understand the problem of
prostitution, and as a consequence, different solutions are advocated. The Swedish
prostitution law of 1998 that criminalizes the purchase, but not the sale, of sex has
been widely debated both in Sweden and internationally (e.g. Ekberg 2004; Kelly,
Coy and Davenport 2009; Svanström 2004; SOU 2010: 49). While the actual law
is gender neutral, its intention was to tackle prostitution through a statement about
prostitution as a phenomenon and practice of gender inequality that is incompatible
with a gender equal society (prop. 1997/98: 55).

Critics of the law argue that criminalization is a misguided method to address
prostitution which worsens the situation for women in prostitution (Östergren
2003). Advocates, in contrast, emphasize the uniqueness of a policy that challenges
patriarchy and addresses the demand, making the buyer responsible for his (or her)
actions rather than accepting male sexual entitlement as inevitable. This chapter
analyses the problem framings of prostitution, traces the origin of the Swedish
model through five broad periods of policy debate, identifies critical junctures that
led to the introduction of the legislation, and explores how gender inequality has
been discussed in different framings of prostitution.

A decade after the introduction of the law an official inquiry has established
that the law has had the intended effects and that prostitution accordingly has
diminished in Sweden (SOU 2010: 49). During the same period Norway and
Iceland have followed the Swedish example and criminalized the purchase of sex.
It is revealing then, that outside parliament prostitution policy continues to be a
hotly contested issue, and the construction of the law as well as its alleged impact
remains questioned (e.g. Dodillet 2010). The ongoing public debate reflects the
nature of prostitution as a policy issue. It can be described as an 'intractable policy
controversy' (following Schön and Rein 1994). These are controversies in which
the differences of opinion are so profound that reasoning and appeal to 'facts' does

not help to solve the conflict. Indeed, what is to be considered as fact is in itself a matter of disagreement. These controversies seldom reach a final resolution.

To explore intractable policy controversies, frame analysis is a fruitful method to understand what the conflict actually is about (Schön and Rein 1994). Frame analysis enables questions to be asked as to whether the controversy is about different understandings about the problem, the cause or the solutions (e.g. Verloo and Lombardo 2007). The division in the debate crosses the simple left-right cleavage and thus political ideology does not present an explanation for diverging opinions. In light of this, frame analysis provides an analytical framework to explore the reasons behind the difference in opinions on the controversial policy issue of prostitution. The focus is on the framing of prostitution in the policy process preceding the introduction of the ban of the purchase of sexual services.

The aim of this chapter is to show how the construction of meaning is essential in order to understand how the ban of purchase of sexual services was adopted and to understand the subsequent debate on the law. The fundamental disagreement on the 'problem' of prostitution manifests in the discussion of the best way to solve the problem, and variation in these constructions makes some solutions desirable and others unlikely. While there are several analyses of the Swedish model from diverse perspectives (Dodillet 2009; Eduards 2007; Ekberg 2004; Svanstrom 2004), in this chapter the policy process preceding the criminalization of the buying of sexual services will be analysed as a struggle of meaning in which various problem framings of prostitution were expressed.

It is often claimed that that the Swedish law was based on a radical feminist idea of prostitution as violence against women (Dodillet 2009; Ekberg 2004; Gould 2001). Analysis in this chapter suggests that the idea of prostitution as violence against women was not, at least initially, the predominant problem framing in the policy process, nor in the claims for client criminalization. I will argue that the institutionalization of an abolitionist frame of prostitution in which prostitution is conceived of as a problem per se that needs to be abolished, before the institutionalization of the problem in terms of gender inequality, was decisive for the final outcome. Finally, the chapter will explain the challenges of, and for, a sex work framing of prostitution.

A Dynamic Frame Analysis

Policy production can be conceived of as a struggle of meaning in which some ideas are institutionalized and others ignored (e.g. Hajer 1995, 2003). In this struggle of meaning are involved a range of actors who are actively deconstructing and reconstructing understandings and discourses. At the same time, prevailing ideas create restricting and facilitating contextual backdrops for the actors' formulation of meaning. Using prostitution as an example, I argue that the policy process should be analysed as a dynamic process in which actors and socially dominant ideas interact (Erikson 2011). The dynamic frame analysis drawn on in this chapter is a constructivist framework developed to allow exploration of this interaction between actors and ideas and the implications of different problem constructions (Erikson 2011). The framework consists of three parts, analysing: ideas; actors; and the interaction between ideas and actors. In this chapter, however, only the aspects of the frame work regarding ideas, and more specifically frame construction and institutionalization, are applied.[1]

The strength of the dynamic frame analysis is that the framing process in which problem representations, causal stories and solutions are constructed, is analysed from an historical institutionalist perspective (Erikson 2011). Consequently, policy frames are analysed with regard to the ideas expressed about prostitution and the level of institutionalization of these policy frames. This is a way of moving one step beyond a descriptive analysis of the debate of prostitution and to capture the relation between different policy frames and policy changes over time.

The policy process was initiated at the beginning of the 1970s through a number of motions on prostitution posed by a few members of the Swedish parliament. From that point onwards, prostitution was repeatedly on the agenda in the parliament, and occasionally within government, until the law was passed in 1998. The trajectory of this process can be broadly divided in five periods on the basis of significant changes in the problem framing of prostitution in Sweden.

- 1970s: Prostitution re-emerges as a political issue
- Early 1980s: An abolitionist frame of prostitution as a problem is institutionalized
- Late 1980s: Prostitution as gendered
- 1990s: Prostitution is institutionalized as a criminal problem
- 1998: Criminalization of the purchase of sexual services is institutionalized.

Here, each period is analysed with a focus on conflicts evident within the framing at the time.

1970s: Prostitution on the Political Agenda

The starting point of the renewed interest for prostitution in the Swedish parliament was the growth in and magnitude of the sex industry, which was attributed to relaxation of legislation in the 1970s (SOU 1972: 36). As with other countries, legislation at the time criminalized brothels and pimping, but neither the buying nor selling of sex. Regarding women in prostitution, the government explicitly expressed that society should only take supportive measures for their protection, mainly within the social service and health care sector and on a voluntary basis (SOU 1981: 71). The problem framing in the institutionalized prostitution policy

---

1   Elsewhere I have also included actors in the analysis as active in the framing process and limited and enabled by the dominant ideas, but this is outside the scope of this chapter. For a more detailed analysis in which all aspects are applied see Erikson (2011).

can be analysed therefore as an overarching *social framing* of prostitution (see SOU 1981: 71 and SoU 1976/77: 5 for an overview of the legislation at the time); akin to other societal problems such as drugs and social deprivation in general. Thus, supportive social measures were proposed as solutions. The seeds of understanding prostitution in an abolitionist frame were therefore sown, since it was viewed as a social problem, and its elimination desirable.

This institutionalized social framing of prostitution was questioned in different ways in the 1970s both by members of parliament in private motions and outside the parliament by the women's movement (i.e. motion 1972: 59, motion 1975/76: 1305, Kvinnobulletinen 1977a, 1977b). For instance, members of parliament from the liberal party proposed legalization of brothels (motion 1972: 59), increased social support for prostitutes to leave prostitution (motion 1972: 330) and stricter criminal sanctions for pimping (motion 1972: 310), in three different parliamentary motions. Outside of the parliament, women's organizations advocated criminalization of the buying of sexual services to tackle men's use of women in prostitution (Hertha 1980; Kvinnobulletinen 1977a, 1977b). During this period, prostitution was included in a governmental inquiry on sexual crimes (SOU 1976: 9). The inquiry proposed changes in the penal code of sexual crimes and the 1976 report led to a strong critique, primarily from the women's movement (SOU 1981: 61). Women's organizations criticized the proposed amendment regarding rape, which was proposed to consider if the women had encouraged the man, and the reduction of pimping to situations in which prostitutes were 'taken advantage of in an improper way' (SOU 1982: 61; SOU 1982: 67, my translation). At the same time as a group of women's organizations demanded a new inquiry on sexual crimes and one on prostitution, in parliament the need for such an inquiry on prostitution was also recognized by members and the Committee on Health and Welfare (SOU 1976/77: 7).

Prostitution was now firmly on the political agenda and the established social framing on prostitution was questioned in terms of both problem construction and associated solutions. The existing legislation was seen as insufficient to meet the expanded sex industry, and the need for a new prostitution inquiry was accepted in order to generate more robust knowledge of the situation.

At this point, three possible framings can be distinguished in the political debate. First, the institutionalized social framing already mentioned above and scrutinized in more detail later. This framing is predominant in existing legislation, official statements from the parliaments committees, and also evident in private members motions. Second, the criminal framing of prostitution, expressed outside parliament by advocates of criminalization, where prostitution was seen as an unacceptable phenomena, with effects so negative for society at large and in particular for women involved, that it should be considered criminal to buy sex (and sometimes sell sex). This criminal framing as it became the focus of subsequent periods will be explored in more detail later. It is worth noting here, however, that criminalization of women in prostitution has rarely featured in policy discussions in Sweden. From the beginning the criminalization that was primarily advocated, was client criminalization, drawing on a gendered problem framing. Third, a normalization framing, advocated in proposals of legalization of brothels. In the motion of Sten Sjöholm, an MP from the Liberal party, the problem of prostitution was described as 'the discomfort, sanitary problems and non-tolerable environmental conditions' (motion 1972: 59, my translation) created by the expansion of the sex industry. Yet Sten Sjöholm saw 'the need for this kind of activity' (motion 1972: 59 my translation), and accordingly he proposed legalization and regulation of brothels.

This framing of prostitution reveals a representation where prostitution as such was not seen as a problem. Instead, the problem was described as the unregulated aspects of prostitution, which can be resolved by containing it within legal and policy frameworks that render it equivalent with other forms of work and thus minimize risk and associated illegal activities. In the framing of prostitution in the previously mentioned inquiry on sexual crime, the same tendency can be noted. This problem framing differs from the social framing and the criminal framing in a fundamental way. The fundamental disagreement centres on whether prostitution per se is a problem, or if the lack of regulation is the problem. As a consequence very different solutions were proposed.

These different problem framings represent two general frames in the prostitution debate at large: an abolitionist frame including both the criminal frame and the social frame, and a normalization frame including a regulation frame. These two frames mark a central dividing line noted by Jenny Westerstrand (2008) in her categorization of the normative discourse on prostitution. The core conflict on prostitution is according to Westerstrand whether prostitution is seen as an acceptable activity which needs to be normalized (normalization position) or if prostitution is seen as an activity that should not be part of society and therefore needs to be tackled (abolitionist position). Within these two overarching frames, many different views of prostitution can be expressed in different ideas about the problem, causes and potential solutions.

Hence in the 1970s, when prostitution reached the political agenda, it remained an open question which path the policy process should take.

Early 1980s: Prostitution is Institutionalized as a Problem

During this period the abolitionist framing of prostitution as a problem per se took precedence. The dividing line was between a social framing of prostitution and a criminal framing of prostitution within the overarching abolitionist frame, with different ideas about origins of the problem of prostitution and about solutions. In the official report of prostitution (SOU 1981: 71), normalization arguments were rejected.

In 1977, the Swedish Government established two different commissions of inquiry that dealt with prostitution: the Prostitution inquiry (SOU 1981: 71); and the Sexual Crime committee (SOU 1982: 61). Both inquiries presented their reports at the beginning of 1980. In the prostitution inquiry there was disagreement within the commission and two different reports were presented, one official and one alternative (SOU 1981: 71; DsS1980: 9).[2] However, all three reports suggested only marginal changes, and accordingly the government did not amend prostitution policy in any significant way. In line with existing prostitution policy the government proposed social measures to prevent prostitution, support prostituted women and a sharpened criminal law to tackle pimping. The social framing was still institutionalized, but in parliament a few women MPs from the Social democrats, the Liberals and the Center party started to raise the issue of criminalization of sex buyers. This claim was also documented in the consultation element of the prostitution inquiry of 1977, mostly by women's organizations. Yet at this stage, the criminalization of the sex buyer was dismissed both by the inquiries, the government and by parliamentary committees. Arguments against criminalization of the clients focused on the risk of diminishing social measures that sought to change attitudes to prostitution and support women in prostitution and the risk that the sex industry would go underground and therefore be more difficult to abolish. Other arguments raised were the difficulty with such legislation in terms of demarcation of the crime and compliance with the ban. It was also suggested by some that it was ethically problematic if only the client was criminalized (DsS 1980: 9).

The core message of all the reports and governmental bills on prostitution, which to a large extent are based on the commission reports, was the framing of prostitution as a social problem. In the reports prostitution was described as a 'social phenomena' (SOU 1981: 71) which should be abolished (SOU 1982: 61). A 1983 governmental bill stated that 'the significance of social measures to diminish prostitution can hardly be overestimated' (prop. 1983/84: 105, 38, my translation). Gender was mentioned in all the reports but whereas patriarchy was problematized in the alternative report of the prostitution inquiry written by Sven Axel Månsson and colleagues, the analysis in the official report talked about gender roles and asymmetrical sexual needs. This approach explicitly endorsed a male biological 'need' for sex (see Coy et al.: Chapter 7). So, within this general social framing it is possible to differentiate between different perspectives. However, in the political debate the dividing line was viewed only between a general social framing of prostitution and a criminal framing, and some of the nuances in the social framing with respect to gender were missed.

A criminal framing of prostitution was expressed in the demands for criminalization. With a few exceptions, criminalization referred only to the client. In these claims the problem of prostitution was described in terms of gender inequality. A social democratic politician, Margareta Persson, described prostitution in a way that captures the core of the argument 'the ancient history of prostitution is the history of men's power over the institutions in society.

---

2   The alternative report, prepared by experts who left the commission, criticized the official inquiry for a lack of scientific analysis and wanted to include some interviews with prostituted women in the report (Mansson and Linders 1984; Olsson 2006).

It is also the history of women's submission' (prot. 1983/84: 152, my translation). However, it would be another decade before this approach was incorporated into law and policy.

Similar to the overarching social framing, it is possible to talk about a wider criminal framing that included more specific discourses. In this framing, prostitution was viewed as a crime and thus requiring a strong law enforcement response, with individuals responsible for their actions. There are similarities between the criminal framing and the social framing, as both are rooted in an abolitionist approach to prostitution. The prominent difference, however, between the social framing and the criminal framing which is whether the cause of prostitution as a problem is attributed to the societal or individual level. More specifically, this was about whether individuals should be accountable for their actions through criminal sanctions or if society was responsible for addressing the problem. This difference was illustrated in the arguments against client criminalization in the alternative report of the 1977 prostitution inquiry (DsS 1980: 9). The report argued that it was in principle wrong to criminalize individuals for a phenomenon that was part of structural, societal pattern (DsS 1980: 9, 699). Both the buyer and the seller in prostitution were thus seen as victims of an unequal gendered system. The government expressed a similar line of argument that 'prostitution causes negative consequences not only for the women. Also the clients' emotional and sexual life can be affected in a negative way through prostitution' (prop. 1981/82: 187, 20, my translation). The government proposed more support for men who paid for sex.

In contrast, the criminal framing of prostitution assigned responsibility to the individuals involved in prostitution. Societal, structural factors were mentioned but demand was highlighted as the direct cause of prostitution and clients, mostly men, were held responsible for their actions. So while gendered social inequalities were acknowledged as significant, the solution in the criminal framing was proposed to hold individual men accountable rather than address constructions of masculinity. Gunilla André, a Centre party politician, argued this in a way that was characteristic of the debate; 'the client has the freedom to chose to buy sexual intercourse or not. What is for the client a voluntary business transaction, is for the prostituted a more or less forced action' (SOU 1982: 61 s. 168, my translation). In the few claims to criminalize both parties in prostitution the same line of reasoning is found when it comes to assigning responsibility to the individuals, with the exception that both the client and the prostituted were seen as equally responsible.

The difference between the social framing and the criminal framing is thus less about how the problem of prostitution is conceived and more about how responsibility is assigned, boiling down to whether or not individual men have responsibility. Again this nuance is often lost within discussion of the overarching abolitionist frame.

During this period the abolitionist frame is institutionalized in the sense that it is no longer questioned and normalization claims are no longer accepted in public policy formulation. All actors in the policy process agreed that prostitution was a problem that needed to be abolished. The debate was limited to the most adequate and effective way to tackle prostitution, which was related to ideas about root cause and responsibility.

This historical abolitionist frame is a prerequisite for advocates of client criminalization and equally hinders opposition to it. From this point on it was difficult to frame prostitution in terms of normalization arguments. The policy trajectory that prostitution should, and could, be eliminated on the basis that it was incompatible with gender equality is beginning to develop. Opponents to criminalization were restricted to arguments that criminalization is not a possible or efficient measure, as the framing of prostitution as a problem per se was no longer up for discussion.

Late 1980s: A Gendered Analysis of Prostitution

By the late 1980s prostitution had become a frequent agenda item in the Swedish parliament due to a series of motions, most of them based around criminalization of the client (JuU 1985/86: 3, JuU 1985/86: 20, JuU 1987/88: 12). During this period gender became a mandatory component in the debate, although the watershed continued to be between the criminal framing and the social framing. A change in the parliament's problem framing can be noted as a story in which men's responsibility and demand were problematized.

In 1988, prostitution was considered in the parliament's Committee on Justice due to arguments from some MPs for criminalization of clients as an effective approach. A discernible shift is that now these motions were not dismissed immediately as in the years before. The Committee on Justice solicited the opinion of the Committee on Health and Welfare on the matter, which in turn consulted concerned social authorities, for example social workers and the police. In their report the Committee on Health and Welfare advised against a client criminalization but offered support for the claim and concluded that:

> Men's demand is, as the committee stated initially, to be conceived of as the driving force in sex trade ... the argument advocated to criminalize men's conduct has certain viability (SoU 1987/88: 3y, my translation).

The conclusion was however that prostitution first of all should be met with 'social policy and not with criminal policy' (SoU 1987/88: 3y). The Committee on Justice agreed and in the final report on the matter made a statement explicitly describing prostitution as problematic in relation to gender equality:

> Prostitution is a phenomenon that cannot be accepted at all. Prostitution leads among other things to women being used and humiliated and it counteracts aspirations of equality between men and women (JuU 1987/88: 12, my translation).

However, criminalization of the client was rejected on the same grounds as before – difficulties in defining and demarcating the 'crime' and potential negative consequences for women in prostitution. When analysing the entire framing of prostitution in these statements and not just the proposed solutions, an important change can be noted. The framing is still a social framing of prostitution, but a tendency towards increased acceptance of the criminal framing is evident. Even though criminalization as a solution is rejected in the report, the story has changed towards a framing in which demand is highlighted and male clients held accountable. Since these statements were passed in the parliament and thus constituted the government official position on prostitution, such changes were significant for the continuing process of policy formulation.

As a result of the debate in the 1980s, gender had become an indispensible analytical element, although differences between various gender analyses were not developed nor discussed at this point. The gendering of the debate meant that men, women and the relations between them in prostitution were brought to light. In connection to this, men's role in prostitution was emphasized in official statements, a crucial precondition for recognizing men's role and responsibility. This was a key to make criminalization of the client an accepted solution to prostitution. The institutionalized abolitionist framing of prostitution and the gendering of the debate served as enabling threads of argument for advocates of client criminalization. These factors did at the same time narrow the debate and made it difficult to frame prostitution in ways which excluded gender or analysed gender in a way that was not compatible with the abolitionist frame. For example, the gendered framing frequently expressed in sex work claims, in which women's choice to sell sex is emphasized, was almost absent in the Swedish debate at the time. This is also a gendered framing of prostitution but the problem of prostitution is constructed in terms of lack of acceptance and respect for women's choice. A possible explanation for the absence of this gendered frame is the difficulty to frame prostitution in that way as the abolitionist frame was institutionalized before gender entered the analytical field of debate. Accordingly, gender analysis was expressed within the abolitionist frame and based on wider social and material inequalities as the backdrop in which prostitution occurs, rather than on individual notions of choice.

1990s: Prostitution as a Criminal Problem

At the beginning of the 1990s, campaigning for criminalization of prostitution increased. No legislative changes were introduced, but each year, stronger support for client criminalization was noted in the parliament. For example, support increased threefold from 23 votes in favour of client criminalization and 294 against in 1984 to 62 votes in favour and 224 against in 1989 (prot. 1983/84: 152; prot. 1989/90: 26). Total criminalization of both seller and buyer was only advocated by a few right wing or Christian democratic MPs (motion 1990/91:

Ju611; motion 1991/92: So231). Thus the dominant perspective reflected a gender analysis about where responsibility should be allocated.

In the autumn of 1992, conflict between two Committees in the parliament resulted in recognition of the criminal framing of prostitution as a potential alternative to the social framing. This event can be conceived as a critical juncture in which a general social framing was set against, and dismissed in favour of, a general criminal framing.

The origin of this conflict was that the Committee on Justice and the Committee on Health and Welfare simultaneously considered a few motions on prostitution (1992/93: SoU2; 1992/93: JuU15). When the jurisdiction over an issue is divided between two Committees, as in the case of prostitution, the Committees normally consult each other. In this case there was no contact between the Committees until it emerged that the Committees had come to contradictory statements regarding prostitution. The Committee on Health and Welfare rejected the need for a new governmental prostitution inquiry from a social framing of the problem (1992/93: SoU2). The Committee referred to an internal inquiry on prostitution carried out by the Ministry of Justice which stressed that prostitution had diminished in Sweden since the 1970s and emphasized the need for, and efficiency of, social measures to confront prostitution. Before this Committee report was passed in the Chamber, the Committee on Justice came to a different conclusion (1992/93: JuU15), and made an announcement on the need for a new prostitution inquiry which should investigate criminalization as a possible measure. As a consequence, the Committee on Health and Welfare had to withdraw their already printed report in the Chamber and change the statement to be in line with the Committee on Justice (prot. 1992/93: 21). This event represented a setback for the social framing on prostitution, while constituting an important step for the advancement of a criminal framing, although one that incorporated elements of social contexts.

At the same time, the established social problem framing was questioned implicitly through the articulated need for a new prostitution investigation and the description of existing social measures as insufficient (1992/93: JuU15). The criminal framing of prostitution in the announcement was, however, very general and included options for both client criminalization and total criminalization. At this point this general and inclusive criminal framing facilitated cooperation between different criminalization advocates; it was this alliance across different perspectives that made the announcement possible. Just a few months after the parliament's announcement, a prostitution inquiry was established with terms of reference to analyse the growth of prostitution in Sweden and particularly shed light on the various problems related to prostitution and its causes. The inquiry was also tasked with investigating criminalization as an appropriate method to counter prostitution objectively.[3]

These events were significant for the recognition of the criminal framing as a legitimate alternative to the institutionalized social framing. That the criminal

---

3   Dir. 1993: 13.

framing was general and inclusive was an important precondition for cooperation in the four-party coalition government. The MPs lobbying for criminalization were, from now on, in a much better position to pursue their claim. It should be noted that a consequence of the general framing was that the advocates of a total criminalization, who approached prostitution from a right wing moral agenda rather than that of gender inequality, could also take advantage of the advancement. However, at this point a more specified criminal framing in terms of a concrete story and focus of criminalization would have been very difficult to pursue. Another consequence of these events was that henceforth all actors in the debate on prostitution had to relate to criminalization as a legitimate alternative. Therefore, I argue that this constituted a critical juncture in the policy process.

Late 1990s: Client Criminalization

In the late 1990s, fundamental dissents between various criminal framings were recognized regarding how to frame the problem and by extension, the cause and who to criminalize. Different ideas about how to understand gendered inequalities and gender relations between men and women that played out in prostitution were a distinguishing feature.

The 1993 Prostitution Inquiry presented their report in 1995 (SOU 1995: 15). Unexpectedly, the inquiry proposed total criminalization of prostitution including both the seller and the buyer. While prostitution was described as contradictory to the idea of equality and equality between men and women in particular, the inquiry argued that criminalization would have positive effects on social norms and make a stance that prostitution was not socially acceptable.[4] The total criminal framing in the report was gendered but the choice of total criminalization was motivated from a discussion in which the relation between the sexes was described as equal in terms of responsibility; reflecting to some degree the achievements in Sweden towards gender equality, but also perhaps a complacency about this and lack of analysis of prostitution as a practice of inequality. The inquiry also emphasized the potential preventative effects of a total criminalization including both buyers and sellers (SOU 1995: 15). A third of the consulted parties suggested only criminalization of the client, among them women's organizations, but also, for example, the official equality ombudsman and the department of social work in Gothenburg.[5]

In the parliament, the proposal of the commission report resulted in intense debate. Advocates from all parties, except the right-wing, claimed criminalization of the client in subsequent motions. Yet most of the political parties were still divided. The left party was the only political party officially in favour of client criminalization. Among the political parties women's sections there existed a joint

---

4   Criminality associated with prostitution and risks of HIV transmission were also mentioned as problems related to prostitution.

5   Dnr S97/81122/IFO.

strategy to work for client criminalization that emerged at the beginning of the 1990s. The women's section cooperated in favour of a client criminalization and in 1996 they tabled a cross-party motion claiming criminalization of the purchase of sexual services (all women's section except the right-wing) (motion 1996/97: Ju718). In the media, prostitution was also a subject of debate. Politicians, researchers and others advocated criminalization of the client instead of a total criminalization (Månsson and Olsson 1995; Sahlin 1995). There were also a few advocates of normalization of prostitution as sex work in the media (Östergren 1998).

During this period the commission of inquiry of violence against women had also finished their work and presented their report, Kvinnofrid (women's peace) (SOU 1995: 60). Unlike the prostitution inquiry the report analysed violence against women from a feminist perspective in terms of gender and power (Wendt Höjer 2002). In 1997, the women's section of the Social Democratic Party received official support for client criminalization at their annual congress (www. Socialdemokraterna.se). Following this, in 1998 the Social Democratic government proposed criminalization of the purchase of sexual services in a bill which was a package of measures to fight violence against women, prostitution and sexual harassment at work. Regarding prostitution the government stated:

> That the arguments for a criminalization are so heavy that it is reasonable to introduce a ban to purchase temporary sexual relations. Thereby is society's attitude in this matter emphasized. Through criminalization, prostitution and its harmful effects can be fought in a more efficient way than previous work to meet prostitution has accomplished (prop. 1997/98: 55, my translation).

In relation to total criminalization (those who buy and sell sex) the government stated that:

> Even if prostitution as such is not a desirable social phenomenon it is not reasonable to also criminalize the one who, at least in most cases, is the weaker party of whom others who wants to satisfy their own sexual drive, take advantage (prop. 1997/98: 55, my translation).

In the bill it was stressed that violence against women and prostitution are related issues, both rooted in gender inequality (prop. 1997/98: 55, 22). However, prostitution was not described as violence against women. The violent context of prostitution had been acknowledged before by advocates of client criminalization (i.e. prot. 1989/90: 26) but the framing of prostitution as violence against women has not been explicit in the Swedish debate. Outside parliament ROKS (the National Organization for Women's Shelters) did frame prostitution as violence against women (interview with Ebon Kram, chair of ROKS 1987–96)[6] but this

---

6   ROKS first proposed that only buyers should be criminalised in 1987 (Gould 2001).

framing was not expressed in the parliamentary debate or in the bill. The bill was voted for by a majority of 181 MPs in the parliament consisting of Social democrats, the Left party, the Center party and the Green party. Half this number, 92 MPs from the right wing party and the Liberals voted for a dissenting motion tabled by the right wing party which rejected client criminalization. The Christian democrats supported total criminalization and abstained from voting (1997/98: JuU13; prot. 1997/98: 115).

Hence, during this period, the dividing line in the political debate was between two different criminal frames of prostitution. Until this point a general criminal frame was the main alternative to the social framing of prostitution and differences within this general frame between different criminalization advocates, were rarely recognized. It is however important to highlight differences between competing criminal frames. The fundamental difference between the client criminalization frame and the total criminalization frame is revealed when analysing the proposals from these variations and their gender analyses. The prostitution inquiry framed prostitution from a total criminal framing perspective (SOU 1995: 15). The analysis emanates from a gender analysis but men (buyers) and women (sellers) in prostitution are regarded as equally responsible for their individual actions as well as both victims of a social system that has tolerated the sex industry. The inquiry argued that the basics for a sex trade are a buyer and a seller and thus both should be seen as responsible. Furthermore, echoing themes from the early 1980s, the inquiry argued that 'the women in prostitution could be seen as victims in prostitution. [...] However, one can question if not also men, who regularly buy sexual services, in some sense are victims' (SOU 1995: 15, my translation). Gender was explicitly acknowledged and prostitution analysed in terms of men who buy sex and women who sell sex as equal. This causal story resembles that of the traditional Swedish way to understand gender relations in terms of consensus and complementary interests (Hobson 2003; Lindvert 2002).

In the client criminalization frame, expressed in the 1998 government bill (prop. 1997/98: 55), prostitution was framed on the basis of a different gender analysis in which the relation between men and women in prostitution is conceived of as hierarchical and men's responsibility is emphasized. This approach identified ongoing material inequalities between men and women. In one of the dissenting opinions to the prostitution inquiry, total criminalization was criticized and it was argued that 'instead it is time that society highlights its rejection against the men who use psychologically and socially vulnerable women (and sometimes men) as merchandise. The sex trade is not a commercial transaction between two equal parties' (SOU 1995: 15, my translation). While beyond the scope of discussion in this chapter, one of the most overlooked aspects of the Swedish model is the commitment to also providing support for those in prostitution, in recognition of these inequalities. Thus within the general criminal frame of prostitution are different framings in which the problem, cause and type of criminalization are identified as possible policy options. In the figure below, some of the most salient are illustrated.

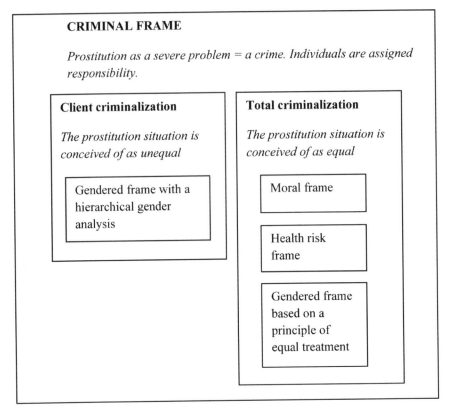

Figure 9.1   Gender in the criminal framing of prostitution

The Path to Criminalization

As the figure shows, the debate mainly centred on the two different gendered frames. Both a total criminalization frame and a client criminalization frame acknowledged prostitution in terms of gender, but their analyses of the power relations between men and women in prostitution differ fundamentally. As a consequence, responsibility and the burden of blame are conceived of in different ways, and different solutions are proposed.

The law prohibiting purchase of sexual services is an institutionalization of a new problem framing of prostitution. Along the journey to this point, the social framing of prostitution was replaced by a client criminal framing of prostitution. Since the 1970s the criminal framing of prostitution has gradually been recognized and the process can be analysed as an institutionalization of a new idea of prostitution. I argue that the process was path-dependent in the sense that the time sequence, and the dynamic interaction between actors and ideas, was important for the final outcome.

The time sequence can be summarized thus: the initial institutionalization of prostitution as a problem per se meant that arguments for normalization became difficult to pursue. The next important step was that prostitution was recognized as gendered. As a consequence, the roles and positions of men and women in prostitution were explicitly analysed and it therefore became easier to acknowledge men's responsibility as in the client criminalization claim. The gendering of the debate in combination with the abolitionist frame, already institutionalized, made certain claims more plausible than others. For example, the client criminalization claims. The prostitution as work claim on the contrary did not fit within the abolitionist frame and became problematic to express when gender inequalities were also added into analysis. These two elements favoured the criminal frame and advocates took the opportunity to pursue it in a critical juncture in the beginning of the 1990s. As a result the criminal frame of prostitution was recognized as a viable alternative to the social frame. These steps enabled the debate between different criminal framings. Finally the total criminal frame was rejected and a client criminal frame was institutionalized through the 1998 ban on the purchase of sexual services. It has been argued that the Swedish prostitution policy is an expression of a radical feminist view of prostitution as violence against women (Dodillet 2009). My analysis shows that the client criminalization claim has a much longer history and that it emanated from other ideas. The claim to criminalize the purchase of sexual services was framed in terms of unequal, hierarchical gender relations but it was not framed as violence against women.

Contemporary Debates

The introduction of the ban of purchase of sexual services did not mean the end of the prostitution debate even if the terms of the debate changed dramatically. The struggle of meaning on prostitution has continued and client criminalization is now questioned from different angles. In the parliament claims have been made for total criminalization (ex. motion 2001/02: Ju291, motion 2005/06: Ju394), for a longer maximum penalty (ex. motion 2008/09: Ju398) and for decriminalization (motion 2010/11: Ju249). There have also been several claims that the ban should be evaluated (i.e. motion 2008/09: A376, motion 2007/08: A409). In the media prostitution has been discussed repeatedly.[7]

An Evaluation of the Ban and Stronger Support for Criminalization

In 2008 a right-wing coalition government commissioned an evaluation inquiry to explore how the ban had worked in practice and how it had affected prostitution and trafficking. The starting point for the inquiry was that the purchase of sexual

---

7 Between 1999–2011 more than 1,000 articles regarding the Ban were found in one of the biggest Swedish press data bases, PRESSTEXT.

services should remain criminalized (Dir. 2008: 44). The decision to formulate the terms of reference in this way served to support of the established problem framing of prostitution in the law since the problem framing was not opened for discussion.

The inquiry completed in 2010 (SOU 2010: 49) and supported the basis of the ban. Findings revealed that the ban had had the intended effects and thus been successful in combating prostitution. One conclusion of the report was that prostitution has increased over the last decade in the other Nordic countries, whereas in Sweden no such development can be noted (SOU 2010: 49). Furthermore, street prostitution in Sweden has been halved. The commission suggested that the reason for this development was the ban. The inquiry also found that more than 70 per cent of the Swedish population supported the law, stronger support than in other Nordic countries. Based on interviews with people involved in prostitution, the inquiry emphasized that client criminalization has not worsened the situation for them. Based on these conclusions the inquiry proposed that the maximum penalty for the purchase of sexual services should be raised from six months to one year. An important reason for this was to encourage police to prioritize the crime. According to the inquiry, monitoring compliance with the ban depended on the priorities set by the police rather than on problems directly linked to the application of the penal provision (SOU 2010: 49, 13ff). As a consequence of the commission, the government proposed in 2011 to increase the maximum penalty for buying sexual services (2010/11: JuU2, prot. 2010/11: 101). This amendment was subsequently passed unanimously.

The terms of reference of the inquiry, the report and its unanimous support in the parliament are important statements for a client criminal frame of prostitution. The problem framing expressed in the ban has been firmly institutionalized in a formal political sense and all political parties now officially support this criminal framing of prostitution. The debate on prostitution has shifted and the framing of prostitution as a criminal problem is now established. Yet, from my preliminary analysis of the contemporary debate, the framing of prostitution as sex work is a new challenge.

The Sex Work Frame as a Challenge

In spite of the evaluation of the ban and the strong support from the political parties both the construction of the law and its effects have repeatedly been questioned in a wider political debate, mostly outside the parliament, that is, in the media (e.g. Dodillet 2010). Claims to decriminalize prostitution have been raised by advocates of a normalization frame of prostitution. Contrary to the criminalization frame, these advocates frame prostitution as a form of intolerance in society. 'Abolish the client criminalization now' (Gunnarsson 2011); 'Stop harassing my dear clients' (Eriksson 2007); 'The ban to buy sexual services punishes the prostitutes' (Östergren 2003), and 'Introduce official brothels' (Molin 2003) are examples of headlines from this debate. As in the past, there is disagreement on the problem construction. The problem framing in the normalization frame can be illustrated by the line of argument used by Helena von Schants, a politician from the Liberal Party. Her view is that prostitution, from a neoliberal point of view, is framed as a choice by adult women which must thus be respected. 'I find it discrimination to infantilize women by denying her judgment, rationality, and responsibility for her actions and the right to her body and sexuality' (von Schantz 2011, my translation). Client criminalization is described as state abuse and driven by moral agendas. The problem according to von Schantz is the lack of tolerance in society towards prostitution. For this reason, she suggests that adequate solutions should address prejudices in society rather than prostitution per se. Her line of argument is common among critics of the ban, in a normalization frame where prostitution per se is not framed as a problem. Instead the problem is constructed as a question of intolerance and prejudices in society. Different aspects are visible within the normalization framing, for example, women's choice or norms of sexuality, as noted by Jenny Westerstrand (Westerstrand 2008). In this normalization frame, women's choices are central aspects of the problem framing. This tendency to focus on the individual women in prostitution has been criticized for a lack of a societal, structural analysis of prostitution (Westerstrand 2011). It could also be interpreted as influenced by the normalization framing.

Before the client criminalization, the normalization frame was almost absent in the Swedish parliamentary debate, and only a few advocates were found in the media. A new trend towards increased support for sex work claims and decriminalization can be noted over the last few years. My analysis indicates that the central dividing line in the prostitution debate in Sweden nowadays is between a client criminal framing and a general normalization frame. The core conflict is still about how to construct the problem of prostitution.

Conclusion

In this chapter I present the importance of analysing different problem framings in order to understand the policy process and debates on prostitution in Sweden. Depending on which problem frame is institutionalized, other ideas about what causes and constitutes problems and solutions are either hindered or enabled. In the policy process preceding the law, important struggles of meaning about the problem of prostitution took place. These struggles concerned the character of the problem, who to blame for it, and how to address and solve it. I have argued that the process was path dependent in the sense that the final outcome was conditioned by previous events. The institutionalization of the framing of prostitution as a problem per se and the subsequent institutionalization of prostitution as a practice of gender inequality favoured the institutionalization of a general criminal frame of prostitution which made client criminalization possible.

The institutionalization of a client criminal framing of prostitution through the ban of purchase of sexual services marked a significant shift in the prostitution debate. However, the struggle of meaning has continued and the sex work framing, based on normalization of prostitution is now challenging the institutionalized problem framing. The contemporary struggle of meaning is about the very foundations of the problem of prostitution. This analysis shows that the introduction of a policy is not the end of a process. The process continues but the conditions change and, with them, the struggle of meaning.

References

Dodillet, S. (2009) *Är sex arbete? Svensk och tysk prostitutionspolitik sedan 1970 – talet*. Stockholm/Sala: Vertigo förlag.

Dodillet, S. (2010) 'Prostitutionsforskare: Utvärderingen av sexköpslagen är en vetenskaplig skandal'. Available at: http://www.newsmill.se/node/25954 [accessed: 12 February 2012].

Ebon, Kram, chair of ROKS (the National Organization for Women's Shelters) 1987–96, interview with author 13 November 2008.

Eduards, M. (2007) *Kroppspolitik. Om Moder Svea och andra kvinnor*. Stockholm: Atlas Akademi.

Ekberg, G. (2004) 'The Swedish Law that Prohibits the Purchase of Sexual Services. Best Practices for Prevention of Prostitution and Trafficking in Human Beings'. *Violence Against Women* 10: 1187–218.

Erikson, J. (2011) *Strider om mening. En dynamisk frameanalys av den svenska sexköpslagen*. PhD thesis. Uppsala: Uppsala University.

Eriksson, J. (2005) 'Sluta trakassera mina kära kunder'. *Expressen*, 27th May 2005

Gould, A. (2001) 'The Criminalisation of Buying Sex: The Politics of Prostitution in Sweden'. *Journal of Social Policy* 30: 437–56.

Gunnarsson, L. (2011) 'Avskaffa sexköpslagen nu!' *UTNT*, 30th April 2011.

Hajer, M. (1995) *The Politics of Environmental Discourse: Ecological Modernisation and the Policy Process*. Oxford: Oxford University Press.

Hajer, M. (2003) 'A Frame in the Fields: Policymaking and the Reinvention of Politics' in M. Hajer and H. Wagenaar (eds), *Deliberative Policy Analysis: Understanding Governance in the Network Society*. Cambridge: Cambridge University Press.

Hertha (1980) *Journal of the Fredrika Bremer Association*. Issue 2.

Hobson, B. (2003) *Recognition Struggles in Universalistic and Gender Distinctive Frames: Sweden and Ireland. Recognition Struggles and Social Movements: Cultural Claims, Contested Identities, Power and Agency*. Cambridge: Cambridge University Press.

Kelly, L., Coy, M. and Davenport, R. (2009) *Shifting Sands: A Comparison of Prostitution Regimes Across. Nine Countries*. London: Home Office.

Kvinnobulletinen (1977a) issue 1, *Journal of the Feminist Organisation Group 8*.

Kvinnobulletinen (1977b) issue 2, *Journal of the Feminist Organisation Group 8*.

Lindvert, J. (2002) *Feminism som politik. Sverige och Australien 1960–1990.* Umeå: Boréa.

Månsson, S.-A. and Linders, A. (1984) *Sexualitet utan ansikte. Könsköparna.* Stockholm: Carlsson & Jönsson Bokförlag AB.

Månsson, S.-A. och Olsson, H. (1995) 'Den röda horluvan tillbaka' in *DagensNyheter*, 14th March 1995.

Molin, B. (2003) 'Inför statliga bordeller' *Expressen*, 16th June 2003.

Olsson, H. (2006) 'Från manlig rättighet till lagbrott: Prostitutionsfrågan i Sverige under 30 år'. *Kvinnovetenskaplig tidskrift* 4: 52–73.

Östergren, P. (2003) 'Sexköpslagen straffar de prostituerade'. *Expressen*, 29th November 2003.

Schön, D.A. and Rein, M. (1994) *Frame Reflection. Toward the Resolution of Intractable Policy Controversies.* New York: Basic Books.

Social Democratic Party (2012) Home page http://www.socialdemokraterna.se/ [accessed: 12 February 2012].

Svanström, Y. (2004) 'Criminalizing the John – A Swedish Gender Model?' in J. Outshoorn (ed.), *The Politics of Prostitution: Women's Movements, Democratic States, and the Globalization of Sex Commerce.* Cambridge: Cambridge University Press.

Verloo, M. and Lombardo, E. (2007) 'Contested Gender Equality and Policy Variety in Europe: Introducing a Critical Frame Analysis Approach' in M. Verloo (ed.), *Multiple Meanings of Gender Equality: A Critical Frame Analysis of Gender Policies in Europe.* Budapest: Central European University Press.

Von Schantz, H. (2011) 'Hur kan man hitta på att kalla Sexköpslagen en liberal lag?'. Available at: www.Newsmill.se [accessed: 10 October 2011].

Wendt Höjer, M. (2002) *Rädslans politik. Våld och sexualitet i den svenska demokratin.* Malmö: Liber.

Westerstrand, J. (2008) *Mellan mäns händer. Kvinnors rättssubjektivitet, internationell rätt och diskurser om prostitution och trafficking.* PhD thesis. Uppsala: Uppsala University.

Westerstrand, J. (2011) 'Ge inte bort sexköpslagen till antifeminister'. Available at: www.Newsmill.se [accessed: 10 October 2011].

Legal Sources

Government Bills (Propositioner)

prop. 1981/82:187
prop. 1983/84:105
prop. 1997/98:55

Commission Reports (SOU, DsS)

SOU 1976:9
SOU 1981:71
SOU 1982:6
SOU 1982:61
SOU 1995:15
SOU 1995:60
SOU 2010:49
DsS 1980:9

Terms of Reference of Government Inquiries (dir) and Comments from the Consultative Procedure (Remiss)

Dir. 1993:13
Dir. 2008:44
Dnr S97/81122/IFO (summary of remiss of the SOU 1995:15)

Parliamentary Bills (Motioner)

1972:59
1972:310
1972:330
1975/76:1305
1990/91:Ju611
1991/92:So231
1996/97:Ju718
2001/02:Ju291
2005/06:Ju394
2007/08:S409
2008/09:A376
2008/09:Ju398
2010/11:Ju249

Proposals of the Parliamentary Committees (Betänkanden)

SoU 1972:36
SoU 1976/77:7
SoU 1987/88:3y
1992/93:SoU2
JuU 1985/86:3
JuU 1985/86:20
JuU 1987/88:12
1992/93:JuU15
1997/98:JuU13
2010/11:JuU2

Parliamentary Protocols (Riksdagens Protokoll)

prot. 1983/84:152
prot. 1989/90:26
prot. 1992/93:21
prot. 1997/98:115
prot. 2010/11:101

Chapter 10

Selling Sex Sells: Representations of Prostitution and the Sex Industry in Sexualized Popular Culture as Symbolic Violence[1]

Maddy Coy, Josephine Wakeling and Maria Garner

Introduction

Sexualization of popular culture, increasingly evident in sexualized imagery and discourses (Gill 2007), is a topical subject of academic and policy analysis and debate (APA 2007; Attwood 2005; Coy 2009a; Papadopoulos 2010). However, several theorists and commentators have suggested that the term 'pornification' (Dines 2010; Paul 2005) more accurately captures the 'porno chic' (McNair 1996) that pervades sexualized media (McRobbie 2008). Anette Dina Sorensen (2005), for instance, argues that 'pornophication' is invading mainstream popular culture in three core ways: the increasing volume and availability of pornography; interest in the porn industry from real life media genres and journalism, giving it credence that she refers to as a 'clean-up tendency'; and the use of conventions of porn in mass culture. In this article we frame the representations of prostitution that we discuss, such as pimp and ho chic, as 'pornification' as they introduce and reify 'pornographic permutations' (McRobbie 2008) that go beyond sexualized imagery to celebrate the separation of sex from intimacy and the reduction of women to body parts as the 'true' story about sex (Dines 2010). At the same time some imagery appears more nuanced, and here the term sexualization might be retained. Where our points refer to themes of both sexualized/pornified media, we reflect this by using both terms.

In the context of what Rosalind Gill (2007) has conceptualized as a 'postfeminist media sensibility' (where the body is endorsed as a site of profit for women, individual choice venerated and differences between women and men re-essentialized as 'biologically natural'), what appear to be contradictory positions

---

1   Reprinted by permission from Elsevier. Originally published in *Women's Studies International Forum* 34 (2011): 441–8.

have emerged over the potential benefits and limitations of sexualization and pornification. Some commentators focus on the opportunity for 'democratization' of sexuality and the apparent opening up of space for women to positively participate in sexualized mass culture (Attwood 2005), while others are concerned with ongoing sexual objectification and narrowing of space for girls and women to resist a sexualized sense of self (Coy 2009a; see also McRobbie 2009).

In the midst of this debate, policy reviews suggest a range of negative impacts associated with exposure to sexualized and pornified media, including: educational underachievement; issues with self esteem and body image; pressure to conform to sexualized femininity, and the (re)production of a masculinity equated with sexual entitlement and conquest (APA 2007; Australian Senate Committee 2008; Papadopolous 2010). For feminist theorist Kathleen Barry (1995), sexualization reduces women to bodies, the culmination of which is found in prostitution where access to women's sexualized bodies is the point of the exchange. It is in this backdrop of sexualized and pornified media that the mainstreaming of the sex industry has emerged as central to much of the policy and academic discussion. Recent collections of essays have explored representations of women involved in prostitution in the news, television and documentary genres (see Mendes et al. 2009, 2010). In this article we explore representations of the sex industry – what Karen Boyle (2010: 113) refers to as the 'mainstream narratives of commercial sex' – in order to demonstrate that the dynamics of prostitution are increasingly found in contemporary globalized media as part of the pornification of popular culture. By the dynamics of prostitution we refer to notions that: women's bodies are commodities in a global marketplace to be bought and sold; women are sexually available for men's sexual pleasure, represented as sexual objects; and that women are empowered by sexualization and objectification (see also Gill 2007). We suggest that these themes are perpetuating a falsely positive perception of global sex industries, and contend that this constitutes a form of symbolic violence (Bourdieu 1990).

Representations of Prostitution in Popular Culture as Symbolic Violence

Popular culture is 'a means by which we learn to engage with the world' (Rose 2008: 52), thus the meanings made available by socio-cultural representations construct perceptions and understandings (Cameron and Frazer 1987). The narratives and representations of prostitution in mainstream media combine to reflect and reconstruct certain ways of perceiving and understanding the sex industry, which we define as symbolic violence.

The concept of symbolic violence refers to unseen forms of domination that are embedded in everyday actions, with such invisibility framed as 'misrecognition' of power inequalities (Bourdieu 1990 cited in Morgan and Bjokert 2006). As defined by Jenkins (1992: 104), symbolic violence is 'the imposition of symbolism and meaning (i.e. culture) upon groups or classes in such a way that they are experienced as legitimate. This legitimacy obscures the power relations which permit that imposition to be successful'. Symbolic violence is thus a means of reproducing gendered hierarchies, of reinforcing gender orders that privilege men and masculinity, and casting women as less than human, without coercion or physical force (Bourdieu 1990). Central to this misrecognition and perpetuation of oppression and domination is women's complicity and engagement in these dynamics (ibid). We thus use the concept of symbolic violence here in a number of ways: first, to reflect our argument that the glamorization of prostitution, for instance 'pimp and ho chic', disguises the harm that women in the sex industry experience and the gender inequality of consumerism that underpins global sex markets (see Jeffreys 2009). Secondly, the argument that prostitution is the 'oldest profession'[2] an ahistorical and inevitable system of exchange between men and women, is an example of how dominant perspectives are presented as 'natural' (Bourdieu 2004). As Morgan and Bjokert (2006: 448) suggest, 'symbolic violence is ... so powerful precisely *because* it is *unrecognizable* for what it is' (original emphasis). Thirdly, we recall Angela McRobbie (2004) who uses the concept of symbolic violence in her analysis of the television programme *What Not to Wear*, on the basis of the individualization that draws sharp lines between women by denigrating 'poor and disadvantaged women' (p. 101), presented and defended as 'just good fun' (p. 100). Some women are thus made 'worth less' in ways that are not widely recognized as hostile, with their complicity. McRobbie draws on Bourdieu to develop 'symbolic violence as a process of social reproduction' (p. 103). This forms part of her wider proposition that as (at least in some regions of the world) women have equality in terms of legal rights and participation in the labour force, popular culture has become a site where unequal gendered power relations are 're-stabilized' (McRobbie 2009). Women's investment in femininity and self-sexualization are portrayed as emblematic of individualized empowerment and choice, hence feminist challenges to the socio-cultural pressures that help shape their decisions/investments are lost, even silenced (ibid).

Following this, we argue that representations of prostitution in popular culture which glamorize the sex industry and fail to acknowledge harm and violence, socially reproduce divisions between women who engage in 'pimp and ho chic' as a temporary identity and the girls/women who, around the globe, are coerced into prostitution by poverty, predatory men, drug use and limited options. The examples of such glamorization that we draw on are also defended in the name of humour, fun and irony, and women's 'freedom' to self-sexualize, as we will go on to demonstrate. These representations of the sex industry, and the discourses that they are both embedded in and reproduce, are thus powerful conduits of the

---

2   The notion of prostitution as the oldest profession is disputed by historian Gerda Lerner (1986), who notes that prostitution only appeared after the establishment of slavery. Bindel and Kelly (2004) also suggest that if there is an oldest profession, it is more accurately agriculture.

perception and appreciation of prostitution as entertainment and leisure rather than the systematic ab(use) of women's bodies. The key discourse is 'superficial empowerment' (Boyle 2010: 99) that does not subvert concrete gender inequalities of violence against women, access to economic resources and political decision making. The message about women's involvement is therefore about 'choice' – if prostitution is a means to personal and financial power, a manifestation of sexual liberation, why would women not choose to participate in it? The mainstreaming of the sex industry has carried these messages into a range of media and socio-cultural sources. These sources, holistically framed as sexualized and pornified popular culture, become *agents* of symbolic violence, which work as an 'indirect cultural mechanism' (Jenkins 1992) of 'invisible' domination, which is legitimized by its location within the field of mainstream mass culture. This location becomes the vehicle for and place of misrecognition, where the harms and violence of prostitution and the unequal gender relations on which it is based, are not only obscured but mimicked, celebrated and consumed as entertainment, a fashion style and leisure. Here, complicity advances into consent, and 'the legitimate culture becomes experienced as an axiom' (ibid: 107).

Harms of Prostitution

Central to framing the glamorization of prostitution as symbolic violence is recognition of the harms women experience in the sex industry: violence, coercion and exploitation as well as the dehumanization of the body as commodity. The disjunctions between women's experiences of prostitution and sanitized versions in many popular media representations (characterized by pimp and ho chic) are most acute with respect to violence; women's experiences of violence in prostitution are either absent entirely and invisibilized by an emphasis on 'fun', or trivialized in the name of humour, as we shall demonstrate. For context, research demonstrates that the majority of women in the sex industry report experiences of physical and sexual violence – one study of 854 people in nine countries found that 63 per cent had been raped since entering prostitution, suggesting that violence is a routine rather than an exceptional event (Farley et al. 2003). Violence and abuse are not confined to specific settings – a quarter (23.3 per cent) of exotic dancers, and over two-thirds (66.7 per cent) of women in prostitution in U.S. drug houses reported sexual violence, while one in five (21 per cent) of women in prostitution on the street, in their own homes and as escorts had been raped more than 10 times (Raphael and Shapiro 2004). A UK study across three cities found almost half of women in street prostitution and over a quarter of those in indoor prostitution had experienced violence in the last six months (Church et al. 2001). Qualitative analysis of women's accounts of prostitution illustrates parallels with their experiences of sexual violence in terms of their sense of violation and disruption of relationship with the body (Coy 2009b). The harms that we refer to throughout this article thus involve these physical, sexual, material and psychosocial layers of abuse.

This pervasive violence reveals the depth of stigma and worthlessness attached to women involved in the sex industry; while such stigma attached to sexual reputation affects all women to varying degrees, it has an acute meaning for women in prostitution since 'the 'prostitute' is the 'end stop' in discourses on good and honest women' (O'Neill 2001: 186). An acute illustration is the way in which language used to describe women in prostitution – whore, 'ho' – persists as a means of denigrating all women, despite its apparent reclamation in popular culture. For example, in May 2011 a British woman described being labelled 'a prostitute' in a civil Anti-Social Behaviour Order (ASBO) as having ruined her 'whole life' (BBC News 2011). The designation of women in prostitution as 'other' and 'lesser' has been cited as justification by serial murderers (Salfati et al. 2008; Smith 1990). Research suggests that women in prostitution are almost 18 times more likely to be murdered than women not in prostitution (Potterat et al. 2004). In the majority of cases, the perpetrator is a sex buyer (Kinnell 2008). One UK study showed that 89 per cent men paying for sex thought women who sell sex were dirty, 91 per cent more sexually available and 77 per cent inferior (Elliott et al. 2002). In this context, portrayals of prostitution in popular culture that reinforce the pornified mythology of women as sluts and 'hos' (Dines 2010), failing to recognize the multiple abuses that women contend with, constitute symbolic violence. For instance, glamorizing prostitution appears, for some, to carry the potential to subvert stigma. However, the sex industry is built on objectification and commodification of women (Barry 1995; Jeffreys 2009), as well as on women's lack of subjectivity and suspension of the self to serve men's desires (O'Connell Davidson 1998; Coy 2008). Glamorization of prostitution in popular culture brings these notions into wider currency. Mainstreaming the idea that women exist as sex objects, even embracing that status, mainstreams a conceptual justification for violence. This is in itself potent symbolic violence, bringing into popular consciousness the sense that as sexual objects women are less than human. Furthermore, glamorizing the sex industry and equating sexualization, pornification and pimp and ho chic with empowerment enacts symbolic violence on women who experience prostitution as harmful, desperate and distressing.

The Mainstreaming and Normalization of the Sex Industry

Across the globe, the sex industry is tightly knitted into corporate culture and generates billions every year that contribute significantly to national and local economies (Barry 1995; Brents and Hausbeck 2007; Jeffreys 2009). Globalization – in terms of extension of free markets and opening up of national borders – has increased both the availability and visibility of prostitution (Marttila 2008). Commercial sex premises proliferate in cities and urban spaces, in the form of strip/lap dancing clubs, sex tours and in some areas licensed parlours, with the anodyne epithet of 'adult entertainment' (Jeffreys 2009). This normalization of commercialized sexual activity is what Marjut Jyrkinen (2005) refers to as

'McSexualization', in recognition of the links with global consumerism. One study of brothels in Nevada draws attention to the use of marketing strategies associated with mainstream businesses and audiences, including the packaging of buying sex as a touristic experience (Brents and Hausbeck 2007). Through this, commercial sex premises embed themselves further into tourism industries, increase their economic and political power, and (re)present paying for sex as a normalized commodity in the 'global cultural marketplace' (Altman 2001: 83). The process of such normalization contributes to the invisibilizing of the gendered consumption of women's bodies by male buyers, thus misrecognizing power inequalities.

As part of 'McSexualization', the paradigm of prostitution has entered popular culture in interlinked, but myriad, ways. Kathleen Barry (1995) argued that the normalization of prostitution would lead to it being a reference point for all other heterosexual relationships, whether or not they involve the exchange of money. In Meagan Tyler's (2008) trenchant analysis of ideal hetero(sex) in self help books recommended by sex therapists, she defines 'the sex of prostitution' as 'synonymous with the servicing of men ... the model of sex which is performed in prostitution rather than the element of monetary exchange' (p. 365). In these self-help books, the key messages are that (hetero)sex is biologically determined and privileges men's desires; for instance, penetrative intercourse is repeatedly acknowledged to offer limited pleasure for women and detailed advice is given to overcome discomfort of oral sex. Similar advice is often used to condition women in prostitution about expectations and appropriate activities (ibid). Thus while the commodification of sex is one feature of the socio-cultural prostitution motif, another is the reframing of (hetero)sex to align with the instrumental model of sex in prostitution that foregrounds male pleasure. Finally, Tyler identifies a major theme in self help texts that mirrors the portrayals of prostitution in popular culture that we discuss: the requirement for women to engage in and embrace the sex of prostitution, just as Rosalind Gill (2007) and Gail Dines (2010) point out the similar requirement in sexualized media and pornography. Ariel Levy succinctly captured this equation with empowerment in her exploration of the mainstreaming of the sex industry:

> Because we have determined that all empowered women must be overtly and publicly sexual, and because the only sign of sexuality we seem to be able to recognize is a direct allusion to red-light entertainment, we have laced the sleazy energy and aesthetic of a topless club or a Penthouse shoot throughout our entire culture (Levy 2005: 26).

Sexualized consumerism actively promotes models of prostitution as a prototype for intimate relationships. There are few cultural references to sex buyers in pimp and ho chic, indicating a selective discourse which minimizes men's accountability and visibility as consumers. Yet the limited representations are revealing. For instance, in 2005, a UK-based lads mag, *FHM*, ran a feature which invited readers to calculate how much sex cost them, by dividing costs such as wine, meals, gifts, by the number of acts of sexual intercourse (Viner 2006). As one journalist commented, 'this aggressively blur[s] the line between girlfriend/boyfriend and prostitute/punter relationships' (Viner 2006) and is also couched in open misogyny since the budgeting advice is 'less than £5 is about the same price as a Cambodian whore … Each shag now needs to be a better purchase than a new CD' (Turner 2005). Research with men who pay for sex demonstrates these themes of 'value for money' and market forces influence their decision making processes (Coy et al. 2007). Sex buyers report seeking quality of service and ensuring that contractual obligations are fulfilled, with the most transparent expression of this sexualized consumerism a comparison of the relative cost of paying for sex to heterosexual dating:

> To go out looking for a girl, it's a lot of expense … paying for sex, it's an agreement between you and the girl, you pay your money and then that's done with. I've taken girls out, I take her for a meal, that cost me £40 … you don't get bugger all after that … [whereas when paying for sex] you can do anything you want for 20 minutes. Everything and anything. For £40 (cited in Coy et al. 2007: 20).

Interestingly a study in Australia reports virtually the same account from one sex buyer: 'I could spend 100 bucks a night taking some bird out, you could do that three or four times you know before you're anywhere … I'd rather come here every now and again and then, pay my money and you know, that's that' (cited in Plumridge et al. 1997: 172). Similar sentiments were also noted in diary accounts of sex tourists to Thailand (Bishop and Robinson 2002). Thus in reproducing these cost benefit analyses in a lads mag, albeit in what is claimed as a 'tongue in cheek' style (that, as Benwell (2004) and McRobbie (2009) note, deflects criticism), *FHM* installs the dynamics of prostitution into the thought processes and relationships of readers. Women in the sex industry are mocked using notions of race and ethnicity (the article also refers to 'Cypriot tarts' for £20 and over £31 'Cuban show girls') that fail to acknowledge the structural inequalities underpinning women's involvement in prostitution. The symbolic violence of these discourses is both the objectification and dehumanization of women to serve men's instrumental sexual desires and the disguising or 'misrecognizing' of gendered, racialized power. This casual normalization of the exchange of women's bodies for money tells a strong story about how prostitution, not just sexualization, has become a lexicon and potential paradigm for heterosexual relationships.

How this is framed as 'entertainment' is of the most relevance in this article. Borrowing from Dee Amy Chinn's (2006) analysis of how lingerie advertisements position women as actively embracing a sexualized self while reinforcing masculine norms, we ask for who are these forms of sexualized entertainment? This is evidenced by research showing that globally the majority of sex buyers are men (Coy et al. 2007; Ward et al. 2005; O'Connell Davidson 1998; Jeffreys 2009). Thus commercial sex is, as Maggie O'Neill (2001: 155) notes, 'with few exceptions ... a market for men'. Accounts from men who visit strip clubs in Scandinavia and the U.S. indicate that many are seeking a space that affirms 'traditional' gender roles based on masculine superiority, free from obligations of gender equality (Frank 2003; Marttila 2008). Yet the framing of prostitution as entertainment obscures these structural power relations and privileges a masculine entitlement to sex (Barry 1995; Coy et al. 2007), by normalizing the sexualization of women's bodies.

Airbrushing Harm: The Glamorization of Prostitution

Here we explore how portrayals of women in prostitution in television and films, with a thematic construction of 'superficial empowerment' (Boyle 2010: 99), propagate notions of 'choice' to explain women's involvement in the sex industry and adoption of 'ho chic' fashion. The most iconic film, *Pretty Woman*, (re)presented a mythology of prostitution whereby women are saved by a rich man, but films such as *Taxi Driver* and *Leaving Las Vegas* also contribute to these perceptions. As Rochelle Dalla (2000) notes:

> Popular images presented on the big screens often portray prostitution as a temporary course of action, where in the end the heroine finds love and happiness and suffers few, if any, enduring scars from her brief stint on the streets; an image not borne out by empirical research and the realities of drug use, homelessness and the multiple challenges of leaving prostitution that women face (p. 352).

In contrast to the fairytale route to prosperity, research shows prostitution actually impoverishes women, if the time out of the employment market and lack of opportunities to develop and update skills/training are calculated over the life course (DeRiviere 2006). The profits from the sex industry for owners of brothels, sexualized dance clubs and escort agencies, however, run into billions – indicative figures suggest that men spend $15 billion a year on strip clubs in the U.S.; trafficking of women is worth $31 billion annually (Jeffreys 2009) and sex industry profits in Japan alone are an estimated annual 4.2 trillion yen (Sassen 2002).

Two examples of representations of women's involvement in prostitution illustrate the discourses of superficial empowerment and entertainment. The first is a 2006 British television situation comedy *Respectable*, set in a brothel, which featured women involved in prostitution to buy new shoes (Hayley) and pay student fees (Kate), and men who pay for sex as timid and seeking kindness (Michael). The series was broadcast for a late night audience, and while not commissioned for a second series in the UK, it was subsequently shown in Germany, Australia and Hungary (Internet Movie Database 2010). In response to feminist critique of the characters and plotlines, producers contrarily claimed that as a comedy there was no requirement for *Respectable* to be realistic, but it was based on real stories from women in prostitution (BBC News 2006). One possible reading of the series is that it attempted to personalize the characters and thus diminish stigma and 'othering'. These fictional characters do not, however, reflect the range of experiences of women in prostitution and there are no references to poverty and coercion. In particular, the representation of an Eastern European woman (Yelena) masks the issue of trafficking of women into the UK from Eastern Europe. At a time when media coverage and government campaigns were urging sex buyers to be aware of women being trafficked from these regions, the portrayal here was of an empowered woman from Eastern Europe in control of her situation. Whether or not individual women like Yelena, Hayley, Kate and men like Michael exist is not our point here (see also Mendes et al. 2010), rather the ways in which these narratives paint a picture of the sex industry which airbrushes out the all negative aspects (see also Cochrane 2006). Similar debate followed the UK dramatization of the novel *Secret Diary of a Call Girl* (Belle De Jour 2005), where a young woman with a university education engages in prostitution for hundreds of pounds an hour, loves sex and enjoys luxury in all aspects of her life. The concern of many critics was not whether or not the character of Belle herself is real,[3] or women with similar experiences exist, but that such glamorization in popular culture diminishes the space to recognize harm, violence and exploitation within the sex industry and places notions of choice and empowerment at the forefront of cultural discourse (Saner 2007, see also Boyle 2010).

The second example is an analysis of the film *Moulin Rouge* (and associated commercial merchandise that has evolved into a genre of clothing named after the film) where notions of 'choice' are also reflected. The film portrays a young 'courtesan' (Satine) for whom prostitution has the potential to be socially and financially rewarding, as women are depicted as able to choose buyers (Della Giusta and Scuriatti 2005). Despite these emblems of empowerment, the virgin/whore dichotomy of femininity is reinforced – as Satine's virginity is her marketing point, her death in the film is inevitable in order to enable her to be the lost love of the two male protagonists (ibid). In dying, Satine cannot be 'despoiled' through prostitution, and can be immortally preserved as 'untainted' and 'pure'. This reveals the ultimate contradiction of the representation in prostitution in *Moulin Rouge* – that while it spawned clothing ranges inspired by the film, the stigma attached to the actual exchange of sex for money is left intact (ibid). Maria Della Giusta and Laura Scuriatti's (2005) analytic focus is on the 'process through which prostitution, which still bears a negative cultural stigma, is deployed to make clothes attractive to buyers' (p. 36). Following the release of the film, women's clothing on the high street and in designer ranges featured corsets, basques, bustiers, chokers and stockings as synonymous with sexy femininity (Freeman 2001). Similar paths from the sex industry to high street fashion are reflected in the mainstream popularity of the 'stripper shoe'

---

3   In November 2009, Dr Brooke Magnanti, a university researcher, revealed that she was the writer of the Belle De Jour novels, and they were based on her experiences of prostitution while completing her PhD.

(Roach 2007), and sales of Playboy bunny branded clothing, stationery and home accessories (Attwood 2005). Sexually objectifying clothing has become trendy and is marketed as empowering, born of both patriarchy and consumerism. Della Giusta and Scuriatti (2005) suggest:

> The use of images of prostitution in fashion and fashion advertising is located at the intersection of these issues: the commodification of women's bodies is a product of non-egalitarian relations, which express themselves at the social, economic and sexual levels, and on which capitalism is ultimately based. The need for a specific role for women as consumers leads to continuously reinventing their subordinate role, and in this sense glamorization of images of subordination is just one tool (p. 41).

The transformation of prostitution into a fashion marketing device is harmful in two ways: the (re)presentation of prostitution as empowering; and the ongoing stigma attached to women in 'real' prostitution (ibid). Catherine Roach insightfully identifies that clothing associated with the sex industry has led to a context where 'it may be acceptable for your average college girl to look like a hooker, but hookers [sic] themselves are not benefitting from this upturn in their popularity' (Roach 2007: 117). However, Angela McRobbie (2008) argues that precisely this assimilation of 'hooker' chic into everyday fashion destigmatizes women in prostitution. While it may be superficially true that women in prostitution are 'less visible as an object of contempt or derision' (McRobbie 2008), we question how the camouflaging of young women as objects for men's sexual release represents power or equality, and why adopting a role so often associated with harm and violence should be celebrated. Metaphors of prostitution are marketed to women as a fun, liberatory way to be sexually adventurous and desirable, while grim realities of poverty, abuse, and coercion are unchallenged. Through this, the sex industry myth of inevitability ('the oldest profession', see Jeffreys 1997) and the male sex right of sexual access to women's bodies (Barry 1995) are implicitly normalized, whilst women in prostitution remain 'other'. Feona Attwood's (2005) analysis of how sex is marketed to women through the lens of fashion, beauty and appearance is also relevant here. She suggests that as sexualized femininity is still largely shaped by patriarchal mores, nascent attempts at an empowering framing of sexuality are constructed around masquerade and theatrical accessories. The incursion of apparel associated with prostitution might therefore be understood as 'trying on the clothes of an adult female sexuality' (p. 402), in the absence of a fully formulated autonomous sexuality for women. However, the promotion and popularity of 'ho chic' links such an adult female sexuality with prostitution, and the motifs and messages associated with commercialized sex without the exchange of money (Barry 1995). While the stigma of prostitution still exists in reality, prostitution is simultaneously being sold as glamorous and emblematic of individual choice in popular culture.

There are also explicit links with the sex industry in some contemporary children's clothing, including t-shirts for babies that have 'pimp squad' or tassels for twirling nipples emblazoned across the front (Coy 2009a). These products normalize prostitution as a light-hearted topic for embellishing clothing, an emblem of edgy, 'cool' fashion, but link children to an industry that is defined as exploitative and abusive when they are involved in it in real life. It is difficult to imagine other contexts and forms of abuse of children that would be subject to 'ironic' promotion in the name of humour. Yet the mainstream cultural backdrop of prostitution as harmless entertainment facilitates this symbolically violent marketing device.

The Language of Prostitution: Mainstreaming 'Pimp and Ho'

Here we explore how the celebration of the pimp and ho vocabulary constitutes symbolic violence. References to pimping in popular culture originated in commercial hip hop music lyrics (Rose 2008) and the term has since become widely used as a verb.[4] The MTV show *Pimp my Ride* introduced pimping as a verb in 2004, as the title of a programme where old cars are restored to a brand new appearance and technical standard with luxury additions (www.mtv.co.uk/shows/ pimp-my-ride). Versions of *Pimp my Ride* are/have been broadcast in the US, the UK, Germany, the Baltic Region, Finland, Italy, the Netherlands, New Zealand, Brazil and through MTV Arabia. Subsequently, 'to pimp' has become a verb that if not exactly mainstream, is associated with youth-oriented popular culture, as a light-hearted way to describe improving an object to make it more valuable. There is an implicit connection here with the traditional use of the word 'pimp' – the value of an object [woman] can be increased by enhancing 'packaging' and negotiating the demands of the market. For instance, one use of the word that is rooted in the gendered dimensions of pimping is the UK website *Pimp my Bride*, which aims to enable women to lose weight before a wedding. Their rationale for choosing this term is revealing: defensively claiming postmodern irony – 'Though the name's a little tongue in cheek, we take your training serious' (sic) (www.pimpmybrideuk. co.uk). *Pimp my Bride* identifies the gendered nature of the concept of pimping when seeking to attract customers – 'We don't just cater to brides to be either, but "Pimp My Groom" wouldn't have worked …'! There are transparent links between the use of 'pimping' as a marketing device and the original meaning of the term, specifically with respect to notions of women as commodities to be made as desirable as possible for marketing purposes.

Popular culture is saturated with exemplars of how the term 'pimp' has become normalized as a marketing device through corporate sponsorship (Lloyd 2010): 'Pimp that snack', a website dedicated to massive enlargements of snacks and chocolate bars; 'Pimp my search' – a website that enables users to create a

---

4   We owe this phrase of 'pimping as a verb' to Professor Liz Kelly, from her presentation at the UK Vice Conference, Gloucester, July 2007.

personalized website with their own logo. Virgin Airlines advertised their upper class passenger facilities with the tag-line 'Pimp My Lounge' (Frith 2006). An extras package for the computer game 'The Sims', featuring clothes, accessories and make-up to enhance players' characters in the game, is called 'Pimp my Sims'. A similar site exists for additions to the software package Safari – 'Pimp my Safari' (www.pimpmysafari.com). The website 'Pimp-text' invites users to 'create your own pimp text' by adding sparkle to fonts for use on social networking sites. The application of the word 'pimp' for products associated with information technology also has an iterative impact for young people that use the Internet on a daily basis (Roberts et al. 2005). One acknowledgement of how entrenched in contemporary youth culture the term 'pimping' has become is the publication of the book *Pimp Your Vocab* in September 2009, a guide to 'teenglish' for adults (Tobin 2009).

A prominent marketing use of the term is the energy drink 'Pimp Juice', named after the rap singer Nell's track and sold internationally, targeted at young people. It is an example of what Eithne Quinn (2000) calls the 'lifestylization' of the 'misogynist, street-heroic figure' (p. 116). While Ice-T claims that 'pimping' denotes a 'fly, cool lifestyle which has nothing to do with prostitution' (cited in Quinn 2000: 124), many of the ways in which pimping has become a verb in popular culture frequently invoke the prostitution-related meaning of the term. For instance, a 2005 Christmas advertising campaign for Selfridges (a UK department store), for example, featured a black man holding a glass of champagne and dressed in 'pimp chic', while women wearing only lingerie posed beside him (Frith 2006), drawing on intersections of race and gender in pimp discourse. In references to pimping and 'hos' that proliferate in commercial hip hop song lyrics, these themes are also apparent – for instance, in P.I.M.P. by 50 cent, the video for which features women being walked on leashes (Levin and Kilbourne 2008), and Three 6 Mafia's (2005) 'It's hard out here for a pimp', which won an Academy Award for best original song, and refers to 'making change off these women'. That a song which valorizes the 'trials' of men who profit from selling women's bodies was re(a)warded by the film industry is extremely telling; despite references to women's fear of murder and poverty, the lyrics reiterate the inevitability of prostitution ('that's the way the game goes') and the sovereignty of the market in securing men's sexual access to women ('you pay the right price and they'll both do you'). Here symbolic violence is evident in the way in which pimping as a verb has become so mainstreamed that it is not only an acceptable topic for popular music songs, but also that the lyrical content explicitly endorses and promotes profiting from women's bodies while disguising (misrecognizing) this through the lens of entertainment.

Pimping has also become a role play game identity, available in board and online game formats. One particular example of hostile attitudes to women in prostitution is found in the 'Pimps and Hos' game, developed in 2004 and marketed on 'adult' board game websites. It is described on one website as 'made for the person with a twisted mind that wants gut busting laughs' (www.pimpcostumes.com).

All the players are designated pimps, and the aim is to 'acquire hos' and pimp them out while travelling around the board (a fictional city named HoTropolis), with the winner being the first to reach $1,500 profit from their 'ho'. Sample cards enable players to infect rival 'hos' with STIs, and 'bitch-slap' women for 'lipping off' – trivializing violence against women and reiterating age old stigmatizing images of women in prostitution as reservoirs of infection. Sexual violence as a core aspect of prostitution is a consistent theme; in contrast to many of the representations that we discuss such violence is acknowledged here, but treated as a legitimate source of humour, as one sample card demonstrates: 'when the guards were tossing your cell for contraband, they find a tube of sex lube; too bad they decided to pound you dry ... Pay the clinic $200 for the soothing cream' (www.guanabee.com). Pimp and ho chic, equated with 'cool', reduce violence and harm to humour, rearticulating physical and sexual violence as a form of symbolic violence by celebrating abusive, predatory masculinity. Free online pimping based games also echo these themes: Pimp War requires players to 'play the part of a ruthless pimp on a quest for power and money. You will become a master at the art of pimping your hos' (www.pimpwar.com). The game is linked to social networking sites and claims to have registered over a million 'pimps' since its 1999 launch (ibid). Pimps Street is similarly transparent about the significance of 'hos' on the site, reminding players that 'to keep hos happy you want to make sure you have a good stock of condoms, crack and medicine and to increase this stock as your hos use them up (during turns, attacks, whoring etc.) and as more hos join your crew' (www.pimpsstreet.com).

As Tricia Rose, author of books about the racialized, gendered dimensions of commercial hip-hop notes:

> Despite the cuddly and fuzzy hat image in some mainstream outlets and celebrated films like Hustle and Flow that attempt to generate sympathy for pimps, pimp ideology and its expression in popular culture are fundamentally exploitative to women (Rose 2008: 168).

To recognize the symbolic violence of the mainstreaming of the term 'pimping' requires recalling the manipulative techniques that men who pimp women use to secure control, including disrupting or destroying identity, violence and drugs (Barry 1995). These are used to form the basis, and humour, of the games discussed above, again mainstreaming notions of women as less than human, existing for men's pleasure and profit. In pornified popular culture, shored up by notions of choice and empowerment associated with prostitution, 'to pimp' has become shorthand for 'to market' something for maximum profit – a usage seemingly devoid of, yet fundamentally based on, the term's semantic origins of exploiting women in prostitution.

Conclusion

References to, and representations of, prostitution across a wide range of sources in contemporary popular culture are indicative of the normalization of commercial sex. In many of these portrayals, commercial sex is associated with female empowerment and entertainment, reflecting a 'postfeminist media sensibility' (Gill 2007), a key notion of which is that women can use their bodies or profit as a means of, and route to, personal empowerment. Yet we argue that the increasing use of prostitution as a motif and marketing device in popular culture obscures empirical realities of violence, exploitation and harm and the structural inequalities on which the sex industry is built. Our analysis also draws attention to the mainstreaming of 'pimp' as a cultural motif, and its defence and normalization through humour and irony even where violence is a core theme. Selling sex may indeed, in marketing terms, sell, but the airbrushing of harm and equation with empowerment lead us to conclude that many contemporary representations of prostitution constitute symbolic violence.

References

Altman, D. (2001) *Global Sex.* Chicago: University of Chicago Press.

American Psychological Association (2007) *Report of the APA Task Force on the Sexualization of Girls.* Washington, D.C.: American Psychological Association.

Amy-Chinn, D. (2006) 'This is Just for Me(n): How the Regulation of Postfeminist Lingerie Advertising Perpetuates Woman as Object'. *Journal of Consumer Culture* 6(2): 155–75.

Attwood, F. (2005) 'Fashion and Passion: Marketing Sex to Women'. *Sexualities* 8(4): 392–406.

Australian Senate Committee (2008) *Sexualisation of Children in the Contemporary Media.* Canberra: Parliament House.

Barry, K. (1995) *The Prostitution of Sexuality: The Global Exploitation of Women.* New York: NYU Press.

BBC News (2006) 'Charity Attacks Five Brothel Show'. Available at: http://news.bbc.co.uk/2/hi/entertainment/5305112.stm [accessed: 10 July 2009].

BBC News (2011) *Plymouth Asbo Woman Angry at Prostitute Accusation.* Available at: http://www.bbc.co.uk/news/uk-england-devon-13274212 [accessed: 11 May 2011].

Benwell, B. (2004) 'Ironic Discourse: Evasive Masculinity in Men's Lifestyle Magazines'. *Men and Masculinities* 7(1): 3–21.

Bindel, J. and Kelly, L. (2003) *A Critical Examination of Responses to Prostitution in Four Countries: Victoria, Australia; Ireland; the Netherlands; and Sweden.* London: CWASU, London Metropolitan University.

Bishop, R. and Robinson, L. (2002) 'Travellers' Tails: Sex Diaries of Tourists Returning from Thailand' in S. Thorbek and B. Pattaniak (eds), *Transnational Prostitution: Changing Patterns in a Global Context*. London, New York: Zed Books.

Boyle, K. (2010) 'Selling the Selling of Sex: The Secret Diary of a Call-girl on Screen' in K. Mendes and K. Silva (eds), Commentary and Criticism: Representation of Sex Workers. *Feminist Media Studies* 10(1): 113–16.

Bourdieu, P. (1990) *The Logic of Practice*. Cambridge: Polity Press.

Bourdieu, P. (2004) 'Gender and Symbolic Violence' in N. Scheper-Hughes and P. Bourgois (eds), *Violence in War and Peace*. Oxford: Blackwell.

Brents, B. and Hausbeck, K. (2007) 'Marketing Sex: US Legal Brothels and Late Capitalist Consumption'. *Sexualities* 10(4): 425–39.

Cameron, D. and Frazer, E. (1987) *The Lust To Kill: A Feminist Perspective on Sexual Murder*. Cambridge: Polity Press.

Church, S., Henderson, M., Barnard, M. and Hart, G. (2001) 'Violence by Clients towards Female Prostitutes in Different Work Settings: Questionnaire Survey'. *British Medical Journal* 322: 524.

Cochrane, K. (2006) 'Five's New Sitcom is about Prostitution. You Know the Funniest Part? The Women All Love their Work'. *The Guardian*, 17th August 2006.

Coy, M., Horvath, M.A.H. and Kelly, L. (2007). *It's Just Like Going to the Supermarket: Men Buying Sex in East London*. London: Child & Woman Abuse Studies Unit, London Metropolitan University.

Coy, M. (2008) 'The Consumer, the Consumed and the Commodity: Women and Sex Buyers Talk about Objectification in Prostitution' in V. Munro and M. Della Giusta (eds), *Demanding Sex: Critical Reflections on the Regulation of Prostitution*. Aldershot: Ashgate.

Coy, M. (2009a) 'Milkshakes, Lady Lumps and Growing Up to Want Boobies: How the Sexualisation of Popular Culture Limits Girls' Horizons'. *Child Abuse Review* 18: 6.

Coy M. (2009b) 'This Body Which is Not Mine: The Notion of the Habit Body, Prostitution and (Dis)embodiment'. *Feminist Theory* 10(1): 61–75.

Dalla, R. (2000) 'Exposing the "Pretty Woman" Myth: A Qualitative Examination of the Lives of Female Streetwalking Prostitutes'. *Journal of Sex Research* 37(4): 344–53.

De Jour, B. (2005) *The Intimate Adventures of a London Call Girl*. London: Orion Publishing.

Della Giusta, M. and Scuriatti, L. (2005) 'The Show Must Go On: Making Money Glamorising Oppression'. *European Journal of Women's Studies* 12(31): 31–44.

DeRiviere, L. (2006) 'A Human Capital Methodology for Estimating the Lifelong Personal Costs of Young Women Leaving the Sex Trade'. *Feminist Economics* 12(3): 367–402.

Dines, G. (2010) *Pornland: How Porn Has Hijacked Our Sexuality*. Boston: Beacon Press.

Elliott, K., Eland, H. and McGaw, J. (2002) *Kerb Crawling in Middlesbrough: An Analysis of Kerb Crawler's Opinions.* Safer Middlesbrough Partnership. Unpublished report.

Farley, M., Cotton, A., Lynne, J., Zumbeck, S., Spiwak, F., Reyes, M., Alvarez, D. and Sezgin, U. (2003) 'Prostitution & Trafficking in Nine Countries: An Update on Violence and Post-Traumatic Stress Disorder' in M. Farley (ed.), *Prostitution, Trafficking, and Traumatic Stress.* Binghamton: Haworth Press.

Frank K. (2003) '"Just Trying to Relax": Masculinity, Masculinizing Practices and Strip Club Regulars'. *Journal of Sex Research* 40(1): 61–75.

Freeman, H. (2001) 'Can-can do'. *The Guardian*, Friday 7 September 2001.

Frith, M. (2006) 'Women and Popular Culture: The Pimp Chic Debate'. *The Independent*, 22nd February 2006.

Gill, R. (2007) 'Postfeminist Media Culture: Elements of a Sensibility'. *European Journal of Cultural Studies* 10(2): 147–66.

Internet Movie Database (2010) *Respectable.* Available at: http://www.imdb.com/title/tt0862615/ [accessed: 30 December 2010].

Jeffreys, S. (1997) *The Idea of Prostitution.* Melbourne: Spinifex Press.

Jeffreys, S. (2009) *The Industrial Vagina: The Political Economy of the Global Sex Trade.* London: Routledge.

Jenkins, R. (1992) *Pierre Bourdieu.* London: Routledge.

Jyrkinen, M. (2005) *The Organisation of Policy Meets the Commercialisation of Sex. Global Linkages, Policies, Technologies.* Economy and Society No 146. Helsinki: Hanken, Swedish School of Economics and Business Administration. Doctoral thesis, available at: http://urn.fi/URN:ISBN:951-555-882-4 [accessed: 4 July 2008].

Kinnell, H. (2008) *Violence and Sex Work in Britain.* Cullompton: Willan.

Lerner, G. (1986) *The Creation of Patriarchy.* Oxford: OU Press.

Levin, D. and Kilbourne, J. (2008) *So Sexy So Soon: The New Sexualized Childhood and What Parents Can Do to Protect Their Kids.* New York: Ballantine Books.

Levy, A. (2005) *Female Chauvinist Pigs: Women and the Rise of Raunch Culture.* London: Pocket Books.

Lloyd, R. (2010) *Corporate Sponsored Pimping Plays Role in US Human Trafficking.* Available at: http://www.thegrio.com/2010/01/corporate-sponsored-pimping-plays-role-in-us-human-trafficking.php [accessed: 18 January 2010].

Marttila, A.-M. (2008) 'Desiring the "Other" Prostitution: Clients on a Transnational Red-Light District in the Border Area of Finland, Estonia and Russia'. *Gender, Technology and Development* 12(1): 31–51.

McNair (1996) *Mediated Sex: Pornography and Postmodern Culture.* London: Hodder.

McRobbie, A. (2004) 'Notes on "What Not To Wear" and Post-feminist Symbolic Violence'. *The Sociological Review* 52: 97–109.

McRobbie, A. (2008) 'Pornographic Permutations'. *The Communication Review* 11: 225–36.

McRobbie, A. (2009) *The Aftermath of Feminism: Gender, Culture and Social Change.* London: Sage.

Mendes, K., Silva, K., Comella, L., Ray, A., Baldwin, D., Orchard, T., Weissmann, E., Thornham, H. and Long, J. (2009) 'Commentary and Criticism'. *Feminist Media Studies* 9(4): 493–515.

Mendes, K., Silva, K., Basu, A., Dutta, M.J., Dunn, J., Attwood, F. and Boyle, K. (2010) 'Commentary and Criticism'. *Feminist Media Studies* 10(1): 99–116.

Morgan, K. and Bjokert, S.T. (2006) '"I'd Rather You'd Lay Me on the Floor and Start Kicking Me": Understanding Symbolic Violence in Everyday Life', *Women's Studies International Forum* 29(5): 441–52.

O'Connell Davidson, J. (1998) *Prostitution, Power and Freedom.* Cambridge: Polity Press.

O'Neill, M. (2001) *Prostitution and Feminism.* Cambridge: Polity Press.

Papadopoulos, L. (2010) *Sexualisation of Young People Review.* London: Home Office.

Paul, P. (2005) *Pornified: How Pornography Is Transforming Our Lives, Our Relationships, and Our Families.* New York: Times Books.

Potterat, J.J., Brewer, D.D., Muth, S.Q., Rothenberg, R.B., Woodhouse, D.E., Muth, J.B., Stites, H. and Brody, S. (2004) 'Mortality in a Long-term Open Cohort of Prostitute Women'. *American Journal of Epidemiology* 159(8): 778–85.

Plumridge, E., Chetwynd, S., Reed, A. and Gifford, S. (1997) 'Discourses of Emotionality in Commercial Sex: The Missing Client Voice'. *Feminism and Psychology* 7(2): 165–81.

Quinn, E. (2000) '"Who's the Mack?": The Performativity and Politics of the Pimp Figure in Gangsta Rap'. *Journal of American Studies* 34(1): 115–36.

Raphael, J. and Shapiro, D.L. (2004) 'Violence in Indoor and Outdoor Prostitution Venues'. *Violence against Women* 10(2): 126–39.

Roach, C. (2007) *Stripping, Sex and Popular Culture.* Oxford: Berg Books.

Roberts, D., Foehr, U. and Rideout, V. (2005) *Generation M: Media in the Lives of 8–18 Year Olds.* Menlo Park, CA: Kaiser.

Rose, T. (2008) *The Hip Hop Wars: What We Talk about When We Talk about Hip Hop and Why it Matters.* New York: Basic Books.

Salfati, C., James, A. and Ferguson, L. (2008) 'Prostitute Homicides'. *Journal of Interpersonal Violence* 23(4): 505–43.

Saner, E. (2007) 'Wrong Call'. *The Guardian*, 20th September 2007.

Sassen, S. (2002) 'Women's Burden: Counter-geographies of Globalization and the Feminization of Survival'. *Nordic Journal of International Law* 71(2): 255–74.

Smith, J. (1990) *Misogynies.* London: Faber & Faber.

Sorensen, A.D. (2005) *Pornophication and Gender Stereotyping in Mass Culture in Denmark.* Paper presentation at the conference 'Nordic Forum', Tallinn, 8 June 2005.

Tobin, L. (2009) *Pimp Your Vocab.* London: Portico.

Turner, J. (2005) 'Dirty Young Men'. *The Guardian*, 22nd October. Available at: http://www.guardian.co.uk/theguardian/2005/oct/22/weekend7.weekend3 [accessed: 3 December 2010].

Tyler, M. (2008) 'Sex Self-help Books: Hot Secrets for Great Sex or Promoting the Sex of Prostitution?' *Women's Studies International Forum* 31(5): 363–72.

Viner, K. (2006) 'It's Not Just on the Streets that the Tide of Prostitution Must be Turned Back', *The Guardian*, Saturday 21st June 2006.

Ward, H., Mercer, C.H. and Wellings, K. (2005) 'Who Pays for Sex? An Analysis of the Increasing Prevalence of Female Commercial Sex Contacts among Men in Britain'. *Sexually Transmitted Infections* 8: 467–71. Available at: www.pimpcostumes.com [accessed: 17 September 2009].

Index

Page numbers in **bold** refer to a figure or table, page numbers in *italic* refer to a note at the bottom of the page.